SOCIAL RELATIONS AND SOCIAL ROLES

Chandler Publications in
ANTHROPOLOGY AND SOCIOLOGY
Leonard Broom, *Editor*

SOCIAL RELATIONS
AND SOCIAL ROLES

The Unfinished
SYSTEMATIC SOCIOLOGY

FLORIAN ZNANIECKI

 CHANDLER PUBLISHING COMPANY
124 SPEAR STREET, SAN FRANCISCO, CALIFORNIA 94105

CONTENTS

PART 1—[THE SCOPE OF SOCIOLOGY]

PUBLISHER'S NOTE

This book contains the last work of Professor Florian Znaniecki. The unfinished manuscript was entrusted to Chandler Publishing Company by his daughter, Dr. Helena Znaniecki Lopata.

Social Relations and Social Roles is as Dr. Znaniecki left it. Footnotes are absent; he had not prepared them when he ceased working. The manuscript has not received the normal publisher's editing, since any editing of a posthumous work entails a risk of violating the author's intention. The work contains some unfulfilled references to material to be covered later; these remain unexcised, since they show the directions in which Dr. Znaniecki believed sociology might go, and the history that might be recovered from a sociological point of view.

FLORIAN ZNANIECKI: HIS LIFE

Florian Znaniecki was born in 1882 near Swiatniki in German-occupied Poland. His father lost his estate in Swiatniki, in the Kujawiak province, when the son was only a few years old and spent the rest of his life managing estates for friends in Russian-occupied Poland. The children (two daughters and the son) obtained from tutors most of their education, including French, German, and Polish. In addition, Znaniecki taught himself English and Russian and gained a knowledge of Greek and Latin in gymnasiums in Warsaw and Częstochowa. An early interest in poetry culminated in the publication of a book entitled *Cheops* when he was in secondary school. His thought turned to philosophy in the gymnasium, when he volunteered to specialize in this field as a participant in a secret learning society. The Russians had severely restricted knowledge transmitted to Poles through the school system, forcing a number of scientifically curious young people to organize underground study groups. Each member contributed knowledge obtained within a field of specialization to other participants of his group. Znaniecki studied in depth the major philosophical works of the world and gave lectures to fellow students in return for information in other subjects. This early enthusiasm for the voluntary search of knowledge persisted throughout his life and was reflected in his professional relations with students.

Znaniecki continued to study philosophy at the universities of Warsaw (B.A.), Geneva (M.A.), Zurich, Paris, and Crakow, obtaining a Ph. D. from the last institution in 1909. It was during these years that he first met the major philosophers and thinkers of Europe. He interrupted his studies briefly to join the French Foreign Legion and to publish a French literary magazine.

His first philosophical publication, entitled *Zagadnienie wartości w filozofji* (*The Problem of Values in Philosophy*), appeared in 1910 and was followed by *Humanism i poznanie* (*Humanism and Knowledge*) in 1912 and by *Evolucja twórcza*, a commentated translation of Henri Bergson's *Creative Evolution*, in 1913. This early interest in social values and in humanistic knowledge was also reflected in several articles published before 1914 such as: "Philosophical Ethics and the Science of Moral Values," "Studies in the Philosophy of Values and the Elements of Practical Realities," and "The Significance of the Evolution of the World and of Man." All of these works were in Polish.

While awaiting a chair in philosophy at one of the Polish universities, Znaniecki worked as the Director of the Polish Emigrants' Protective Association. It was in this capacity that he met the well-known American sociologist, W. I. Thomas, who had started the investigation of the backgrounds of immigrants in the United States by studying the Polish segment of this population. Thomas asked Znaniecki to come to America to assist in the project. Znaniecki agreed (taking the last train to leave Poland before World War I). He then devoted his time to writing, in English, "The Principle of Relativity and Philosophical Absolutism," which appeared in *The Philosophical Review* in 1915.

After working with the Polish immigrant material for some time, Znaniecki wrote an introduction to the projected volume, on the basis of which Thomas asked him to be a full collaborator. *The Polish Peasant in Europe and America* was the result of this combination of theoretical interest in values and of sociological research. Although publishing the philosophically oriented *Cultural Reality* in 1919, Znaniecki became increasingly convinced of the value of inductive thought and research through his cooperation with Thomas and changed his identification to that of a sociologist. He retained, however, an interest in values and knowledge as bases for human behavior.

While in America, Znaniecki (whose first wife had died) met and married Eileen Markley, a Connecticut-born lawyer trained at the University of Chicago, with degrees from Smith and Columbia. He converted her into a sociologist. Eileen helped Znaniecki with *The Polish Peasant* and *Cultural Reality* as well as with all his later books and articles.

After World War I, the University of Poznan offered Znaniecki a chair in philosophy, changing it at his request to a chair in sociology. Feeling obliged to help in the intellectual reconstruction of Poland, he accepted and returned to his mother country in 1920. Sociology had not been offered in Poland before this time, nor had it been taught in most European universities. With the help of his new students, Znaniecki founded the Polish Sociological Institute and started the *Polish Sociological Review*. The major function of the Institute was empirical research and, over the years, its members collected numerous manuscripts prepared by peasants and workers, as well as those of highly educated Poles. A single competition for workers' autobiographies drew three hundred manuscripts, over one hundred of which the Institute published, at least in part. Most of these primary documents were burned by the Nazis. However, they had served as a training reserve for young Polish sociologists and as a base for the development of theoretical formulations of the Institute's founder.

Znaniecki remained in Poland most of the time between the two world wars, and continued to write both in Polish and English. (See Bibliography.) During this period *The Laws of Social Psychology* (1925) was published in English. He accepted Columbia University's invitation as visiting professor for two years in 1932, and produced *The Method of Sociology* in 1934. *Social Actions* was published in 1936, after his return to Poland.

World War II broke out while Znaniecki was on the high seas, heading for Poland after a summer of lectures at Columbia. (The lectures resulted in the publication of *The Social Role of the Man of Knowledge* in 1940 by the press of that university.) The ship was detained in England. After some delays and uncertainty as to the right course of action, it became obvious that return to Poland was impossible. Poland was occupied by that time by the forces of Nazi Germany and of Communist Russia, and Znaniecki had the honor of being placed on the blacklists of both governments. He therefore returned to America, where, thanks to the middle-of-the-term action of J. William Albig, then head of the Sociology Department at the University of Illinois, he obtained an immediate professorship. With the help of his wife's relatives, he attempted to locate his family in Poland. His wife and daughter, after a short stay in a concentration camp, managed to escape the country and joined him in America. His son by the first marriage, the poet and novelist, Juliusz Znaniecki, was unable to leave. Taking an active part in the Polish underground and in the Warsaw uprising, he was taken by the Nazis to the Dachau concentration camp, from which he was released two years later by the American forces.

Znaniecki's main interest in the definition and analysis of the object-matter and method of sociology continued at the University of Illinois. With the assistance of students he studied social roles and social groups on campus. The unpublished "The Social Role of the University of Illinois Student" was written in 1942. During this period of his life he published a number of articles; *Modern Nationalities* (1952), a study of the evolution of national culture societies; and *Cultural Sciences* (1952), a theoretical work dealing with sociology and its relations to other sciences. He was elected president of the American Sociological Society in 1953, and was hard at work on what he half-humorously called his *magnum opus* (with the temporary title of *Systematic Sociology*) when he died in 1958.

Znaniecki's Sociology

Znaniecki's work, both as a creative thinker and as an enthusiastic teacher, can best be understood as a constant progressive clarification of the scientific problems he considered basic to sociology: The nature of the social systems which are its subject matter and the methodology by which they can be analyzed. The methodological emphasis upon the need to study cultural data as they appear to the people involved in social interaction and not to the outside observer was formulated as early as 1912 in his *Humanism and Knowledge*. The divisions of sociology were first explained in 1934 in *The Method of Sociology* and the final systematic presentation of his ideas was to be contained in the *Systematic Sociology*: a work designed not to deal with new problems, but to present the final crystallized expression of his forty-year concentration upon sociological theory, with few actual references to the

monumental research which led to its formulation and modifications.

The definition of sociology as a cultural science whose function
is to study systems of social interaction based upon patterns of
values and norms of behavior, through the use of the "humanistic
coefficient," was developed in its final form in *Cultural Sciences*.
This book, published by the University of Illinois Press in 1952, was
actually to have been only an introductory chapter to *Systematic
Sociology*. However, all the years of interest in sociology and its
relation to other sciences, both social or cultural and natural, resulted in such a lengthy analysis that it had to be published as a
separate volume.

In this book, as well as in the short introduction to the manuscript that followed, Znaniecki explained that sociology is an objective, inductive, and generalizing *science* whose subject matter
calls for a method different from that of natural sciences. The
function of sociology, according to him, is not the study of society
in the Spencerian or Comtian sense, nor the study of "human
nature," but the investigation of organized, interdependent interaction among human beings. The various forms of cooperative
interaction he defined as social systems. Sociology must proceed
through induction to the analysis of the various forms of social
systems with the goal of developing a taxonomy of such systems.
Only then will sociologists be able to make causal, functional,
ontogenetic, and phylogenetic generalizations which are, according
to Znaniecki, the aim of all sciences.[1]

The four social systems which are the object matter of sociology,
in Znaniecki's final theory, are: social relations, social roles, social
groups, and societies.

Znaniecki's interest in social relations can be found in all his
major works. In addition, two articles separated by almost thirty
years were devoted exclusively to the topic. In 1928 he presented
a paper on "The Sexual Relation as a Social Relation and Some of
Its Changes" at the First International Congress of Research in

---

[1] See Chapter 1, pp. 3–20. See also the numerous articles dealing with
sociology listed in the bibliography, as well as *Cultural Sciences*.

Sex.[2] The fully developed theory of social relations was stated in "The Dynamics of Social Relations," published in 1954 in *Sociometry*.

Znaniecki's theory of social groups, which is integral in his major works, can first be found in "Group Crises Produced by Voluntary Undertakings" in Kimball Young's *Social Attitudes*, published in 1931. "Social Groups as Products of Participating Individuals" appears in the *American Journal of Sociology* in 1939. An extensive discussion of groups forms the "Social Organization and Institutions" chapter in the Gurvitch and Moore *Twentieth Century Sociology* (1945).

The theory of societies was first expressed in English in the contribution to *Twentieth Century Sociology*. Its more developed explanation is contained in *Modern Nationalities* (1952). However, this theory, dependent as it was in his system upon the theories of social relations, social roles, and social groups, had not been fully crystallized at the time of his death.

THE DEVELOPMENT OF ZNANIECKI'S ROLE THEORY

The creative growth of Znaniecki's theories can best be illustrated through the gradually introduced modifications of the theory of social roles. His interest in the place of values in human behavior antedates even *The Polish Peasant*. The cooperation with Thomas led him from the philosophical, deductive analysis of the cultural base for social interaction to research and induction. The place of education in the preparation of persons for social interaction was developed in Polish in *Socjologia wychowania* (*The Sociology of Education*) (1928 and 1930). "The Social Role of the Unemployed," published in a book in honor of Professor I. A. Blaha by the Czech *Sociologicka revue*, uses this concept as a tool of analysis. *The Social Role of the Man of Knowledge* (1940) expresses not only the increasingly developed role theory but also Znaniecki's interest in systems of knowledge in societies, and the

[2] Published in *Verhandlungen des I. Internationalen Kongresses für Sexualforschung*, Vol. IV, pp. 222–230 (Berlin-Köln, Marcus and Weber, 1928).

manner in which they evolve through the development of new roles. The unpublished "The Social Role of the University of Illinois Student" developed in detail the concept of social person. The "Social Roles of Innovators," published in the *Midwest Sociologist* in 1955, contains many of the ideas about the evolution of roles which were to be developed in *Systematic Sociology*.

Within this last work, Znaniecki modified considerably his original theory of social roles, and of their relation to other systems of social interaction. The first four-fold division of social systems, which are the province of sociology, appeared in 1934 in *The Method of Sociology*. In it he divided "the data of sociology" into categories to be studied through: (a) the theory of social actions, (b) the theory of social relations, (c) the theory of social persons, and (d) the theory of social groups. By 1958, in his presidential address to the American Sociological Society, Znaniecki had reformulated these divisions into the systems which were to appear in *Systematic Sociology*: social relations, social roles, social groups, and societies.

Znaniecki had crystallized his theory of social relations, the analysis of basic relations in communities and the theory of social roles, by 1958. He was in the midst of tracing the evolution of major social roles in societies when he died. A complete and excellent analysis of the total sociological theory of Florian Znaniecki can be found in Hyman Frankel's unpublished Ph. D. dissertation, *The Sociological Theory of Florian Znaniecki* (University of Illinois, 1959).

HELENA ZNANIECKI LOPATA

Works of Florian Znaniecki

Books in English

The Polish Peasant in Europe and America (with W. I. Thomas). First edition, 5 volumes, Boston: Badger, 1918–1920.

Cultural Reality. Chicago: University of Chicago Press, 1919; pp. xv, 1–359.

The Laws of Social Psychology. Chicago: University of Chicago Press, 1925; pp. viii, 1–320.

The Method of Sociology. New York: Farrar & Rinehart, 1934; pp. xii, 1–338.

Social Actions. New York: Farrar & Rinehart, 1936; pp. xix, 1–746.

The Social Role of the Man of Knowledge. New York: Columbia University Press, 1940; pp. 1–212. Translated into Spanish as *El papel social del intelectual*, Mexico, 1944, and, according to Columbia University Press, into Japanese.

Cultural Sciences. Urbana, Ill.: University of Illinois Press, 1952; pp. i–viii, 1–438.

Modern Nationalities. Urbana, Ill.: University of Illinois Press, 1952; pp. i–xvi, 1–196. Unpublished outline translated by Vincente Herrero and published as "Las sociedades de cultura nacional y sus relaciones." Mexico: El Colegio de Mexico, No. 24 of *Jornadas*, a series of social studies, 1944; pp. 3–80.

Systematic Sociology. The present volume.

Articles and Other Publications in English

"The Principle of Relativity and Philosophical Absolutism." *The Philosophical Review*, Vol. XXIV, 1915, pp. 150–164.

"Experiences of an Immigrant" (anonymous, autobiographical). *Atlantic Monthly*, 1918–1919.

"The Object-Matter of Sociology." *American Journal of Sociology*, Vol. 32, No. 4, January, 1927, pp. 529–584.

"The Poles." *Immigrant Backgrounds*, H. Fairchild, ed., in honor of W. I. Thomas. New York: Wiley, 1927; pp. 196–212.

"The Sexual Relation as a Social Relation and Some of Its Changes." Excerpt from *Verhandlungen des I. Internationalen Kongresses für Sexualforschung*, Vol. IV. Berlin-Köln, Marcus and Weber, 1928; pp. 222–230.

"Social Research in Criminology." *Sociology and Social Research*, Vol. XII, 1928, March-April, pp. 307–322.

"Education and Self-Education in Modern Societies." *American Journal of Sociology*, Vol. 36, No. 3, November, 1930, pp. 371–386.

"Group Crises Produced by Voluntary Undertakings." *Social Attitudes*, Kimball Young, ed. New York: Holt, 1931; pp. 265–290.

"The Analysis of Social Processes." *Publications of the American Sociological Society*, Vol. 26, No. 3, August, 1932, pp. 37–43.

"The Sociology of the Struggle for Pomerania." Torun: Baltic Institute (The Baltic Pocket Library), 1934; pp. 1–57.

Comment added to Herbert Blumer's *Critiques of Research in the Social Sciences, I.* New York, 1939, pp. 87–98.

"Social Groups as Products of Participating Individuals." *American Journal of Sociology*, Vol. 44, 1939, pp. 799–804.

"The Social Role of the Unemployed" (in English). *Sociologicka revue*, Brno, 1939 (volume in honor of Prof. I. A. Blaha); pp. 239–251.

"The Changing Culture Ideals of the Family." *Marriage and Family Living*, Vol. III, Summer, 1941, pp. 58–62, 68.

"Sociometry and Sociology." *Sociometry*, Vol. V, No. 3, 1943, pp. 225–233. Translated into French in *Cahiers Internationaux de Sociologie*, Vol. I, October, 1946, pp. 106–119.

"The Impact of War on Personal Organization." *Sociology and Social Research*, Vol. 27, January-February, 1943, pp. 171–180.

"Social Organization and Institutions." *Twentieth Century Sociology, a symposium.* G. Gurvitch and W. Moore, eds. New York: Philosophical Library, 1945; pp. 172–217.

"Controversies in Doctrine and Method." *American Journal of Sociology*, Vol. 50, No. 6, 1945, pp. 514–521.

"Sociological Ignorance in Social Planning." *Sociology and Social Research*, Vol. 30, No. 2, November-December, 1945, pp. 87–100.

"William I. Thomas as a Collaborator" (speech at memorial services at University of Chicago). *Sociology and Social Research*, Vol. 32, March-April, 1948, pp. 765–767.

"Methodological Trends in Sociological Research." *Sociology and Social Research*, Vol. 33, No. 1, September-October, 1948, pp. 10–14.

Comment on John L. Thomas' article "Marriage Prediction in *The Polish Peasant.*" *American Journal of Sociology*, Vol. 55, No. 6, May, 1950, article pp. 572–577, comment pp. 577–578.

"European and American Sociology after Two World Wars." *American Journal of Sociology*, Vol. 56, No. 3, November, 1950, pp. 217–221. Translated as "Europäische und amerikanische Soziologie nach zwei Weltkriegen." *Universitas.* No. 6, 1951, pp. 497–504.

"The Function of Sociology of Education." *Educational Theory*, Vol. 1, No. II, August, 1951 (publication of the John Dewey Society of the College of Education, University of Illinois), pp. 69–78.

"The Present and Future of Sociology of Knowledge." *Soziologische Forschung in Unserer Zeit* (in honor of Leopold von Wiese's seventy-fifth birthday). Köln, Westdeutscher Verlag, 1951; pp. 248–258.

"Should Sociologists Be Also Philosophers of Values?" *Sociology and Social Research*, November-December, 1952, pp. 79–84.

"Basic Problems of Contemporary Sociology." *American Sociological Review*, October, 1954, Vol. 19 (presidential address, American Sociological Society, Urbana, Ill.), pp. 519–524.

"The Dynamics of Social Relations." *Sociometry*, November, 1954 (paper read in section on theory at the 1954 meetings of the American Sociological Society).

"The Creative Evolution and Diffusion of Knowledge." *Three Columbia Centennial Lectures*. New York: Polish Institute of Arts and Sciences in America, 1954.

"The Social Roles of Innovators." *Midwest Sociologist*, Winter, 1955, pp. 14–19 (paper read at Midwest Sociological Society Meeting in Omaha, 1953).

"Important Developments in Sociology." *Sociology and Social Research*, Vol. 40, No. 6, July-August, 1956, pp. 419–420.

"Social Roles." *Estudios Sociologicos Internacionales*, Vol. II, Instituto "Balmes" de sociologia, Madrid, 1961, Consejo Superior de Investigaciones Cientificas; pp. 745–779. (Summary of the manuscript contained in this volume, made by Helena Znaniecki Lopata but attributed by the Spanish publisher to Mrs. Florian Znaniecki.)

BOOKS PUBLISHED IN POLISH

Cheops: Poemat Fantastyczny, Warsaw: J. Fiszer, 1903; pp. 4–84. (*Cheops: A Poem of Fantasy*)

Zagadnienie wartości w filozofji. Warsaw: Przegląd Filozoficzny, 1910; pp. 2–115. (*The Problem of Values in Philosophy*, published by *The Philosophical Review*)

Humanism i poznanie. Warsaw: Przegląd Filozoficzny, 1912; pp. 2–231. (*Humanism and Knowledge*, published by *The Philosophical Review*)

Evolucja twórcza. Warsaw: Gebethner & Wolff, 1913; pp. x–310. Translation and discussion of Henri Bergson's *Creative Evolution.*

Upadek cywilizacji zachodniej: Szkic z pograniczą filosofji kultury i socjologji. Poznań: Kimitet Obrony Narodowej, 1921; pp. xiii, 1–111. (*The Fall of Western Civilization*)

Wstęp do socjologji. Poznań: Poznańskie Tow. Przyjaciół Nauki, 1922; pp. 2–467. (*Introduction to Sociology*)

Socjologia wychowania. Warsaw: The Ministry of Education of Poland; Vol. I, 1928, pp. 1–312; Vol. II, 1930, pp. 1–372. (*The Sociology of Education*)

Miasto w świadomości jego obywateli. Poznań: Instytut socjologiczny, 1931; pp. 1–141. (*The City Viewed by Its Inhabitants,* from the study of the city of Poznań by the Polish Sociological Institute)

Ludzie teraźniejsi a ciwilizacja przyszłości. Lwów-Warsaw: Książnica-Atlas, 1935; pp. 1–379. (*People of Today and the Civilization of Tomorrow*)

ARTICLES AND OTHER PUBLICATIONS NOT IN ENGLISH

"Etyka filozoficzna a nauka o wartosciach moralnych." *Przegląd Filozoficzny,* 1909. ("Philosophical Ethics and the Science of Moral Values")

"Statystyka wychodztwa." *Wychodzca Polski,* z. 1 and 2, 1911. ("Emigrant Statistics")

"Wychodztwo a położenie ludności wiejskiej zarobkującej w Królestwie Polskim." *Wychodzca Polski,* z. 3, 1911. ("Emigration and the Economic Status of the Agricultural Population of the Polish Kingdom")

"Studia nad filozofji wartości i elementy rzeczywistości praktycznej." *Przegląd Filozoficzny,* 1912, pp. 1–27 ("Studies in the Philosophy of Values and the Elements of Practical Realities")

"Znaczenie rozwoju swiata i człowieka." *Swiat i Człowiek*, Vol. IV, 1913, pp. 283–356. ("The Significance of the Evolution of the World and of Man")

Organizacja obywateli pracy. Poznań, 1920, pp. 1–14. ("The Organization of Workers")

Preface to Berkan, Wladyslaw, *Życiorys słasny.* Poznań: Materiały Instytutu socjologicznego w Poznaniu, I, 1923; pp. iii–xvii. (The preface to one of the autobiographies collected and published by the Polish Sociological Institute)

"Szkice a socjoloji wychowania." Kraków: *Ruch pedagogiczny*, Nos. September-October, 1924, pp. 145–159, and November-December, 1924, pp. 209–219. ("Outline of Educational Sociology")

"Stany Zjednoczone Ameryki Połnocnej." *Nauka Polska*, Vol. IV, 1924, pp. 487–508. ("The United States of America")

"Co jest psychologia społeczna?" *Przegląd współczesny*, No. 38, pp. 370–386, and No. 39, pp. 51–87, 1925. ("What Is Social Psychology?")

"Przedmiot i zadania nauki o wiedzy." *Nauka Polska*, Vol. V, 1925, pp. 1–78. ("The Subject and Problems of the Sociology of Knowledge")

"Die soziologischen Ursachen der gegenwärtigen Krise der Demokratie." *Demokratie und Parlamentarismus, Prager Press*, 1 January, 1926.

"Zadania syntezy filosoficznej." *Przegląd Filozoficzny.* Vol. XXX, z. 2, No. 3, 1927, pp. 103–116. ("Problems of Philosophical Synthesis")

"Prąd socjologiczny w filozofji nowoczesnej." *Księga pamiątkowa ku czci w Heinricha*, Kraków, 1927. ("The Sociological Trend in Modern Philosophy")

"O wyborze zawodu." *Młodzież Sobie*, Poznań, R.I. No. 3, 1927, pp. 26–28. See shortened form in *Młodziez Sobie*, 1930, No. 3, pp. 3–4. ("On Choosing a Career")

"Sammlung u. Verwertung des soziologischen Materials." *Zeitschrift für Völkerpsychologie und Soziologie*, Vol. III, 1927, pp. 274–293.

Preface to Mirel, Franciszek, *Elementy społeczne parafii rzymsko-katoliciej*. Poznań: Fiszer i Majewski, 1928; pp. ix–xix.

"Początki myśli socjologicznej." *Ruch Prawniczy, Ekonomiczny i Socjologiczny*, R. VIII, 1928, pp. 78–97. ("The Origins of Sociological Thought")

"W sprawie rozwoju socjologji polskiej." Poznań: *Programi samoobrona*, 1929, pp. 1–24. ("The Process of Development of Polish Sociology")

"Potrzeby socjologji w Polsce." *Nauka Polska*, Vol. X, 1929, pp. 486–498. ("The Needs of Sociology in Poland")

"Podstawy i granice celowego działania wychowawczego." *Zagadnienie oswiaty dorosłych: Dwie Konferencje*, Warsaw, 1930, pp. 17–32 and 200–217. ("Foundations and Limitations in the Goals of Education"—for the conference dealing with "The Question of Adult Education")

"O szczeblach rozwoju społecznego." *Ruch Prawniczy, Ekonomiczny i Socjologiczny*, R. X, 1930, pp. 285–296. ("The Rungs of Social Evolution")

"Forming the Educand," From Vol. I of *Socjologia wychowania*. Extrait du *Bulletin International de la Société Scientifique de Pédagogie*, Warsaw-Lwów, 1930, Kaiążnica-Atlas, pp. 1–16.

"Siły społeczne w walce o Pomorze." *Polskie Pomorze*: Toruń, 1931, Vols. I and II, pp. 80–108. ("Social Forces in the Struggle for Pomerania," in joint volumes)

"Studia nad antagonizmem do obcych." *Przegląd socjologiczny*, 1931, z. 2–4, pp. 1–54. ("Studies in the Antagonism to Strangers")

"Kultura amerykańska." *Ruch Prawniczy, Ekonomiczny i Socjolo-*

giczny, R. XII, z. 1, 1932, pp. 36–39. ("American Culture")

"Polska w kryzysie swiatowym." *Dziennik Poznański*, No. 279, December 3, 1933. ("Poland in the World Crisis")

"Persönliche Erziehung und soziale Kultur." *Kölner Vierteljahrhefte für Soziologie*, 12, 1934–1935, pp. 328–356. (A translated section from *Ludzie teraźniejsi a ciwilizacja przyszłości*)

"Les Forces sociales en Poméranie." Toruń: L'Institut Baltique, 1934, pp. 1–55. (Translation of "Siły społeczne w walce o Pomorze" [1931])

"Kierownictwa a zwolennictwo we współpracy twórczej." *Kultura i Wychowanie*. Warsaw, 1934, R. I, z. 4, pp. 277–294. ("Control versus Freedom in Creative Cooperation")

"Teoria sobkostwa i towarzyskosci." *Przegląd socjologiczny*, Poznań, Vol. III, 1935, pp. 83–108. ("A Theory of Selfishness and Sociability")

"Socjologia walki o Pomorze." Toruń: Instytut Baltycki, 1935, pp. 1–48. (Translated from English, "The Sociology of the Struggle for Pomerania" [1934])

"Stefan Czarnowski, 1879–1937." *Przegląd socjologiczny*, 1937, Vol. V, pp. 3–4. (obituary)

"Uczeni polscy a życie polskie." *Droga*, 1936, No. 2–3, pp. 101–116, and No. 4, pp. 255–271. ("The Educated Pole and Polish Life")

"Znaczenie socjologiczne badań Ludwiga Krzywickiego nad społeczeństwami niższymi." *Krzywicki, Ludwik*. Warsaw: Instytut Gospodarstwo społecznego, 1938, pp. 217–248. ("The Significance of Ludwig Krzywicki's Sociological Studies of Primitive Societies")

Preface to Chałasinski, Jósef, *Młode pokolenie chłopów*. Warsaw: Państwowy Inst. Kultury Wsi, 1938, pp. ix–xvii.

"Tworczość naukowa Stefana Czarnowskiego." *Czarnowski, Stefan.* Warsaw-Poznań: Społeczeństwo-Kultura, 1939, pp. xxix–xxxvii. ("The Scientific Productivity of Stefan Czarnowski")

"Stan obecny technologii spoleczneji." *Ruch Prawniczy, Ekonomiczny i Socjologiczny,* R. 19, No. 3, 1939, pp. 317–327. ("The Present State of Social Technology")

[THE SCOPE OF SOCIOLOGY]

CHAPTER 1

WHAT IS SOCIOLOGY?

This is a question which many thousands of people have been asking for a long time: scientists and scholars who are not sociologists, religious, political, military, and economic leaders who wonder if it might be useful or harmful from their point of view, and college students who are trying to decide whether to take courses in sociology. Sociologists themselves have no unanimous answer. Their conceptions of sociology differ considerably; they agree in some respects as to what sociology is or ought to be, but disagree in other respects. We shall survey their agreements, notice their main disagreements, and endeavor to discover whether these disagreements can be settled and how.

1. Agreements and Disagreements Among Sociologists

When we study the works of famous sociologists published during the past hundred years and the sociological textbooks used in colleges during the last twenty years, we see that, however much these works differ in content, the majority of the authors accept certain common principles on which their conception of sociology is based.

In the first place, they agree that sociology falls into the category of "sciences," not into that of "arts," in the sense in which these terms are used in the current title "College of Arts and Sciences." Some critics doubt whether sociology deserves to be called a science. Comparing it with such universally recognized sciences as physics and chemistry, they show how defective it is—inexact, speculative, full of errors and controversies. But in answer to these critics, sociologists insist that no science is perfect. Every science grows gradually, through cooperative contributions of many scientists, and improves slowly in the course of its growth; old methods become discarded and more efficient ones introduced. Numerous theories once accepted as true are proved later to be erroneous; and each innovation raises fresh controversies. If sociology is more defective than physics and chemistry, it is because it began to develop much later; several hundred years ago those older sciences were at least as speculative, inexact, full of errors and controversies as sociology is now.

Secondly, sociology is conceived as an *inductive* science. This means that every sociological theory is supposed to be derived from the discovery of some kind of observable factual order among the data of human experience, that every sociological problem should initiate a search for some kind of factual order hitherto unknown, and that the results of this search must be tested by further factual evidence. In this respect, sociology is like biology or astronomy, which investigate factual order among such empirical data as living organisms or stars and planets. It differs from theology and metaphysics, whose doctrines cannot be tested by factual evidence. It differs also from "deductive" sciences, like formal logic and pure mathematics, whose theories are not derived from the investigation of empirical data, though they are used in the course of such investigations. Logic is essential in planning investigations and systematizing the results of inductive research; and mathematics is necessary to measure whatever has to be measured in the empirical world.

Thirdly, sociology is conceived as a *generalizing* science. It does not limit itself to the study of particular data or combinations of data, but by comparative research tries to discover what such data or combinations have in common and to draw generalizations applicable to many of them. Here again its task is like that of natural sciences, e.g., zoology or chemistry. Thus, zoologists, after observing and analyzing particular animals and comparing the results of their observation, divide animals into general classes and subclasses and generalize about their relationships with their natural environment; chemists, after analyzing and comparing particular samples of matter, draw generalizations about chemical elements and compounds. Thus, sociology differs from purely descriptive, or so-called idiographic, studies, e.g., detailed descriptions of particular geographic areas, each of which differs from others in its location, topography, climate, fauna, and flora, or descriptions of particular historical events (such as World War I) or of the lives of particular famous individuals or masterpieces of literature.

Fourthly, sociology is conceived by the majority of sociologists as an *objective*, or strictly theoretic, science. Its task is to investigate what really is, not to judge what ought or ought not to be. In this respect, sociology is supposed to be like theoretic physics and astronomy, and to differ from such disciplines as ethics, politics, and aesthetics. Of course, this does not prevent its results from being applied for the realization of ethical or political goals, just as the results of theoretic physics are applied to the realization of practical goals by electrical and mechanical engineers. Indeed, students of sociology are usually more interested in social work, social administration, education, prevention of crime and correction of criminals, improvement of community life, prevention of war, etc. than in sociological theory. But sociologists, like other scientists, are aware that the effective solution of practical problems depends upon adequate theoretic knowledge.

However, although sociologists share this basic conception of sociology as a science, they disagree as to the kind of data and facts which constitute the proper object-matter of sociological investigation and as to the best methods to be used in this investigation. We shall postpone the discussion of methods, since the choice of methods depends on the kind of problems which scientists are trying to solve. Disagreements about the object-matter of sociology are, however, of primary importance. No such disagreements exist among natural scientists: Everybody agrees that botany is the science of plants, zoology the science of animals, astronomy the science of stars and planets, geography the science of the surface of the earth, although some data and facts may be cooperatively studied by specialists in several sciences—e.g., biochemists investigate chemical processes occurring within organisms, and certain physical theories are applied to astronomical facts and chemical elements.

2. SOCIOLOGY AS THE SCIENCE OF SOCIETY

When the term sociology was introduced by Auguste Comte more than a hundred years ago, he conceived it as the science of "society." In other words, its task was to investigate societies as wholes, compare them, and draw generalizations about them. This conception predominated in the nineteenth century; the first thorough, systematic sociological work—Herbert Spencer's *Principles of Sociology*—was a general theory of all kinds of human societies, from the simplest to the most complex. This theory is still very influential, as it is accepted by most of the authors of sociological textbooks.

According to this conception, society has three essential characteristics: (1) It is a collectivity composed of a large number of human beings of successive generations, inhabiting a geographically circumscribed territory; (2) It is organized, in the sense that the activities of its participants are interdependent and integrated in such a way as to enable the society as a whole to last for a long period of time; (3) It is united by the common culture which its participants share.

The study of such territorially circumscribed, organized collectivities originated in classical antiquity, though from a different point of view. Greek and Roman thinkers were primarily interested in *political* collectivities, or—as we call them—states. They studied Greek city-states, e.g., Athens and Sparta, and large kingdoms, such as Persia, Egypt, Macedonia, the Roman Republic, and later the Roman Empire. They assumed that political organization under common government is the foundation of all social unity and order. During the Middle Ages, theologians and most social philosophers considered the Church rather than the State to be the foundation of social order. But when secular thinkers revived classical theories, they accepted their assumption of the basic importance of political organization. Until the second half of the eighteenth century, nearly all the influential works of social thinkers were political.

This emphasis on politics was largely due to the fact that most of the thinkers were more interested in practical problems than in objective theoretic research. They wanted to improve human lives, to introduce a more perfect order into their collectivities or to prevent deterioration of the existing order, to promote unity and cooperation, and to counteract divisions and conflicts. Inasmuch as the government of a state exerts powerful control over the people inhabiting the territory of this state, it seemed obvious to social thinkers that only through the agency of the government could their ideals be realized. Consequently, they devoted most of their attention to the functions of governments, evaluated various kinds of governments from the point of view of their ideals, tried to ascertain how governments became better or worse, and how undesirable governments could be eliminated and desirable governments developed.

However, even in classical antiquity some philosophers, historians, and geographers were interested in other, nonpolitical aspects of the lives of the peoples inhabiting various areas: language, religion, art, customs, mores, material techniques—in short, to use the modern term, their *cultures*. This interest grew as European explorers, merchants, travelers, conquerors, and colonists became acquainted with the peoples outside of Europe. Each of these peoples had a distinct culture, obviously different from the cultures with which the explorers were already familiar. Eventually, cultural differences between inhabitants of various areas within Europe (not always coextensive with state territories) also began to attract the attention of social thinkers. Finally, the eighteenth-century philosophers who built general theories about the historical development of mankind included in their theories not only political organization, but also religion, philosophy, science, technology, economics, literature, and art.

Consequently, when under the influence of natural sciences the program for an objective science of human society emerged, the initiators of this program, while taking for granted that a common government is indispensable for the existence of such a society, were aware that it is not sufficient to unite it. For they knew that most of the activities which the people inhabiting a territory perform, even when subjected to governmental control, are not parts of the political organization, but have some organization of their own, following cultural standards and norms which are not established by legislation.

The language which these people use (either only spoken or both spoken and written) has definite phonetical, semantical and grammatical rules. Furthermore, they take part in well-regulated, organized religious rites and ceremonies. Most of them participate in various kinds of technical production and economic exchange, also in accordance with specific norms. They conform with certain customs and mores in their private lives. They share various conceptions of nature and mankind developed by intellectual leaders and judged to be true according to accepted principles. Some of them write and others reproduce lyric poems, stories, dramas, and musical compositions in accordance with their aesthetic standards and norms. Some produce aesthetically standardized paintings and sculptures which others observe and appreciate.

Thus, the science of society, or sociology, as Comte and his followers conceived it, came to include, besides the study of governmental functions—legislative, administrative, juridical, military—also studies of the religion, technical production, economic exchange, organization of family life, education, language, literature, art, and knowledge found within the population of each separate, politically circumscribed territory.

This was obviously a very difficult task when the society under investigation included millions of people and had a rich and complex culture—for instance, the society composed of all the inhabitants of France, the society composed of all the inhabitants of Germany, or the society composed of all the inhabitants of the United States. As a matter of fact, most of this investigation was carried on by such specialists as political scientists, students of law, economists, religionists, linguists, historians of literature, and of art. But for the sociologist these were, so to speak, merely auxiliaries. Sociology, and only sociology, could integrate their results.

A similar, but easier, task was faced by investigators of so-called primitive societies, with a small population, a simple political organization, and a less developed culture, e.g., the Arunta in Australia, the Polynesian or Melanesian islanders, the Hottentots or Masai in Africa, the Zuñi or Kwakiutls in North America. While investigators of such small societies now call themselves cultural anthropologists, rather than sociologists, their works are included under sociology, according to those sociologists who still accept the concept of society as defined by Comte and Spencer.

However, since sociology was supposed to be a generalizing science, the next problem was: How to compare particular societies and draw generalizations about them? And here the nineteenth-century sociologists who modeled the conception of their science upon natural sciences, instead of waiting for the results of comparative research, assumed in advance that all societies in order to survive, must possess common characteristics similar to those which enable biological organisms to survive. A multicellular organism is a combination of anatomically differentiated and structurally connected parts, or organs, each composed of many cells, and each performing a specific physiological function essential for the existence of the organism as a system. To survive, a society must also be like a multicellular organism, according to those sociologists. Some of them—Lilienfeld, Schäffle, Izoulet—tried to prove that a society really is an organism, structurally and functionally, only much larger and more complex than an individual organism, since its cells are human beings, who are themselves multicellular organisms. Such theories have been discarded, for it is obvious that the functions of individual participants in a society are not rooted in biology, but in cultural history; their actions are not innate, but learned, and the standards and norms which they follow are parts of their cultural heritage.

Herbert Spencer took this into consideration, and his theory of society as a system which, though not an organism, is analogous to an organism, still influences many present sociologists. He called the functions which certain parts of the population of a society perform, and which are considered essential for the existence of the society, *institutions*. This term is still widely used. Spencer listed six institutions which he found in all societies: two of them, ceremonial and professional, are now usually left out, but the other four—domestic, industrial, political, and ecclesiastical—are listed in most present textbooks, though under somewhat different names. Other institutions have been added in recent times by such authors as Joyce O. Hertzler, Lloyd Vernon Ballard, Constantine Panunzio. Indeed, in one way or another, all the main components of culture have been included under the concept of institution.

3. CAN SOCIETIES, AS DEFINED BY NINETEENTH-CENTURY SOCIOLOGISTS AND THEIR FOLLOWERS, BE CLASSIFIED?

If sociology is a science of society in the sense in which this term has been used by most sociologists, then the primary task of sociologists is to develop a *taxonomy*, or systematic classification of societies, for all other sociological generalizations must depend upon it. This is what biologists have been doing. They achieved a systematic classification of organisms which enabled them to reach other kinds of generalizations: causal, about changes in organisms; functional, about relationships between organisms and their environment; ontogenetic, about the growth of individual organisms; phylogenetic, about the evolution of new varieties of organisms.

Spencer's is still the only consistent attempt to develop such a taxonomy. He used the evolutionary approach, borrowed from biologists. According to him, all societies, like all organisms, are products of evolution, and evolution follows the same universal laws. Every society can be classified as representing a certain stage of social evolution. Although this theory has been invalidated by factual evidence, no other systematic classification of societies has been substituted. On the contrary, the more thorough the study of particular societies, the more obvious the impossibility of developing any systematic classification of all of them. For the total life of the people who participate in a society depends upon many factors, natural and cultural.

First, since every society occupies a certain territory, the lives of its participants depend in considerable measure upon the size of the territory and the geographic conditions under which they live. These not only differ from society to society, but change considerably in the course of time. A few examples will illustrate this. Compare, for instance, the present size of the territory of China with that of Luxemburg, or the geographic conditions of Brazil, Saudi Arabia, and Finland. Consider the change in size of the Roman Republic from the fifth to the first century B.C., or that of Russia from the fifteenth to the end of the nineteenth century A.D. Review the changes which occurred during the last century and a half in the geographic distribution of the population of the United States and the environmental conditions under which the people in its many sections have been living.

Secondly, societies differ in the number and demographic composition of their populations. Manifestly, a tribal society with less than a thousand people is unlike a society of more than a hundred million. A society composed of relatively homogeneous people who for generations did not mix with outsiders, be it small, like many Melanesian or Amerindian tribes, or large, like the eighteenth-century Japanese society, is difficult to compare with a heterogeneous society composed of peoples of many different origins, like the Roman Empire, the United States, or the Soviet Union.

Political differences are also obvious. A modern society, with a highly complex and specialized governmental organization, is hardly comparable with a primitive society where political control is in the hands of a small group of heads of clans or large families, under the leadership of a chief. A society where a totalitarian regime tries to control the entire life of its members is different from a democratic society where the functions of the government are limited and controlled by the people. Furthermore, a number of smaller political societies with separate governments can be integrated into one. This is well exemplified by the history of the Roman Empire, of the Ottoman Empire, of Austria under the

Hapsburgs, of Russia from the fourteenth to the twentieth century, and of modern Italy and Germany during the nineteenth century.

On the other hand, some large societies may be again subdivided into separate smaller societies, like the Roman Empire, the Ottoman Empire, colonial Spain, and Austria. Some societies may even cease to exist in the political sense, like the Polish society, which was divided in 1795 between Russia, Prussia, and Austria, but later—in 1918—began to exist again.

Cultural differences are many, and they do not coincide with territorial, demographic, or political boundaries. A society whose members use a written language differs considerably from one where only oral language is used. Obviously societies with diverse religions also vary. Well known are the differences between societies with highly developed machine industries and those in which handiwork is the only method of technical production. A society where considerable scientific research is carried on by intellectual leaders certainly differs from one without scientific research. Societies where the young generation acquires knowledge in schools on all levels, from the primary grades to universities, manifestly differ from societies where no schools exist.

Furthermore, the same language may be used in several political societies, e.g., Italian during the seventeenth and eighteenth centuries in all states within the Italian peninsula; English in Great Britain, the United States, and Ireland; Spanish in Spain and Latin America. On the other hand, within the same political society many languages may be found: more than a hundred in Russia, more than twenty written languages and several hundred local dialects in India, and at least forty languages in the United States among the immigrants. The same holds true of religions: Islam is shared by ten political societies; Roman Catholicism is the dominant religion in more than twenty-five societies, and one of the several religions in most of the others; while Judaism dominates one, but exists in many others. A society with only one well-integrated religion differs considerably from a society where, as in the United

States, nearly two hundred and fifty separate and distinct religions coexist. And every one of these components of culture undergoes some changes in particular societies, which may be variously connected or hardly connected at all with territorial, demographic, or political changes.

In view of the vast diversity of natural backgrounds, political organizations, and cultural components of particular societies, the only generally recognized distinction now made is that between small, primitive, or preliterate societies and large, civilized, literate societies. Students are coming to the conclusion that each society, viewed as a whole, is unique, although they try to define certain types which particular societies approximate in various degrees. Thus, Ruth Benedict distinguished two opposite types of preliterate societies and an intermediary type which did not fit into either. Toynbee drew a few rather vague general conclusions about civilized societies from a comparative survey of twenty-one civilizations. Howard Becker tries to divide societies into a number of types distinguished by different combinations of certain basic characteristics. This is quite far from the ambitious generalizations of Spencer and his followers, and farther still from the systematic taxonomies developed by biologists and chemists.

4. Sociology as the Science of Man

Another conception of sociology, radically opposed to the one promulgated by Comte, started at the initiative of biologists and psychologists, who objected to the insufficient attention which sociologists were paying to the human individual. Their objection was in some measure justified. Comte in his classification of sciences omitted psychology altogether; Spencer considered individual biology and psychology essential only at the earliest stage of social evolution, before society fully developed. Durkheim and his followers thought that a man's psychological life was entirely a product of society. Whereas, according to the opposite view, only human individuals really exist, society as a system of institutions being merely an arbitrary construct of philosophers. Thus, a human collectivity is an aggregate of human beings and must be explained by the nature of those beings, or—to use a popular term—by human nature. The foundation of sociology is the biopsychological study of man as an entity, since the common nature of human beings requires and conditions their participation in collectivities, and what these collectivities are depends on the nature of their participants.

In this respect, human beings resemble many animals; consequently, studies of animal "societies" were made in the expectation that they would provide a key for understanding human societies. The biological interdependence between human individuals, so far as the satisfaction of their basic needs is concerned, led to the concept of *symbiosis* and, more recently, to the development of human ecology. Many psychologists used for a long time the concept of biologically rooted "instincts" as basic forces which make human individuals live together. Later, behaviorism resulted in a complete rejection not only of societies in Comte's sense, but of human groups in general as superindividual realities; since only individuals exist, their aggregates exist only as combinations of mutual responses to mutual stimuli. Even some of the psychologists who do not try to reduce human psychology to human biology claim that, inasmuch as society is produced and maintained by its individual participants, a thorough knowledge of psychology is not only essential, but sufficient to explain its existence.

But individualism, whether biological, psychological, or a combination of both, is also a failure. It cannot account for the existence of the common culture shared by participants in a collectivity, on which the life of every individual as an organism, as well as his psychological development, depends; nor for the vast diversity of cultures, which is obviously incompatible with the doctrine of the universal psychological similarity of human nature; nor for the continuous historical growth of new cultures, while the biological nature of the *genus homo* remains fundamentally unchanged. However, the need to investigate individuals cannot be ignored, even by sociologists.

5. Sociology as the Science of Social Interaction

A third, relatively new conception of the task of sociology is much less ambitious than the other two. Instead of beginning with the assumption that the total life of the people who compose a territorially circumscribed, politically organized society is integrated, or with the assumption that every human collectivity is merely a combination of individual human beings of an essentially similar nature, sociologists limit their task to comparative studies of certain specific phenomena which are observable in many diverse collectivities and yet are not reducible to human biology or psychology.

Sociologists are not the first or the only ones who find specialization necessary for scientific purposes. Other scientists have specialized in comparative studies of such culturally patterned activities as technical production, exchange and consumption of technical products, religious cultus of supernatural beings, speaking a language, creating works of literature, art, music, philosophic or scientific knowledge. These cultural scientists have discovered that the specific activities which they investigate, though they may differ in various collectivities or societies and change in the course of time, manifest enough fundamental similarity to make generalizations possible.

Obviously a sociologist cannot compete with those specialists in their respective realms, but at best learn some of the more important results which they have achieved. Can he contribute something original to human knowledge? Quite a few modern sociologists have been concerned with this problem—Tarde, Simmel, Max Weber, Cooley, von Wiese, Ross, Mead, and myself. Though their solutions differ in some respects, they have found one kind of human actions which have not been adequately investigated either by psychologists or specialists in the various realms of culture. These actions have been called *social*. Most of them are also culturally patterned and supposed to follow certain standards and norms. But the objects with which they deal are not economic values, or technical instruments and products, or divine beings, or works of art and literature, or philosophic and scientific ideas: They are *men*.

Some of these actions deal with human individuals, others with human groups; and a social action may be performed individually or collectively. For instance, a minister of religion may try to convert an individual sinner, or preach to a whole congregation so as to make all its participants repent their sins. On the other hand, the congregation as a whole pays the minister's salary and may try to influence the local Board of Education so as to have religion taught in the public schools.

Now, men as objects of actions differ fundamentally from all other objects, in that they are also conscious agents. They experience and evaluate the men who act upon them, and perform or tend to perform actions of their own in consequence of the actions to which they have been subjected. In other words, human agents not only act upon others, but *interact* with others. Therefore, quite a few sociologists consider that the main task of sociology is to investigate such interactions. Some of them define sociology as the science of human relations, or social relations, in the sense of relations between interacting human individuals or groups.

Of course, studies of social actions and of relations in this sense are not new, but date back as far as three thousand years ago. The same may be said about studies of animals, plants, or stars. What is new, is the consistent effort to make such studies scientific according to modern conceptions of science. This need not imply that the knowledge gathered in the past is altogether unreliable, only that it must be tested by scientific standards. Thus, we may say that sociological knowledge, as here defined, just like zoological, botanical, or astronomical knowledge, has been slowly growing for centuries.

Of course, there are important differences in the ways human agents interact. Popularly speaking, what any one of them is doing to another may be "good," "helpful," "desirable," or "bad," "harmful," "undesirable" from the other's point of view. We shall call the first kind of interaction social *cooperation*; the second kind, social *conflict*.

Social thinkers have devoted more attention to social conflict than to social cooperation. Thus, among the most important works of Greek and Roman historians are accounts of various wars: Herodotus studied the Greco-Persian War, Thucydides the Peloponnesian War, Caesar the Gallic War and the Civil War. And, to this very day, wars are a matter of primary interest to historians and contemporary observers. Marx and his followers believed class conflicts to be the most influential social forces in human history; and other social philosophers consider interindividual conflict the primary and universal kind of human interaction. Hobbes, for instance, stated that originally "Man is a wolf to man." Social Darwinists insisted that struggle for survival is a universal characteristic of the human species, just as of other animal species. Even quite recently, some sociologists formulated a general theory that interhuman relations begin with competition, result in conflict, gradually lead to accommodation (which limits conflict), and, last of all, to assimilation (which implies full cooperation). The study of crime, or criminology, still remains one of the most popular branches of sociology.

Many other thinkers, however, have given priority to the study of cooperation. At first they did so for ethical reasons—e.g., Plato, Aristotle, the Stoics, the Epicureans, Confucius and his followers, and quite a few religious thinkers, Buddhists and Christians. In modern times, thinkers have found objective reasons for this priority, inasmuch as cooperation among the participants in a human collectivity is essential for its very existence. Moreover, investigation of the origin of interindividual conflicts indicates that many of them are due to external influences which disturb such cooperation as already existed, while intergroup conflict presupposes close cooperation within each conflicting group. This means that, without adequate knowledge of social cooperation, no scientific generalizations about social conflict are possible.

We shall try to show in this work that investigation of social cooperation is indeed the primary task of sociology; investigation of social conflict, a secondary task.

6. SOCIAL COOPERATION AND SOCIAL SYSTEMS

Social cooperation may be carried on by two individuals—e.g., two lovers, two friends, two business partners—and by thousands—e.g., the managers and workers in an automobile factory or faculty members, students, and nonacademic employees of a modern state university. It may last a few hours or many years. It can include relatively similar actions or widely diversified, specialized actions. In any case, however, the cooperation is effective in so far as those who participate in it conform with certain social standards and norms. It presupposes that every participant will evaluate positively those fellow participants with whom he interacts, that he will do something which contributes to what the others are doing, and refrain from doing anything which might disturb actions of the others. This means that the actions of cooperating individuals are *interdependent* and *organized* in such a way as to enable them altogether to achieve results which are expected to be valuable to all of them.

We have called such an organized combination of actions of cooperating agents a *social system*. This term was introduced by Spencer, who considered society as a whole to be a system. And he pointed out that "A society in the sociological sense is formed only when . . . there is cooperation. . . . Cooperation . . . is at once that which cannot exist without a society and that for which society exists." And cooperation implies organization.

While, as we have noticed, the Spencerian concept of society—in the sense of the totality of people inhabiting a circumscribed territory, politically organized, and sharing an integrated, institutionalized culture—has proved scientifically unproductive, it cannot be denied that the inhabitants of every large territory form many distinct *limited* social systems of various size, duration, and complexity, each based on organized cooperation. But the old problem still remains: Are those numerous and diverse social systems components of a much larger, more inclusive system, whether called society or by some other name?

Two different approaches to this problem have been used. Some sociologists start with the hypothetic theory that such an inclusive system does exist; they define it and try to prove their theory by showing that all the multiple smaller systems are subordinated to this one larger system. Unfortunately, they have not reached any general agreement as to the nature of the larger system. For instance, according to some theorists, every society has an economic system which dominates all the other systems; the antithesis between capitalistic and communistic societies is based on this theory. Certain theorists postulate, instead—as most classical thinkers did—that every society has a political system to which all other systems (including the economic ones) are subordinated: This is the main basis of the well-known distinction between totalitarian and democratic societies. A few theorists assume the existence of a dominant ethical system or *ethos*, and define every society according to its ethos.

Other sociologists, however, are now using what may be considered a strictly inductive approach. Instead of starting with the study of what is supposed to be the dominant, most inclusive system, they begin with a comparative study of various relatively small and simple systems, and then proceed to investigate their factual integration into increasingly large and complex systems. Although this approach is rather slow and requires a vast amount of empirical research, it has proved highly productive from the scientific point of view. Consequently, it will be used throughout this work.

We may mention right here that we shall begin with a study of the systems of cooperative interaction between two individuals, popularly called *social relations* or *interpersonal relations*; investigate the integration of such relations into *social roles*, i.e., systems of cooperative interaction between a particular individual and several others; go on to the integration of the social roles performed by a number of individuals into organized *social groups*; and, finally, consider the integration of many diverse social groups, not into one kind of society, but into several different kinds of *societies*.

Many social systems, large and small, have already been studied by historians, political scientists, ethnologists, cultural anthropologists, and sociologists in various human collectivities, past and present, throughout the world. Some investigators have tried to reach generalizations about them: divide them into classes and subclasses, find causal laws of changes which they undergo, discover the connections between them, and explain the origin and spread of new varieties of systems. Serious obstacles, however, have impeded the development of a general sociological theory based upon these studies: lack of scientific objectivity, superficial observations, practical difficulties in obtaining reliable information, *a priori* doctrines which make investigators ignore data and facts that do not confirm their doctrines, the use of defective methods in comparative analysis, tendencies to reach sweeping generalizations without testing them by factual evidence. Nonetheless, as we shall see, considerable scientific progress has been achieved.

CHAPTER 2

THE FIELDS OF SOCIOLOGICAL RESEARCH

1. THE CONCEPT OF FIELD OF RESEARCH

How do the sociologists who specialize in the study of social interaction obtain the factual evidence upon which their theories are based?

Social interaction always occurs in the space in which the people who interact are located. This is obvious when the interaction is physical and consists in outward behavior of the agents which affects their bodies or some material objects they are using; but it is also true when it is intellectual, or mental, and consists in symbolic communication of ideas which influence their attitudes and actions. Thus social interaction is in some degree conditioned by spatial proximity. It is apt to occur more frequently and repeatedly among people within a relatively small area who can easily meet face-to-face, see and hear one another, than among people scattered over a large area where they rarely meet. Of course, with the growth of rapid transportation of men and material objects and the development of such means of communication as writing, printing, the telegraph, the telephone, radio, and television, the size of the area within which people can frequently and regularly interact has been steadily increasing. But even now there are geographical limits beyond which regular social interaction is quite scarce.

Consequently, many sociologists nowadays select for investigation collectivities of people located in definite spatial areas where they expect to find a considerable amount of social interaction. This kind of investigation is often called *field research*. The term research means that investigators are searching, trying to discover some data and facts hitherto unobserved or inadequately observed, and intend to test their conclusions by further observation. "Field" means the area within which research in this sense is carried on.

Such a choice of spatial areas for purposes of research is nothing new. For some time natural scientists have been making a similar choice, sometimes calling the area selected a field. Thus, geologists investigated sections of the surface of the earth which they believed had not yet been thoroughly studied, and tried—often successfully—to find something new within each of these sections. More recently, oceanographers studied certain parts of the oceans and made important discoveries. Botanists and zoologists went into relatively unexplored regions of Africa, South America, Asia, the Arctic, and the Antarctic, and actually discovered hitherto unknown varieties of plants and animals. Paleontologists selected certain limited areas, dug under the surface, and frequently found fossil remnants of now extinct forms of life.

We shall use the term *fields of sociological research* to denote all those spatial areas within which sociologists have investigated or are investigating social interaction. Unfortunately, the word field has been used by some social thinkers in a figurative sense, to denote a specific kind of *data* which scientists study, wherever they may be found, rather than an area where many different kinds of data coexist. We see no justification for this use. A zoologist would hardly call all insects, wherever they live, a field of zoology; for him, they constitute an object-matter of entomology as a branch of zoology. Just so, crimes as a distinct kind of social phenomena are not a field, but an object-matter of criminology as a branch of sociology.

Now, spatial areas where scientific research goes on—whether called fields or something else—can differ widely in size. For instance, botanical research is carried on not only in those rather large unexplored geographical areas mentioned above, but also in such small fields as agricultural plots, woods, gardens, even sections of a hothouse, selected and circumscribed for purposes of observation and experimentation. On the other hand, almost the whole surface of the globe can be considered the field of research for botanists who investigate those elementary forms of plant life which are not limited to particular areas, but may be found wherever environmental conditions make their survival possible.

The same holds true of sociology. The fields of sociological research also differ much in geographic size, in the number of people included within them, and in the multiplicity and diversity of active relationships among these people. Such differences are important, for—as we shall see—an adequate knowledge of some kinds of organized social interaction can be gained only by methodical studies of human collectivities which fall within fields of a certain limited size.

We shall survey briefly the main fields of sociological research, from the smallest to the largest.

2. COLLECTIVE MEETING PLACES

Studies of local gatherings or collective meetings are among the oldest and most popular. For, when a number of people meet together in the same place for a shorter or longer period, this usually (though not always) means that they have some common purpose. Investigators who are interested in this purpose can try to discover what they are doing or intend to do. Moreover, a meeting, while it is going on, is accessible to direct observation, in so far as an observer can see the people, notice their movements, hear and understand their oral communications.

Thus, classical thinkers were interested in observing political meetings. The Greek *agora* and the Roman *forum*, where people congregated for political discussions and collective activities, were well-known fields of observation. In modern times, meetings of legislators in state buildings, of political party leaders in selected centers, and of diplomatic sets in capitals have been observed in detail, either by certain participants or by outsiders allowed to witness them. For centuries, the meetings of royal and princely courts were closely observed, since whatever was going on between participants in a court could influence the political functioning of the state.

Also from classical antiquity on, battlefields were subjected to thorough investigation, mainly for political reasons. A battle could be an event of crucial significance for a state, affecting its structure, functioning, expansion or reduction, perhaps its very existence. Obviously, military tacticians were always interested in observing present battles and reconstructing past ones. Ancient historians, beginning with Thucydides, devised effective methods of collecting results of the observation of several competent, independent witnesses, combining them into a composite picture of a certain battle as a process of collective interaction. In modern times, when battles often include hundreds of thousands of participants, extend over large areas, and last for lengthy periods, direct observation must generally be supplemented by other sources of knowledge.

Public mass performances, occurring in limited spatial areas and within limited time periods, have also interested social observers. Some of these were considered significant as manifestations of social unity and order, such as triumphant marches of victorious armies, city festivals, and royal coronations. Other mass gatherings—crowds and active mobs—on the contrary assumed importance because of their disturbing effect on existing order. Ancient political scientists observed these gatherings, but only toward the end of the nineteenth century was systematic investigation initiated by some sociologists (Tarde and Le Bon).

Observation of theatrical gatherings, including actors and audiences, is also rather old, and continues to this day. Meetings of intellectuals for the purpose of philosophic or scientific discussion began to be described by Plato; and in modern times, we find numerous descriptions of scientific congresses. Religious meetings have for a long time been a matter of considerable interest, but impartial observation was at first rather rare. When the observer was a fellow believer, he noticed only what was important from the point of view of his religion, whereas unbelievers were seldom admitted. Only during the last seventy-five years have objective studies of religious meetings developed—e.g., studies of religious revivals, of public festivals, and of the conduct of participants in the course of church ceremonies.

From the fifteenth century on, many companionate meetings of guests in the residences of upper-class hosts have been observed and described in great detail.

No doubt many of these studies of social interaction among people congregating in certain places have agglomerated a considerable amount of reliable information which can be used for sociological hypotheses. Only in recent times, however, did some sociologists and social psychologists develop exact scientific methods for carrying on such studies, following the model of research used by biologists and physical scientists. In accordance with this model, the size of the field of research must be determined by the capacity of the investigator to observe and define exactly all the relevant facts occurring during a certain period of time and to check the results of his study by repeated observation. Furthermore, the field should be, as far as possible, *closed*, i.e., isolated from the outside world in order to exclude all kinds of unobservable and unpredictable influences. And, finally, the investigator should have the opportunity of *experimenting*, introducing certain changes and observing their consequences. In short, the field should be under the control of the investigator, like a physical laboratory or a small botanical plot.

Among the fields that approximately satisfy these requirements we may mention camps of various kinds—summer camps, trailer camps, small military camps; groups of workers in separate divisions of an industrial plant; and especially groups of children in nurseries, kindergartens, and primary schools. Indeed, a small educational grouping of children seems most satisfactory from the methodical point of view, for it meets periodically under conditions which can be controlled; it is spatially isolated during definite periods; its participants can be subjected to various experiments; moreover, techniques of observation have been devised so that the children are unaware of being observed and consequently unaffected by observation.

Recently, closed, controlled fields have been formed by investigators exclusively for the purpose of carrying on specific experiments. For instance, in order to ascertain by direct observation the relationships between leaders and followers, or the way in which social groups perform certain collective activities, college instructors initiate various kinds of interaction among small sets of college students who meet apart from the total college population.

Yet, observations within such small fields are never self-sufficient. For the individuals who participate in a political meeting, in a battle, in a mob, in a companionate upper-class entertainment, in a religious ceremony or revival, in a military camp, kindergarten, or experimental group performance are also participating or have been participating in various social systems outside of this field. In so far as, in interacting with one another, they follow certain standards and norms, they must have learned most of these before they congregated; and if, during the congregation, they learn something new, this means that some other participants in the congregation who learned it before have transmitted it to them. The very fact that an observer can control a social field has important sociological implications; for he has obtained control only because he is a participant in some influential social system or systems, and his investigation is therefore recognized by other participants as positively significant.

For instance, an investigation of a children's grouping in a kindergarten or school implies that the investigator has been admitted as a participant into a socially ordered system of educational interaction. Observations carried on in a college class or psychological laboratory presuppose the existence of the college as a social system, with an order of its own in which both the investigator and the subjects of his investigation participate. The existence of a wide and complex social order is a necessary condition of controlled observation in a summer camp, a military barracks, or a social work center. And when an observer for experimental purposes begins to function as organizer and leader, the effectiveness of his experiment depends upon the pattern of leadership which his followers, as a consequence of their previous participation in social life, have been prepared to accept.

Thus, what an observer of the interactions of people congregated in a certain place will discover depends on how much he already knows about their cultural background and the standards and norms with which they have learned to conform. If he knows little, many of their actions will be to him inexplicable and unpredictable: for instance, he cannot explain or predict the actions of participants in a religious ceremony, if the religion which these participants share is unfamiliar to him. During his observation, he can discover something, indeed; but to gain full knowledge, he must after the ceremony spend a long time investigating the standards and norms of the believers and the social organization of the group of which they are members. Whereas, if the investigator knows or thinks he knows all that is essential about the cultural background of the people who congregate, occasionally or periodically, in a certain place, then what he aims to discover during his observation is how or why individuals who are supposed to follow the same cultural standards and norms differ in their actual conduct. And this is a psychological, rather than a sociological, problem.

It is significant, therefore, that most of the conclusions drawn by modern investigators from the observation of gatherings of people are classified under psychology or social psychology. Thus, studies of crowds or mobs led to a general theory called "psychology of crowds." Recent studies of the behavior of children in nurseries, kindergartens, and schools are included under the heading "experimental social psychology." Most of the experiments in leadership and group cooperation among college students have been initiated by psychologists.

The main advantage of such studies from the sociological point of view is that they enable investigators to measure the influence of certain psychological factors upon social cooperation. For instance, this is what sociometrists, following the initiative of Moreno, are doing.

3. Community Habitats

Much more productive scientifically, because resulting in the discovery of many new social systems, have been the studies of social interaction between participants in *communities*.

We call a community any human collectivity which has the following characteristics:

(a) The people who compose it live within a separate area, large enough to include a considerable number of inhabitants, but not too large to prevent each one from meeting at least occasionally every other inhabitant and identifying him personally. Such an area is the common *habitat* of these people.

(b) It is composed of individuals of both sexes and of various age levels; and in the course of its duration its composition changes through births and deaths.

(c) It obtains the necessary means of subsistence by the active efforts of its own participants.

(d) Its participants have a common culture, speak the same language, accept the same standards of values and norms of conduct.

(e) Its participants are conscious of belonging to it, in contrast with the territorial "outsiders" and cultural strangers who do not belong.

Numerous human collectivities possess these characteristics in various degrees, though differing in other respects. We must distinguish two main types of communities, the "primitive," or "tribal," and the "rural." The term community was originally applied to only the second type; the first was usually termed a society. And yet, from the point of view of sociological research, both types are sufficiently similar to be included under the concept of community. Moreover, during the last hundred years, a new type of community has emerged, due to purposive efforts of social leaders. It might be called a *planned* community.

Any sociological investigator who visits the habitat of the people constituting a community, as above defined, and stays long enough to observe many cases of interaction between particular inhabitants can gradually discover whatever social systems are maintained by them and eventually also what kinds of social conflicts occur among them, especially if he has an opportunity to communicate with them, so as to obtain adequate information about the standards and norms with which they are expected to conform. Nonetheless, it took centuries to develop adequate scientific studies of tribal communities, on the one hand, and of rural communities, on the other hand.

A tribal community differs from others in two important respects. In the first place, its solidarity and its separation from outsiders and strangers is based on the belief that all its participants, and only they, are descended from the same distant ancestors and constitute a tribe in the sense of a united, exclusive hereditary group. This belief in common descent has in the course of history been accepted by hundreds of thousands, even millions, of people. Originally, however, it applied only to a numerically limited collectivity of people, among whom social cooperation had been going on for generations, and where every living participant could be identified as a descendant of predecessors who had been active, solidary participants during their lives. A tentative statistical survey of tribal communities, based on information gathered during the seventeenth, eighteenth, and nineteenth centuries, indicates that few of them numbered more than three thousand people, and many of them less than a thousand.

In the second place, the majority of those tribal communities which have been investigated were in the past, and a few of them still are, politically independent, not subjected to the rule of any larger state. This was due to the fact that the areas which they inhabited were distant from the political centers of powerful governments, difficult to reach, or even unknown. Even when, from the fifteenth century on, geographic explorers discovered such territories, their governments often showed no interest in them, for they seemed politically and economically useless—as, e.g., the Arctic territories of Asia and America or the territory of Central Australia. As late as the beginning of this century some areas of Central Africa and South America were still beyond the active rule of any modern government. Even after such a rule had been assumed, the tribal communities inhabiting these areas sometimes preserved a certain degree of social autonomy.

Now, every independent tribal community, living within a

limited area, controls this area. Even if some of them migrated from one area to another, after migration they tried to assume control of the new habitat and to settle there permanently.

Often the participants in a tribal community occupied several durable village centers within the area controlled by the community as a whole. But sometimes they divided into a number of smaller groups which scattered over the area and moved frequently from place to place; such groups, being interconnected by bonds of tribal solidarity, periodically congregated in some local center for a few days or even weeks. This is, for instance, what Australian tribes and some Amerindian tribes regularly did. And the whole habitat of a tribal community was in most cases separated from the habitats of other tribal communities by definite boundaries which could be crossed only under certain conditions. Thus, interaction between participants in a community and participants in other communities was limited, and every community remained rather self-sufficient socially. An investigator could, therefore, ascertain what kinds of social cooperation existed among its members without having to study other human collectivities.

This does not mean, however, that the community was *culturally* isolated. Some cultural products and patterns spread in the course of time from one community to another by what anthropologists call "cultural diffusion." We shall later be concerned with the territorial expansion of numerically growing tribes through conquest and through voluntary unification with neighboring tribes.

Certain Greek and Roman thinkers were interested in the contemporary tribal communities which lay outside the borders of politically organized societies, but they did little first-hand research of their own and mainly collected all kinds of indirect information. Along with European exploration of distant lands and consequent colonial expansion, interest in tribal communities steadily increased. At first, knowledge about them was quite inadequate; geographic explorers and travelers had only brief contacts with them, and the conclusions they drew about their life and culture were based on very superficial observations. Later, closer and more lasting contacts were established, resulting in increasingly detailed factual information. But those who initiated and carried on such contacts were traders, missionaries, colonists, governmental agents and administrators whose interests were (and still are) practical rather than theoretic. Their observations and conclusions were therefore biased. A familiar manifestation of this bias is the common name "savages," which is persistently and popularly applied to all inhabitants of tribal areas, in contrast with the "civilized" invaders who entered their habitat and assumed control of their lives.

When anthropologists and, later, sociologists began to develop general theories of lower, or primitive, societies, they had to use such materials as were available, and did use both the superficial descriptions of travelers and the more thorough, but seldom unprejudiced, information gathered by practical agents. But, as their theories were intended to be scientific, these authors and critics did their best to estimate the reliability of the materials they used. Under their influence, subsequent investigations of tribal communities tended to conform more and more with scientific standards; and their productivity increased, as the investigators became aware of the vast cultural diversity of tribal communities.

At first, anthropologists classified them either by the way in which the participants acquired their means of subsistence (e.g., by hunting, pastoral, and agricultural activities) or by their racial traits (e.g., Negro, Mongolian, Amerindian). Investigators assumed in advance that any particular community which they approached would prove to be essentially like others of the same class. Such assumptions frequently impeded new discoveries. Gradually, however, investigators who spent long periods of time in close contact with the people living in tribal habitats learned to subject their preconceptions to methodical doubt and to search for the unexpected. Each tribal community was then approached, not as a particular variant of a class already known, but as a field of research still largely unknown. Consequently, during the last half century students of tribal communities (most of which were already familiar to travelers, geographers, merchants, missionaries, and administrators) made more new discoveries than had been made during the whole period of colonial expansion. By now, as a result both of this research and of the gradual disintegration of original tribal cultures, these fields are becoming gradually exhausted, though considerable possibilities still remain.

Rural communities, unlike tribal communities, are not politically independent or culturally exotic in the sense of being outside the realm of modern civilizations. Their habitats are located within territories of large organized states, and they are subjected to some influences from highly developed literary cultures, religious and secular. Their investigation was initiated, on the one hand, by folklorists, who were interested in the old traditional cultures or folk cultures which had survived in certain areas, in spite of the influence of modern literary cultures, and, on the other hand, by social thinkers who were interested in local, especially agricultural communities which remained for centuries socially integrated and partly separated from one another, in spite of the unifying power of a state government.

The folklore, which started in the second half of the eighteenth century, was at first as much a collector's hobby as a scientific study. Folklorists were seeking for curious, peculiar cultural phenomena, such as were found mostly in rural areas. They collected tales, legends, myths, poems, songs, musical tunes, dances, products of decorative art, costumes, and technical implements. They described ceremonial customs, magical practices, and technical performances.

The expansion of this interest, however, coincided with the growth of cultural nationalism, which tended to unify socially all the people who spoke dialectical variants of the same language— French, English, German, Italian, Polish, or Russian—and who presumably shared other essential components of the same culture. Ideological leaders of cultural nationalism assumed that cultural differences among these people—class and occupational differences, urban-rural and regional differences—were later products of secondary importance, and that their cultural similarity was due to the fact that most, if not all, of them were descendants of an essentially homogeneous ethnic group (often called a tribe). The data which folklorists collected apparently had their roots in a distant past and could be considered survivals of the original cultural products and patterns which the given *ethnic group* had shared in earlier stages of its history. Folklore became, thus, partly merged with ethnography.

During the nineteenth century, increasing thoroughness of observation and exactness of comparison resulted in a gradual narrowing down of fields of ethnographic research. Sweeping generalizations about common and distinctive ethnic patterns of original French, German, Anglo-Saxon, Italian, or Polish culture gave way to specialized studies of traditional regional cultures. For instance, about twenty different regional cultures were distinguished in France, more in Germany and in Italy.

The final stage was reached when ethnographers, without ceasing their regional studies, began to investigate traditional folk cultures as they functioned within relatively small old local collectivities comprising at most several neighboring villages and hamlets, sometimes only one large village or a small town with its rural environment. The people of such a local collectivity usually manifested some degree of social solidarity and separateness from the outside world, the more so the better preserved and integrated their traditional culture; for even seemingly insignificant cultural differences between themselves and the inhabitants of more distant areas appeared important to them. And the ethnographers who studied cultural survivals within such a collectivity usually found that many of them were still functioning vitally, affecting the active life of the people, even when the latter already participated in some measure in political, religious, and economic systems of the larger modern society within whose boundaries their small area was located. Gradually during this century ethnologists became aware that the old approach, which consisted in collecting and classifying products and patterns included under the general category of folk culture, was entirely inadequate for understanding the significance which these products and patterns have for the social life of the people who preserve and use them. This awareness opened the way for new sociological research which has already led to many unexpected discoveries.

The second line of intellectual interest which led to methodical investigation of local collectivities or communities was initiated by historians and political scientists. The very term community seems to have originated in studies of Western medieval village communities, which were characterized by common possession and use of certain pieces of land, a large amount of common economic control and cooperation, and some degree of administrative autonomy. Analogous communities were found in Eastern Slavonic countries, in India, and in China. Some administrative autonomy still survives in the French *commune*, the Germanic *Gemeinde*, the Polish *gmina*, the Anglo-American township. Social historians and contemporary observers gradually found that economic cooperation and administrative autonomy were often only partial manifestations rooted in the common folk culture which ethnographers had discovered. Most of the participants were born within the habitat of the community and brought up to share this culture; and the personal life of every participant was closely intertwined with the personal lives of others.

When colonial expansion started, colonists who brought with them the same traditional culture usually tried to settle in spatial proximity and gradually formed a more or less integrated, solidary community. Thousands of such immigrant communities with distinct cultures were founded in rural areas of the United States, Canada, and Brazil, and many of them still survive. Thus, rural communities with distinct folk cultures have proved rich fields of sociological research.

With the development of industry, trade, and transportation, changes occurred in rural communities which attracted considerable attention from social thinkers. On the one hand, the size of communities increased when several smaller communities became socially centered around the same town. On the other hand, however, the population in many rural areas was becoming disintegrated, losing its traditional unity, and lagging culturally behind the populations of other areas. Social leaders and reformers tried to counteract this disintegration and to promote cultural progress by starting a new, more efficient community organization and inducing the people to participate in it. This ethical interest contributed to the development of *rural sociology* as a discipline which investigates not only the old traditional type, but also the new type of *planfully* organized communities.

4. CITIES AS FIELDS OF RESEARCH

Cities have always attracted more attention from social thinkers than tribal or rural communities, for the obvious reason that all culture above the preliterate level, popularly called "civilization," grew up in cities.

Thus, the political organization of a city always was, and still is, much more complex than that of a tribal or rural community, and was usually formalized in a system of legal norms; indeed, the term politics is derived from the Greek term *polis*, which means city. Ceremonial religious cultus in temples controlled by groups of priests developed fully in cities. Writing was invented in cities, mostly by priests; and, until recent times, when literary education spread into rural areas, all literature, sacred and secular, was created by writers who learned it in cities. The specialized craftsmanship developed in cities went far beyond the rural craftsmanship, and so did the fine arts. Only in cities could large-scale trade and banking be organized, and most of the machine industry was invented and became concentrated in cities. All the sciences grew in urban centers; and the transmission of literary culture and scientific knowledge to the young generation by organized school education started and expanded in cities.

Obviously, therefore, investigations of civilization, past and present, have to study the functions of those inhabitants of cities who actively participated or are participating in the various realms of culture—politics, law, religion, literature, craftsmanship, art, trade, banking, industry, science, and education.

The early authors of works about cities did not do much objective research. When they described their own cities, they thought that they already knew everything essential about them. When they visited other cities, they tried to learn what seemed important from the point of view of their own interests. Since most Greek and Roman thinkers were primarily interested in political organization, this is what they investigated—typically Aristotle, who studied the political constitutions of the Greek cities. Later, throughout centuries, the politicians who visited capital cities, especially the foreign envoys, also concentrated on the study of governmental groups. Traveling merchants were mostly interested in the groups which dominated the economy of the cities they visited. Traveling aristocrats described in detail the life of the upper urban classes, and little else. Scholars, scientists, men of letters, and artists established contacts with local associations of specialists in their respective realms of culture.

Only in recent times did an objective, scientific approach to cities begin. It was started by those historians who traced back the evolution of certain cities and compared their past with their present. However, a historian does not carry on firsthand observation of the lives of the people who inhabit a city; he relies on documentary evidence. Such evidence is of great importance for scientific purposes, but it is not a substitute for direct field research. This research was initiated by sociologists who, following the example of cultural anthropologists and students of rural communities, have been attempting to investigate all kinds of social interaction going on among the inhabitants of a city.

Obviously, this task is very difficult. It is undoubtedly possible for a sociologist with enough time and opportunity to study rather thoroughly the social life of inhabitants of a town with a population not exceeding two or three thousand, especially if he is familiar with the culture which they share. But in a modern city with a large population the stream of social intercourse among the inhabitants is so complex and rapid, their activities are so specialized, and the standards and norms which they follow so varying, that it is impossible for an individual investigator to cover such a wide field.

Consequently, this kind of research must be carried on cooperatively by a number of investigators for a long period of time. To mention a few well-known examples. The study of the city of Chicago, with a population of 400,000–500,000, initiated by Park and Burgess more than thirty-five years ago, is still going on under the guidance of professors of the University of Chicago, with the cooperation of numerous assistants and students; and new discoveries are being made all the time. The Lynds' cooperative investigation of Middletown, with 50,000 population, required a number of assistants; and after ten years it was resumed in order to ascertain the most important changes which had occurred during that time. The most systematic of all such studies—that of Yankee City, with only 18,000 population—initiated by W. Lloyd Warner (orginally a cultural anthropologist) with the cooperation of J. O. Lord and the help of many assistants, lasted for years.

The term *urban sociology*, coined to denote such studies, is often misunderstood. It does not mean a special division of sociology dealing with a definite category of social systems, like, for instance, sociology of the family, which specializes primarily (though not exclusively) in studies of families as groups composed of parents and children, or sociology of religion, whose main task is a comparative study of various kinds of religious associations, or industrial sociology, which investigates mainly the social organization of the workers and managers engaged in industrial production. For the city is not and never was a united social system. Only Plato, a philosopher, planned an integrated, perfectly organized city; and he was fully aware that no real city resembled it, though he hoped that eventually such a city would be created.

The common characteristic of all cities is the permanent agglomeration within a limited, circumscribed habitat of a population much more numerous than the people of a tribal or rural community, which might spread over an area of the same size; and this population represents all ages, diversified occupations, several social classes, and sometimes several different cultures. The preliminary task of urban sociologists is, therefore, to study the geographic location of the city, its inner spatial structure, the number, composition, and changes of its population, as well as the ecological distribution of its inhabitants within the urban area. But having done that, they treat the city not as an integrated whole, but as a limited field of research. They investigate various social roles in which inhabitants of the city are engaged—roles of craftsmen, industrial workers, managers, engineers, small and large merchants, bankers, physicians, pharmacists, priests, scientists, artists, teachers, journalists, publishers, politicians, policemen, etc. They study class gradations, class solidarity, and class conflict. They investigate the municipal government and its division, families, churches, schools, factories, department stores, labor unions, ethnic groups, various kinds of clubs, criminal gangs, boys' gangs, etc.

Such research has certainly resulted and will result in many valuable discoveries. In the first place, while cultural patterns of social cooperation in traditional communities are relatively stable, in cities they are continually changing. For instance, families in urban areas were found to differ more from the old type than rural families. Relations between social classes in cities have also been changing rapidly in recent times. Sociologists and social psychologists have observed that the total personal lives of individuals in a modern city are less integrated and more subject to unexpected change than the lives of participants in a tribal or rural community. Secondly, and this is even more important, as occupational specialization increases, new varieties of social roles evolve in the cities. Moreover, new kinds of social groups have been organized during the last hundred years and continue to be organized in cities.

5. METROPOLITAN REGIONS

However productive scientifically the investigation of cities, sociological research should not be confined to them. A city, even though spatially and demographically limited, is obviously not isolated socially. There are many connections between its inhabitants and the inhabitants of larger areas. Its study raises problems which can be solved only by carrying the investigation far beyond its spatial limits.

For a city is a social center whose influence extends at least over surrounding rural communities, usually also over more distant towns, frequently over other, less influential cities. The scope of this influence depends upon several factors: geographic location, means of transportation and communication available to inhabitants, size, cultural development, and social organization.

Many social thinkers have recognized the significance of this influence, for they found that the growth of cities, their cultural development, and their social expansion have resulted in the gradual unification of many small, separate communities into larger and more complex collectivities to which the term "society" is often applied. Take a well-known modern example. Within the vast territory which is now controlled by the government of the United States, the numerous rural communities and small towns which multiplied in the course of westward colonial expansion became integrated into what is called American society, in consequence of the formation, growth, and increasing influence of new cities.

Students of the city as a social center usually investigate that city which is most influential, as compared with other cities, within a certain territory. Such a dominant city was called by the Greeks a *metropolis*. The term originally meant "mother city," the city which gave birth to colonies inhabited by descendants of those citizens who had migrated into more or distant areas and settled there. But modern writers apply it to any powerful city which dominates a relatively large territory. Such a territory is sometimes called a *region*. The general term region, however, has several meanings: It is used in a different sense by students of so-called regional cultures, on the one hand, and by demographers and governmental statisticans, on the other hand. To avoid confusion, here we shall use exclusively the specific term *metropolitan region*. We define it as an area whose inhabitants are subjected to the influence of a city which functions as a metropolis in the sense of the *main center of urban culture* in that area. This influence varies in accordance with the cultural activities of which the metropolis is the center. What kind of influence and how wide the region of any particular city can be ascertained only by sociological investigation.

The best known and seemingly the easiest to investigate is the influence of a *political* metropolis, the capital where the government of a state is located. Individual rulers or leaders who permanently or temporarily live in the capital have subjects or followers far beyond its narrow limits. Administrative groups (including the police) organized in the metropolis have subgroups in other cities or towns throughout the entire region subjected to its control. When the state has an army, the supreme command of the army is usually located in the capital. The general laws promulgated by legislators functioning in the capital apply to the lives of inhabitants of the entire metropolitan region, and the decisions of judges active anywhere in the region can be modified or invalidated by the supreme court located in the capital.

However, the range of influence and the degree of power of a political metropolis can change, as many historical examples show. The metropolitan region may increase in size in consequence of military conquest, as the region controlled by the capital city of Rome did from the fourth century B.C. to the second century A.D. It may also increase through colonial expansion, as the region of the city of Washington did in the course of the nineteenth century. Or it may decrease under the impact of foreign invasion, as in the case of Constantinople from the fifth to the fifteenth century. Or the political center of the same region may move from one city to another, as the government of Poland moved from Poznań to Kraków, then to Warsaw, and the government of Russia from Moscow to St. Petersburg in the eighteenth century and back to Moscow in the twentieth century. The degree of political control exerted by a metropolis also depends on the type of government: The capital of an absolute monarchy or autocratic dictatorship obviously exerts more control than the capital of a democratic republic. And in a union of states the control is divided between the capitals of particular states and the common capital of the entire union.

But not every influential city is a political metropolis. A city may be primarily or even exclusively a religious center, or what may be called an *ecclesiastical* metropolis. It has a high priest, a bishop, an archbishop, a patriarch, or a pope, who exerts influence over subordinate priests or ministers throughout the region where people who share the same religion live. It contains dominant groups performing special functions on behalf of the church and its members—administrative, theological, educational, juridical, economic, political—each of which has subgroups in other cities or towns within the region. Consider again the case of Rome. After the fall of the Western Roman Empire, when Rome ceased to be a political metropolis, it became an ecclesiastical metropolis; and its region expanded westward beyond the limits of the Empire; first of all, over Western and Central Europe, later throughout Spanish, Portuguese, and French areas of the American continents.

A city can be primarily a center of industry, commerce, and banking; then it may be called an *economic* metropolis. It includes dominant individual industrialists, merchants, and financiers who exert influence upon many businesses throughout a more or less large region; and some industrial, commercial, and banking groups organized within it have subgroups in more or less distant cities within the region. Quite a few cities in the late Middle Ages were little more than economic centers; and in modern Europe we may mention such big cities as Antwerp, Hamburg, Liverpool, and Manchester, none of which are capitals. In the United States, most of the political capitals are purposely separated from the cities which are economically powerful. Thus, the relatively small cities of Albany, Springfield, and Sacramento are respectively the capitals of the states which include such great cities as New York, Chicago, and San Francisco. On the other hand, Washington, D.C., politically one of the most powerful capitals in the world, can hardly be compared in economic importance with New York or Chicago.

Some cities have been mainly educational, literary, artistic, or scientific centers. We call such a city an *intellectual* metropolis. Athens is a famous example. While orginally it was a capital and a religious center of a rather small area, and later its political influence spread for a time beyond this area, it finally became the intellectual metropolis of a much larger region, and remained influential long after it lost all political power. The small cities of Oxford and Cambridge were for centuries the most important intellectual centers of England. During the Renaissance, the range of intellectual influence of Florence was much wider than the range of its political influence as capital of Tuscany. Poland had no capital after it was partitioned between Russia, Prussia, and Austria, but for more than a century five cities—Kraców, Warsaw, Poznań, Wilno, and Lwów—remained intellectual centers of Polish culture. In the United States, such widely influential educational and scientific associations as Harvard, Princeton, the University of Michigan, and the University of Illinois are located in small cities outside of political and economic centers.

An intellectual metropolis exerts its influence in various ways. If it has a highly developed university, it trains intellectual leaders in every realm of culture, including the teachers on lower educational levels, and its influence is manifested wherever its former students function. If it is a literary center, with authors whose works are published, the influence of these authors spreads as far as the readers of their works. If it has a scientific or artistic academy, an opera, a symphony orchestra, such an association may affect scientists, artists, or musicians, as well as their followers, in many other cities and towns.

Sometimes a city combines the characteristics of a political, ecclesiastical, economic, and intellectual metropolis. Babylon is perhaps the oldest example. Rome during the first two centuries of the Empire was still the center of an old religion, an influential economic center, and the intellectual center of Latin secular culture. In modern times, Paris has been the capital of France, a secondary center of the Catholic Church, an important economic metropolis, and a widely influential center of philosophy, literature, and art. Recently, Moscow is becoming a political, economic, and intellectual metropolis with a region larger than that of any other city.

Of course, when the regions of influence of several cities which function as political, ecclesiastical, economic, and intellectual centers overlap and include inhabitants of the same territory, the problem arises: What is the connection between their functions? Do they mutually supplement or interfere with each other? And when the range of influence of one metropolis expands over a new area, does this result in conflict with another metropolis? If so, how is the conflict settled?

Although the discussion of these problems must be postponed until later, one general remark may be pertinent now. As we mentioned before, the social unification of numerous small local communities into larger and larger collectivities, or societies, was due to the growth of cities and their expanding influence. This was possible because in the long run cooperation between cities within certain large geographic areas proved stronger than conflict. Take two interesting historical examples.

First, that of Italian cities, capitals of relatively small states. For nearly eight hundred years, political and economic conflicts went on between them. Since the time of the Renaissance, however, there has been continual intellectual cooperation among them in literature, knowledge, and art. Eventually, beginning with 1870, they became politically united and integrated. Second, the United States. The early religious and political conflicts between them have practically disappeared; another Civil War would now be impossible. Economic conflicts between metropolitan regions are slowly but steadily decreasing, and intellectual cooperation already includes nearly all educational, scientific, literary, and artistic centers.

But how do investigators obtain factual material about the social life in metropolitan regions? Of course, some first-hand observations of the relationships between prominent leaders and social groups in a metropolis and the inhabitants of certain sections of the metropolitan region were made and described already in classical antiquity, e.g., by Polybius, who studied the political and military expansion of Rome, and by Strabo, who surveyed the cultural influence of Rome upon inhabitants of distant areas in the western parts of the Empire. Since then similar observations were made and recorded, and they continue to be made. But such observations are obviously insufficient. Fortunately, other kinds of materials were and are available, especially written *documents*. Writing was invented in cities, as we know, and spread from the urban centers.

These documents include, first of all, standards and norms intended to regulate the conduct of people subjected to the influence of the metropolitan center: legislative enactments and legal codes, administrative orders, military rules, standards and norms formulated by ecclesiastical authorities, economic leaders, technologists, logicians, methodologists, aesthetes, and linguists. Many long-lasting social groups, especially in modern times, have written constitutions from which conclusions about their organizations and functions can be drawn.

Numerous documents contain descriptions of various events which occurred within the region—chronicles, reports of subjects to rulers, court decisions, summaries of observations of group meetings, and recently reports of journalists. Valuable documentary sources are to be found in individual biographies and autobiographies. Social communication and interaction between individuals who are not in direct contact with each other are expressed in letters. Other, more recent types of documents are pamphlets and periodicals which contain all kinds of propaganda and advertising. Also significant are written and printed works used in education, now generally called *textbooks*.

Historians have in the course of centuries developed adequate standards by which the reliability of these documents can be judged.

6. THE MODERN WORLD AS A FIELD OF RESEARCH

Even the most thorough study of the social systems in a metropolitan region, however, leaves important sociological problems unsolved. For instance, certain religions are shared by groups of people inhabiting several continents; and recently communism has similarly gained small and large groups of adherents in nearly every country throughout the world. Look at the world-wide spread of scientific discoveries and many technical inventions. In some of the larger cities within the United States nearly fifty different nationalities are represented by groups, many of whom maintain some social contacts with the peoples in those distant countries from which they and their parents came. Most of the familiar and difficult sociological problems which now require a solution have sprung from the two World Wars, the formation of the League of Nations and later the United Nations, with the possibility of a third World War at any time. All this means that the modern world as a whole is becoming a new field, the widest possible field for sociological research. But many obstacles will have to be overcome before such research can be adequately carried on; and not enough sociologists are capable and willing to cooperate on such a wide scale.

CHAPTER 3

HUMANISTIC VERSUS NATURALISTIC APPROACH TO SOCIOLOGICAL FIELDS

1. NATURALISTIC PRESUPPOSITIONS IN STUDIES OF HUMAN COL-
   LECTIVITIES

Every scientist who approaches a field of research must have definite standards for selection of those data and facts which he intends to investigate as presumably relevant to the problem which he wishes to solve. For the number and diversity of the data which he can experience and of the facts which he can observe within a large field—a metropolitan region, a city, or even only a community habitat—is so vast that, if he selects them arbitrarily without any standards, his investigation will lead him into a bewildering chaos.

Now, many investigators of long-lasting human collectivities assume that they should study first the *natural* objects and processes which they observe within their fields, following the methods and using the results of natural sciences.

Such an investigator usually starts with the geography of the area within which the people of a particular collectivity live. Of course, if he does not reside in this area, but has to travel in order to reach it, he must know in advance its geographic location in relation to other areas. Once he enters it, he tries to observe its topography, its climate, its flora and fauna, and the appearance and spatial distribution of human dwellings and other buildings, if any. Sometimes, indeed, the area has already been studied by geographers; then he supplements the results of their studies by his own observations. Most of the works of anthropologists, rural sociologists, urban sociologists, and regional sociologists begin with such geographic descriptions.

In investigating the people within this geographic area, he studies them, first, as human bodies, since this is how they are originally experienced by him. He takes into consideration their similarities and differences in sex, age, and other physical characteristics, some natural, as when they appear to belong to a distinct race or several races; some artificial, e.g., the kind of clothes they wear. Most descriptions of tribal and rural communities include such observations. He tries also to ascertain, so far as possible, the ecology of the people, i.e., their qualitative and quantitative distribution among the particular localities into which the whole territory is divided. He cannot help observing their spatial mobility, and attempts to find out how frequently, at what times, in what numbers, in what direction, and how far they move. In recent times, the results of statistical surveys of the population of rural areas, cities, and regions have made these tasks of investigators relatively easy.

The third kind of objects and processes which an investigator who uses a naturalistic approach selects for study refers to the problem of how the people who inhabit a given geographic area satisfy their biological needs. He observes what kind of food they eat, how they adapt themselves to the climate, what kind of home they use, how they protect themselves from external dangers. Since the sexual "impulse" or "drive" is one of their biological needs, he also tries to find out how this impulse is satisfied. And since the collectivity cannot last unless children are born and reared, he investigates how their survival and growth are insured.

Inasmuch as participants in a human collectivity obtain most of their means of subsistence by certain technical performances, the investigator observes how they are doing it, or—in popular terms—how they "make a living." In an economically self-sufficient community, this depends on the natural resources located within its area, from which raw materials are derived, and on the tools and methods used to prepare these materials for consumption. In a community which has to import certain materials, tools, or products from elsewhere, the problem is what the inhabitants do to obtain these imported goods. In any case, in most studies of communities, cities, and regions, considerable attention is devoted primarily to material techniques.

Such a selection appears at first sight well justified. Since the regular satisfaction of biological needs constitutes an indispensable condition of the very existence of every long-lasting human collectivity, it seems obvious that investigators should study the data and facts mentioned above as thoroughly as possible.

Unfortunately, the idea that those data and facts should be investigated as natural phenomena, before studying anything that is going on among the people living in a certain area, has proved scientifically defective. It was originally rooted in the doctrine that the total life of every human collectivity is determined by natural forces, because men are essentially natural beings, a distinct class of animals. However, human collectivities differ in many respects, and considerable disagreement has developed among theorists as to what natural factors determine these differences. Formerly certain geographers claimed that, because men, like other living beings—animals as well as plants—must adapt themselves to the natural conditions in which they live, all the important differences between human collectivities are primarily due to differences in their natural geographic environments. But this geographic determinism was obviously invalidated by observing that, as material culture developed, men could change their geographic environment. Compare, for instance, the present life of the inhabitants of Manhattan Island with the life of its inhabitants four and a half centuries ago.

In opposition to geographic determinism, many anthropologists and demographers asserted that, inasmuch as within the human genus are found a number of species and subspecies, popularly called "races," each with some distinct hereditary traits, all the important differences between human collectivities must be due to their racial composition. This racial determinism has also been completely invalidated, since racially different peoples can share the same culture, and racially similar peoples can develop different cultures. Nor is a combination of geographic and racial factors sufficient to explain cultural similarities and differences.

In recent times, however, another justification of this naturalistic approach has been promulgated by those epistemologists who claim that sensory experience is the only reliable source of scientific knowledge.The geography of an inhabited area, the bodily composition, spatial distribution, and physical mobility of its population, the material goods which the people consume, the technical equipment used to produce or import these goods, and the processes of their use are all accessible to sensory experience. Moreover, they can be reliably recorded for future observers by means of maps, models, drawings, photographs, and statistical tables. Successive observations and records allow investigators to trace any qualitative and quantitative changes. A study limited to these data is strictly objective, in the sense that its results, such as they are, seem entirely independent of all subjective ideas, beliefs, attitudes, and tendencies of the people who compose a collectivity.

But this is precisely the fundamental weakness of the naturalistic approach. For the people who participate in a human collectivity are not only biological organisms: They are also conscious thinkers and agents, just like the observer himself. It is impossible to explain what they are doing or to predict what they will do without taking fully into consideration their ideas, beliefs, attitudes, and active tendencies. Almost all the data which the investigator experiences are also experienced by them, indeed, were probably experienced by them long before he arrived. This includes the area which they inhabit, its topography, its climate, all the objects, animate and inanimate, in this area, their bodies, everything they consume and produce, and all the tools they use. Whatever those data may be to the observer as a natural scientist, to them practically they are meaningful *values*; and how they treat these values depends not on what he thinks, but on what they think about them.

Consequently, through his study the investigator must always try to discover how anything he observes within his field of research is experienced and evaluated by those human agents who are actively interested in it. We call this the *humanistic approach*. And in the course of this approach, he will find that the valuations and actions of conscious human agents are not naturally determined, but *culturally conditioned*.

Indeed, every investigator ought to be conscious of the need for this approach before he enters his field. For he himself becomes an empirical datum to the people whom he observes and is subjected to their valuations and actions. He cannot predict what they will do to him or explain what they have done until he has learned something about the standards by which they evaluate him. And, inasmuch as his research requires some actions on his part, he is sooner or later bound to discover that these people expect his actions to be guided by definite norms and that, unless he follows these norms, they will react in a way that may not only interfere with his research, but make continued stay in this particular field impossible.

Investigators who already belong to the collectivity which they study or are familiar with the social standards and norms of the people within their fields of research find it relatively easy to adapt themselves to these requirements, and in any case are apt to consider whatever social difficulties they may have to face in the course of their research as minor practical troubles. But a comparative historical survey of reports about the experiences of "outsiders" who entered or tried to enter various occupied areas shows that their treatment by "insiders" raises sociological problems of primary importance for the understanding of the meaning which things within this area have for its occupants. We shall survey briefly some of these problems.

2. Spatial Data as Human Values

The first sociological problem arises when we consider the conditions under which an observer can enter bodily into a geographic area and move from place to place within this area. From the point of view of natural science, a geographic area is simply a geometrically circumscribed portion of space within which material objects are located and natural processes occur. Given an organism capable of moving by its own power or with the aid of a propelling machine, its moving into and within a geographic area implies only a lack of such material obstacles to its movement as can be neither removed nor circumvented, and the existence of physicochemical conditions—air, temperature, light—necessary for its survival and orientation.

But a human individual intending to move into and within an *inhabited* geographic area is bound to find sooner or later that it is not enough to plan his movements only on the basis of his knowledge of material objects and physicochemical conditions within this area, for unpredictable happenings initiated by human agents are apt to occur. Travelers have found that many areas are surrounded by man-guarded boundaries, and then everybody approaching these boundaries from the outside is compelled to stop before crossing them; such was the case, for instance, in ancient and medieval city areas and now in modern state areas. Sometimes travelers meet no guarded boundary, but are stopped as they advance into the area; this is what usually happens to travelers coming into tribal territories. In other cases, travelers are compelled to stop before entering the central part of an area, e.g., an agricultural village. In still other cases, travelers are immobilized in a certain place within an area and prevented from moving elsewhere.

Furthermore, various things can happen to the traveler who is stopped. Sometimes the obstacles are removed and he is allowed to proceed or even helped in his movements; but he may be turned back or even forcibly deported. Sometimes all his possessions are taken away. He may be imprisoned, forced to labor, tortured, or killed.

In the light of all these possibilities which travelers have had to face in the course of known history, the expectation of a modern American traveler that, in moving into the area of a rural community or a city, he will not be stopped, but allowed to proceed undisturbed, raises as much of a problem as any of the former. Even more puzzling is the fact that some travelers are not only free to enter, but are furnished (for a consideration) the opportunity to use ready mechanical contrivances—trains, buses, ships, airplanes—for quick, safe, and efficient entry into the areas of their choice. History shows that freedom to enter and move around within the area of any American community or city was not originally implied as obvious; on the contrary, it developed as an explicitly granted privilege. And even now the privilege is not extended to some classes of travelers—fugitives from justice, vagabonds suspected of petty thieving, aliens—and any traveler can be deprived of it if he transgresses certain norms of conduct, such as the rules for motor traffic. Historical works on travel and transportation show how many complex social forces were and still are involved in the slow development of the astounding opportunities which a modern American traveler has of reaching by mechanical means nearly every area within the limits of the United States.

Investigators who formerly were inclined to take these opportunities for granted were shaken in their complacency during the last war, when this relatively new freedom was again curtailed; and military posts, war prisoner camps, Japanese settlements, and industrial centers organized for war production became inaccessible to visitors without special individual permits, which were often difficult to obtain.

Furthermore, even when an investigator is not impeded by human agents while entering the geographic area of a community, city, or region, he will soon discover that his freedom of movement extends only to certain small sections of this area: public roads, streets, squares, parks, commons, an occasional "no-man's-land." By far the largest part of the area is closed to trespassers. Every portion of space is under the control of some individual or group; and nobody is allowed to move or stay within it who has not been granted the right to do so by the controlling agent. An investigator who tries to move into such a space without permission takes some risk. Risks vary and range from a polite questioning to the death penalty, which has often been meted out in past centuries to infidels entering sacred places and in this century, under the Nazi and Bolshevik regimes, to strangers venturing into forbidden areas.

None of these various ways of treating an observer who moves into or within a geographical territory inhabited by a human collectivity can be either predicted or explained in terms of a natural order of material objects distributed in this territory or of physical, chemical, or biological forces active in it. But if the investigator gives up his naturalistic dogmatism and redefines his problem from the humanistic point of view, he will discover observable facts on which prediction and explanation of these happenings can be based. He needs only to ask how the movements of a human individual entering or crossing the area where a community or a city is located, or any particular section of this area, appear in the active experience of the people who compose the community or city. By combining and comparing their social actions which bear upon this moving individual with the symbolic expressions of their evaluative and normative attitudes, he will be able to understand and anticipate their conduct. But he must be able to do this investigation with entire objectivity, by strictly inductive methods, without letting his own convictions and assumptions, however sure he may be of their validity, interfere with his research.

If he can do this, he will find eventually that the inhabitants of the area he visits have a very different conception of "space" from the one he has acquired from geometry, geography, and astronomy; or at least that, even if they know and accept this conception as an ideological construct, it represents to them a pure abstraction with little bearing upon their actual spatial experiences, except at relatively rare times, when for some practical purposes they carry on one-dimensional, two-dimensional, or three-dimensional measurements. What they actually experience is not one universal abstract "space" as nonquantitative continuum, but many distinct concrete, qualitatively diverse, often partly overlapping *spaces* as empirical values irreducible to a common denomination.

Now, nearly every spatial value within human reach is claimed as a possession by some social group, sometimes by several groups which share its ownership for different purposes or at different times. For instance, while a meeting is in progress in a public hall or square of a city in Illinois, the group which has arranged the meeting has possession of this particular space. But the same space is a permanent value of the incorporated city as an organized group; it is also an integral component of the more extensive spatial value controlled by the State of Illinois as an organized political group; and, finally, it is one of the many, diverse components of that most extensive spatial value—the territory over which the United States as a politically organized society has supreme control. Hardly any land physically accessible to men can be found nowadays which is not claimed by some social group.

When a concrete space is experienced as a group value, any individual who stays within or even moves across this space is experienced as an agent who is thus sharing the use of this value with the group. Sharing a group value is a right which group members normally possess; but for outsiders it is a special privilege which must be explicitly or implicitly granted by the group. Even group members do not always have equal rights to share the spatial values of their group. Some of them have special rights to certain places within the group-controlled space from which others are excluded. Temples have inner sanctums where only priests are allowed to stay; the office of the president of a corporation or a college is reserved for him, and nobody is admitted to it except by the president's permission; the father of a patriarchal family has his own special seat at the dinner table.

We are familiar with rights to use portions of space for economic purposes. Thus, a farmer has the right to control his land, a craftsman the right to control his workshop, a merchant the right to control his store. But even under individualistic economies, such rights are not absolute, as is proved by the fact that individual ownership of space can be taxed and cannot be transferred except by group sanction. While many spatial values have a utilitarian significance, and the possessive claims of social groups or of individual members of these groups are economic in character, this is not the universal significance of these values.

A space may be extremely valuable socially, though economically useless; and even when economically useful, the prohibition or the permission to use it may depend altogether on other, noneconomic considerations. Comparative studies indicate that the most important spatial values were originally religious, not utilitarian. Usually, the most valuable part of a group area was its center, which was also a focus of sacred power. The Acropolis of a Greek city or the Capitol of Rome could not be used for any utilitarian purpose. The story of Jesus driving money dealers out of the precincts of the Temple shows that their economically useful activities were considered a profanation of the sacred center of Jerusalem and Judea. The Chinese system of spatial valuation was essentially founded upon a differentiation of spatial values into sacred (positively or negatively) and profane areas; and only profane areas could be utilized to satisfy economic needs. Even a profane area, however, had to be religiously protected against evil magico-religious powers which might, without this protection, come from the outside and make it impure, negatively sacred, unfit for economic use, and even dangerous to stay in or to move across. The outside boundaries of tribal areas, of village community areas, and of city-state areas were consecrated to protective gods, often marked by altars or symbols of gods, carved or uncarved stones, images, sacred trees, etc. Beyond the boundary, evil forces roamed uncontrolled.

Any stranger from beyond the boundary was, therefore, a possible bearer of magico-religious danger, which by his mere presence could infect the spatial values of the community; and if he entered or even approached the holy centers, his nearness would profane those centers. It was altogether a minor matter whether or not he used any of the economic values within the area—ate fruit, shot game, or caught fish. Indeed, if he did, it might neutralize any danger inherent in him, on the principle that by sharing the food of the community he established a bond between himself and its members. Often he was explicitly offered food before being allowed to proceed; this made the community safe from him and gave him the privilege of being temporarily admitted into the community territory.

This religious holiness still survives in many spatial values, such as churches, cemeteries, and memorials. And in some of the most widely spread religions the custom persists of consecrating certain spaces destined for secular use—homes or public buildings. Moreover, even spaces which are no longer considered holy still may be socially sublimated. The social center of every city, as distinct from its business center, is composed of the public buildings reserved for important group functions. A college campus is sublimated space devoted to the function of educating the young; within it, on a still higher level of sublimation, are buildings the inner space of which is given over to teaching and research; and the highest level of sublimation, next to the chapel, surrounds the inner offices of the president and the deans. A traditional "family home" has a certain degree of institutional sublimation, which makes it safe against the intrusion of strangers. Some residential areas are sublimated because of the high social status of their inhabitants and are protected against the penetration of shops, which would profane them.

Thus, the investigator of an inhabited area is inevitably and continually reminded that his presence in a particular place at a particular time is not merely a geographical, but a social phenomenon, and that every movement he makes in space, as well as every moment he remains without moving, is fraught with social implications. By entering or trying to enter a given area, he has willingly or not provoked some reaction of the agents to whom this area belong as a social, if not as a religious or economic value; he has become, knowingly or not, a potential participant in the general social life of this collectivity and probably also in one or more of the smaller groups of which it is composed. He cannot foretell what will happen to him, unless he knows enough about the social order of this collectivity to understand, in terms of the active experience of the inhabitants to whom the spatial values into which he is intruding belong, what this order and his intrusion mean to them.

3. The Humanistic Approach to the Population

After the investigator has succeeded in redefining humanistically his geographical conceptions of his field of research, he will be logically led to redefine his demographic conception of the people who inhabit this area, as he realizes fully that these people are to each other social values, not merely biological organisms, and that their presence in the area is ultimately dependent on their mutual valuations.

The demographic composition of a human collectivity located within an area at any given time is inexplicable, unless we know the standards and norms by which individuals and groups who were active within this area before that time tried to regulate the collective life of its inhabitants. The need for such knowledge becomes manifest as soon as the investigator compares the present composition of the collectivity with its past composition, and finds that this composition has changed. Comparative studies of communities, cities, and regions, not as static cross sections, but in the course of their duration, indicate that changes in human populations, unlike changes in the fauna and flora of uncultivated geographic areas, are not direct manifestations of natural forces, discoverable by biological research, but symptomatic manifestations of complex and varying cultural factors discoverable by humanistic research. While these changes can be measured statistically, their measurement will not lead to valid causal generalizations which can be confirmed by verified predictions, unless and until the cultural factors on which they depend have been investigated.

The population living in a community habitat, a city, or a region changes when it gains new participants and when it loses previous participants. As we know, it can gain new participants by birth or immigration, and lose previous participants by death or emigration. Its numerical gain or loss is accompanied by qualitative changes in its composition. We shall first survey changes due to immigration or emigration, because here the influence of cultural factors can be most easily ascertained.

(a) Cultural Conditions and Consequences of Immigration

Inasmuch as every investigator who enters a field of research from outside is an "immigrant" who intends to become, at least temporarily, a participant, his own experiences often provide the key for the understanding of immigration as a social process.

In comparing immigration into various community habitats, cities, and regions at various historical periods, we discover that this process occurs in two different ways. Immigrants may be voluntarily admitted into a particular area as potential participants in the collectivity which inhabits this area, or they may enter the area by force or threat of force.

Most scientific investigators belong to the first type of immigrant. In order to be admitted voluntarily, an investigator must initiate personal contacts with some socially influential inhabitants, and be positively evaluated by them; he is expected not only to refrain from doing anything conflicting with the norms by which the conduct of participants is supposed to be guided, but to do something which those who admit him consider desirable. When he seeks admission, he is apt to discover that to be recognized as an investigator is hardly the right way to go about it. In tribal and rural communities, scientific research is entirely unknown; even in cities, only a small minority understand and appreciate what a scientist wishes to do. Ordinarily, "insiders" are apt to be suspicious of an "outsider" who manifests too much curiosity. Consequently, an investigator, in order to be accepted, must learn what standards participants apply in evaluating newcomers and what they expect them to do.

A survey of such evaluations and expectations shows that they differ widely in various collectivities. Moreover, within the same collectivity different valuations and expectations are applied to immigrants according to their presumed importance as future participants, and these differences affect considerably the social life of immigrants in relation to inhabitants. We shall discuss in detail these valuations and expectations in our comparative study of social roles. Meanwhile, we may mention a few typical examples.

Newcomers who are presumably endowed with positive religious sacredness have always been considered highly valuable; they are eagerly admitted, in the expectation that their presence will benefit the whole community. Thus, in ancient Greece socially important travelers were supposed to be guarded by certain gods (especially Zeus) and goddesses. In medieval Europe and to this day in Islamic countries, pilgrims returning from holy places were welcomed everywhere as bearers of holiness. When missionaries are voluntarily admitted to tribal communities, it is because they are expected to exercise beneficent religious powers. On the other hand, when they are rejected, this usually means that their power is considered dangerous, if not explicitly maleficent. Peaceful representatives of foreign powers—envoys and diplomats—have in the course of history proved valuable additions to the communities where they are stationed, and in modern times upper-class visitors are welcomed as guests and eventually as settlers in both rural communities and cities. The admission of foreign merchants has also a long tradition, although at first they were allowed to stay only for a limited time.

We are familiar with historical and sociological studies of mass immigration of people from rural areas into cities, as well as with the penetration of new immigrants from distant countries into American rural communities and cities already settled by older immigrants. It makes a considerable difference to the demographic composition of an inhabited area whether racially or culturally different outsiders are excluded or admitted without discrimination, or allowed to enter freely but socially isolated to prevent miscegenation, or admitted only as slaves or indentured laborers. And if a collectivity admits foreign innovators—technicians with needed skills, prophets of new religions, teachers of new knowledge, merchants who import new goods from abroad, industrialists who initiate new products—its culture is apt to change much more rapidly than the culture of a collectivity which keeps foreign innovators away; and this change in turn will effect future population changes.

Immigration by force is exemplified in modern times by Spanish, Portuguese, French, and British colonial conquests, the expansion of the Russian Empire up to the end of the nineteenth century, the German *Drang nach Osten*, and recently by Japanese, Italian, German, and Russian military invasions of areas which the invaders wished to control permanently. In all these instances, control of the territory was assumed and maintained by temporary or permanent immigrants—soldiers, politicians, bureaucrats, and privileged settlers. Less conspicuous, but still significant, has been the immigration of governmental agents into rural communities and cities which were already parts of a state, for the purpose of strengthening their control by central authorities.

This forcible immigration is obviously not a natural process. It implies that the organized social group to which the immigrants belong is more powerful than any group which the original inhabitants can form. To explain why such a group invades an inhabited area, we must know what this area and its population mean to its members. The effects of forcible immigration depend on how the immigrants evaluate and treat the natives and how the natives react to the conduct of the immigrants. Considerable research has been done in such fields, and we shall briefly survey it later. Here a few examples, showing the importance of cultural rather than natural factors, may be given.

The invading group often superimposes its own possessive claim to the invaded territory over the claims of the original settlers, as did the Spanish in Central and South America and the French and British in various regions of Africa. Furthermore, the invaders have to introduce some order of their own, regulating relations between themselves and the original population and often imposing definite obligations upon the latter. Frequently, they also attempt to substitute some of their standards and norms of social interaction for those which existed before. The British have tried to do this in most of their colonial areas, under the assumption that the new social order would be better for the inhabitants than their old order; and this is what the Bolsheviks did when they imposed the communist economic and political order upon the peoples they conquered or reconquered. In many cases, the invaders tried to impose their culture upon the inhabitants of the territory they invaded: their religious culture, as when Christian conquerors converted "pagans"; or their national culture, as when Austrians and Prussians germanized and Russians russified conquered "foreigners."

Reactions of original inhabitants to changes initiated by invaders differ widely, ranging from voluntary acceptance to violent rebellion. And it is impossible either to explain or to predict their reactions without adequate knowledge of the cultural background and social solidarity of the natives, and of the way in which they experience and evaluate the invaders, interpret their methods, and anticipate their future conduct.

(b) *Cultural Conditions and Consequences of Emigration*

Some inhabited areas have emigration as well as immigration; others only emigration, without immigration. Now, emigration is as incomprehensible as immigration, unless we know what it means in the active experience of the emigrants and of the inhabitants of the area from which they emigrate. Fortunately, a considerable amount of material bearing on this problem has been collected, and quite a few studies have already been made. Here also we must distinguish between voluntary and compulsory emigration. Voluntary emigrants have a positive goal which they hope to attain. They are not merely *moving away* from the area in which they formerly lived; they are *moving toward* some area which appears to them in anticipation as more valuable than their own. The choice of their future habitat depends, first, on their standards of valuation; second, upon what they believe they know about areas outside their own and the inhabitants of them; third, on what they believe they know about the ways and means of reaching those areas.

Voluntary emigration, like immigration, is selective; only here the selective factors are the evaluative attitudes and active tendencies of local individuals toward outside areas and their people, not the attitudes and tendencies of the local people toward individual outsiders. Emigrants who seek religious or political freedom as the supreme value differ personally from those who seek only economic advance. Emigrants moving from rural areas to cities differ from pioneers participating in the formation of new communities. Emigrants who intend to return to their original habitat after having gained abroad the means to improve their social conditions at home differ from those who intend to settle abroad permanently. Among the former there is a considerable difference between, say, British gentry who emigrate to the colonies as governmental officials, and return home after retiring on a pension, and peasants or workers of Eastern or Southern Europe who formerly emigrated to America with the intention of returning, after having gained enough money and prestige to rise in their domestic class hierarchy.

The selection character of compulsory emigration, or expulsion, is even more obvious. The expulsion of religious dissenters—Jews and Moors—from Spain was based on different standards of selection from those used in expelling warlike Indians from territories into which white settlers were moving, while letting peaceful Indians remain. Forcible transportation of convicts into colonial areas, as used by the British and the French, differed from forcible expulsion of political and intellectual leaders and their followers who did not conform with demands made by the government in power.

The two standards of selection have been indiscriminately used for more than two centuries by rulers of Russia. Common criminals as well as political opponents and nonconformist intellectuals were sent to Siberia by the Tsarist government and are now being sent by the Communist government; only the number of those compulsory emigrants, especially of those subjected to forced labor, increased greatly between 1910 and 1950. The Nazi method of transporting nonconformist leaders from their communities or cities to concentration camps is familiar. And if we include under compulsory emigration the leaving of one's habitat to escape the danger of death or various forms of persecution, we shall find that during the last quarter of a century the vast majority of compulsory emigrants were political and intellectual nonconformists. Obviously, it is impossible to explain this expulsion without adequate knowledge of the social life and the culture of the collectivities from which they were expelled and of the standards of conformity and nonconformity which the groups which expelled them used in evaluating individuals. Nor can the consequences of this emigration for the inhabitants of the area from which the emigrants were compelled to move be discovered without a thorough study of the functions which they performed in those areas before leaving.

Thus, human migration, viewed naturalistically as a movement of living bodies from one geographic area to another, is a mere symptom of two different, complex combinations of cultural forces, one combination functioning in the area from which the migrants move, the other in the area into which they move. Moreover, the very process of migration is affected by cultural factors. In studying long-distance mass migration, the investigator must take into account valuations and active tendencies, individual and collective, bearing upon the very space which separates the old and the new habitats, as well as the processes of travel and transportation back and forth across that space. Otherwise, it would be impossible to account for such spectacular phenomena as the development of American travel techniques from the Indian trail and the log or birchbark canoe to its present vast and complex organization.

(c) Cultural Factors in Population Changes Through Births and Deaths

But leaving migration aside, how about demographic studies of those natural processes of birth and death on which the long-time duration of every spatially located collectivity and its numerical size manifestly depend? Is not the validity of these studies conclusively demonstrated by the high probability of prediction of future trends?

Here again, however, comparative studies of community habitats, cities, and regions with different cultures and changing patterns of social interaction indicate the dependence of those natural processes on cultural factors. Births and deaths are highly significant events to the participants in collective life, and they try to control them in accordance with their standards of valuation by various techniques, some of them ineffective, others indubitably effective. Newborn children are newcomers, potential participants in the life of the collectivity into which they are born. Like immigrants, they may be wanted or unwanted by the active participants. If wanted, all known means are used to stimulate conception, to facilitate birth, and to help infants survive. Moreover, if accepted, they are subjected to a cultural preparation before they become active participants—a longer and more thorough preparation than immigrants receive. If unwanted, limitation of sexual intercourse, contraception, abortion, and infanticide are resorted to. And whether children are wanted or not, how many children, what kind of children, and whose children depend on family patterns, religious systems, economic standards, class hierarchy, political organization, etc.

Attitudes toward death also vary widely. Individuals who are positively valuable, according to existing standards, are generally protected against death; individuals who are of little value are unprotected; and those negatively valued are excluded from their communities or even put to death. But sometimes the most valuable individuals—warriors, priests, prophets, and physicians—are expected to risk death or even sacrifice their lives voluntarily. In some communities aging persons were put to death before they lost their powers, for the sake of their future in the other world; sacred kings were killed, in their own interest and that of their subjects, before they lost their sacredness.

The acceptance by religious, social, and intellectual leaders of the principle that all human lives are valuable and should be protected helped to stimulate the rapid progress of modern medicine and hygiene; and this progress, which has produced such important changes in population trends, is a purely cultural process. On the other hand, within the very Western culture which developed these ethical standards and scientific techniques, we have recently witnessed a historically unprecedented, planful killing of millions of individuals from many areas, without distinction as to their sex, age, their cultural achievements, or their personal valuation by other community members, only because a powerful group valued them negatively, according to standards of a prehistoric, scientifically absurd mythology of "race."

Thus, the predictive validity of a population study, apart from migration, is dependent entirely on the assumption that cultural factors on which the rates of births and deaths depend will remain uniform and stable during a certain time among the population of the given territory; and the conclusions of the investigator refer only to the particular case under investigation. From such a study no generalizations whatsoever can be drawn which would be applicable to the population of other territories or of the same territory at other periods, unless preceded by a comparative study of their diverse and changing cultural factors.

(d) *Cultural Factors of Ecological Distribution*

The ecology of a community, as mapped by an anthropogeographer at a particular moment of its duration, is also inexplicable, and its future changes unpredictable, without full understanding of the standards and norms in accordance with which participants in the community intentionally regulate the spatial conditions of social participation in various kinds of cultural systems. As we saw above, every portion of space accessible to active human experience is a social value, an object of possessive claims of one or several groups and of one or several individuals who have been granted rights to use it permanently or temporarily. These groups and individuals use it for culturally patterned activities, and their usages often overlap.

A religious group which requires periodical ritualistic meetings and frequent personal contacts between its leaders and other members tends to obtain possession of a spatial area fitted for these purposes. If its members belong to it entirely and exclusively, they will live permanently as residents within the area controlled by the group, as medieval monks lived in their monastery. But if they belong also to other groups and have to reside in or near places controlled by the other groups, the religious group will obtain possession only of a spatial center for its church and for the residence of its minister, as accessible as possible from the homes of most of its members. Jewish ghettos were formed when both Jews and Christians or Jews and Mohammedans wanted to prevent defiling contacts with members of an "impure" out-group; strictly secular, religiously indifferent social intercourse, however, was allowed. As beliefs in the magico-religious impurity of outsiders weakened, ghettos either disappeared or remained only as manifestations of a tendency to cultural separatism.

High-class families, which try to prevent their members and especially their children from frequently meeting face-to-face members of low-class families, tend to form exclusive residential districts; and yet low-class individuals who function as servants live in those districts, and craftsmen and salesmen visit them. Foreign invaders, endeavoring to control native inhabitants by force, form exclusive military and administrative centers from which their coercive activities can effectively spread over the whole area; nonetheless, family homes, economic centers, religious meeting places, and recreational districts remain.

To reconstruct fully the ecology of an inhabited area, it is necessary to investigate first the possessive claims of various groups and the ecological rights of various individuals, and find out how these groups and individuals use their spatial values. Families, clans, secret associations, religious sects, cooperatives for technical production, governing sets, political parties, occupational associations, ethnic groups, class groups, business corporations, neighborhood groups, schools, leisure-time associations, gangs, sexual cliques, and gamblers' circles, all use spatial values for their own purposes, and all influence the permanent location, temporary concentration, and movement of the people of a community. So do individuals whose roles include rights to occupy certain places within the community—priests, administrators, judges, policemen, doctors, lawyers, merchants, craftsmen, industrial managers, innkeepers, and bankers. After all these groups and roles have been studied, the ecology of the community will prove merely a kind of composite picture of the combined effects which the dynamic functioning of all these diverse and overlapping social systems have had, up to a given static moment, upon the spatial distribution of habitations and centers of interaction. An ecological map of a community drawn before such a thorough study of its social dynamics may be practically useful to a newcomer, but its scientific significance is problematic.

4. Humanistic Redefinition of Human Needs

Not only the geography and demography of a community, but its economy, must be approached from the point of view of its participants as conscious agents. The logical necessity of this approach will be realized by every investigator who reflects objectively about his own personal experiences and those of other investigators. He soon discovers that the satisfaction of his own biological needs in the course of his investigation depends altogether on the conception of those needs and the practical interest in them which participants manifest.

The records of observers of human communities, be they ordinary travelers or scientific investigators, indicate a wide diversity in the ways in which their biological needs are satisfied. Usually, this satisfaction is contingent on permission to enter the community area. If forbidden to enter or driven out, the biological survival of the travelers was likely to be a matter of indifference or even of negative interest to community members. If their very presence polluted the spatial values of the community, their use of any objects belonging to community members for the satisfaction of their needs could not be tolerated. The Roman ban prohibiting even the use of community water and fire to excommunicated persons was a striking manifestation of this attitude.

Sometimes, however, a stranger, while not allowed to enter an area, was nonetheless granted food or some other value he needed for survival, either as an outright gift or in exchange for some gift he had to offer. This was done usually to counteract any evil influence he might otherwise try to exert from the outside upon those who refused to admit him. Thus, when foreign beggars were not admitted to a home, temple, village, or town, they were often given alms at the gate to prevent them from cursing the inhabitants. At other times, travelers compelled to remain outside of a tribal or state territory were allowed to offer to guardians at the border or to send to rulers through the medium of the guardians gifts in exchange for food. In short, an outsider who was considered personally unworthy of being admitted into an area of the community might still be worth propitiating or be a bearer of goods worth acquiring in exchange for products of the inhabitants.

If the outsider was admitted, this normally meant that his person was considered valuable enough to be granted the means of subsistence. Sometimes this meant nothing more than permission to use directly the natural objects located within the community area and therefore belonging to the community. Strangers admitted to areas of tribes that lived on wild game and uncultivated plants—some Indians, Eskimos, and Australians—were often simply allowed to take what they needed of subsistence values by hunting, fishing, gathering edible plants, using water and firewood, making their own shelters, and guarding themselves against any natural or supernatural dangers that might threaten them. But this presupposed that they had the necessary equipment and skill. If they were unable to support themselves by drawing directly upon natural resources or to protect themselves by their own devices, they could survive only by being given a share in goods already prepared for consumption by the natives, or in whatever devices the natives used for their own safety against destructive agencies. This applied especially to strangers coming into areas where the chief means of subsistence were gained by planful, long-term techniques—agriculture, animal husbandry, and elaborate industrial production—and where there were collectively prepared devices for safety. Since the newcomer, even when he had started such technical activities, would have to wait a long time for their results, his life in the meantime depended on the willingness of the natives to support and protect him.

And here we find a highly significant social custom almost universal, though with many secondary variations: the custom of *hospitality*. Wherever this custom prevails, a visiting stranger is treated as a guest by the natives who have admitted him bodily into the space which they possess. They function individually or collectively as his hosts, giving him shelter, food, and protection against any danger that may threaten him—natural forces, wild animals, magico-religious evils, or human enemies. Hospitality is dependent upon the social valuation of the person of the guest. As we have seen, he may be positively valued on various grounds: his own magico-religious powers, or the protection of some powerful divinity, or his apparent physical superiority and bravery, or his mastery of arts and crafts, or his superior experience and knowledge, or his status as representative of an important group, or his personal fame. Sometimes, however, he is of no importance whatsoever, an insignificant individual, utterly helpless; and it is his very helplessness which apparently makes him an object of positive interest.

The needs of the guest are defined for him by his hosts; first, in terms of their own cultural standards, i.e., of what they traditionally consider human beings need; second, in terms of his personal worth—the more socially valuable he is in their eyes, the greater his needs are supposed to be. He is offered the kind of food they eat, the kind of shelter they use; he is protected from dangers which they believe threaten him. The gradation of his needs according to his importance is manifest by the difference in the hospitality offered to a bishop and a beggar, to a baron and a juggler, to a master and his servant, to an ambassador and a private tourist, or to a famous hero and an unknown person. A favored guest may even be offered a way of satisfying his sexual need—sometimes with his host's wife or daughter, sometimes with a lower-class woman.

The guest is not expected to define his needs differently from his hosts or to request something they do not believe he needs. However, when the guest is known to have different standards, and his personal worth is high, his hosts may be willing to humor him. Thus, the hosts of an envoy from a powerful foreign country try to learn and satisfy his wants, however odd they may seem, and a holy ascete can refuse all luxuries offered to him.

But, no matter how the custom of hospitality may vary in different collectivities and change, depending on the relative importance ascribed to guests and their hosts, an investigator to whom this custom is applied is logically bound to redefine for the purposes of his research the biological concept of human needs. He must cease to take for granted that all human beings are necessarily activated by the same objective natural needs and that he as a scientist truly knows the needs of the people of the collectivity he studies. For he finds that what they actually endeavor to obtain often differs considerably from what, according to him, they really need: They frequently "want" what he thinks they do not "need," or do not "want" what he thinks they "need."

And he cannot dismiss their conception as unreal. If they believe that he, like every human being, needs food endowed with positive magical qualities or needs protection from evil magico-religious forces, this belief of theirs is a hard fact, a component of the real, objective situation he has to face; while his own conviction that he, and every human being, needs food of a definite chemical composition, unless understood and accepted by his hosts, does not enter into the situation. Nor is his situation exceptional. He will find, for instance, that the children in the community are similarly made to accept the judgments of adults as to what they really need and are taught to adapt their wants to these judgments. The concept of "real needs," "objective needs," does not help him explain or predict the actions he observes. These actions are conditioned not by human needs as such, but by *human needs as defined and standardized by human agents.*

A comparative survey of standards practically applied in different collectivities and in the same collectivity at different periods is apt to shake the investigator's conviction of the universal validity of his own standards. Take only the matter of food, and compare the standards of the Eskimos, by which all human beings need primarily meat and animal fat, with those of the Hindus, according to whom no human being needs meat or animal fat; or the attitude of Polynesians with that of Mohammedans toward pork; or the high valuation of milk by the Todas with its rejection by the Chinese; or the wide differences and changes in the valuation of various alcoholic drinks as good or bad for human health. Nor are these variations limited to culturally backward communities: Compare the varying standards of nutritive needs which have been applied in Western countries during the last hundred years by physicians of different schools and by various groups of cultists and faddists.

5. Redefinition of the Process of Satisfying Needs

If the visiting observer does not allow intellectual or practical prejudices to interfere with his thinking, he is bound to ask how the socially standardized needs of community members are satisfied. According to the popular conception, rationalized in classical economic theories, every human individual originally and essentially strives to satisfy his own needs; and only because and inasmuch as he cannot achieve this by his own efforts does he try to obtain the aid of others by offering something in exchange. But this is not what usually happens to the visiting observer, if admitted as a guest. His hosts primarily and originally assume the responsibility of satisfying his needs, however they may define them. Because they are doing so, he is expected to express his appreciation of the hospitality he receives.

This expression may be purely verbal; but it may also take the form of gifts—objects or services—offered to his hosts. The guest's ability to offer valuable gifts enhances his prestige; his willingness to do so, if he can, manifests his appreciation. The matter of acceptance of the guest's gifts by a host, however, is complicated by considerations of the host's own personal worth in comparison with that of his guest. A host whose prestige is high might lower it, if he accepted valuable gifts from a guest with a prestige equal or inferior to his own; whereas a host of relatively low prestige might gain more by receiving valuable gifts from a superior guest. These considerations eventually lead to dual class standards of hospitality. When a high-class host of independent means entertains visitors, any offer of economically valuable gifts on the part of the latter would be considered an insult; whereas the status of an innkeeper or hotelkeeper is raised in proportion to the amount of money which his visitors are willing to pay for the shelter and food he offers.

An investigator who reflects about these facts and compares what happens to him and other investigators visiting various fields of research will have to ask himself: Is this treatment exceptional or does it manifest the existence of some cultural patterns which are applied by inhabitants of these fields not only to strangers, but also to other inhabitants? And if he tries to answer this question by observing social interaction between inhabitants in the field which he is investigating, he will discover many other facts which will make him doubt the traditional view that the essential aspect of the economic life of a human collectivity is, popularly speaking, how individuals make a living. Instead, he may reach the conclusion that it is more important to find out how individuals are *granted a living*.

In more exact terms, the general problem of biological survival of participants in a collectivity involves three specific problems. First, who are the agents whose actions tend to satisfy what they consider the needs of a particular individual, and what do they do for him? Second, what is he doing to satisfy his own needs? Third, what is he doing to satisfy the needs of other participants, and who benefits by these activities of his?

The primacy of the first problem as compared with the second is indicated by the existence of participants who live almost entirely by the aid of others. To this category belong small children, invalids, in some collectivities persons endowed permanently or temporarily with an exceptional degree of positive sacredness—Indian Yogies and other holy ascetes, some highly sacred inactive kings, and sacred victims destined for religious sacrifice—or the exceptionally impure, magically or socially, as adolescent girls isolated from social intercourse, and prisoners in solitary confinement.

Of course, an individual belonging to this category does something to satisfy his needs, since even eating food that has been prepared for him requires a minimum of activity; but this activity represents only the completion of an active process initiated and carried on, not by himself under the urge of his biological impulses, but by others as an active expression of social tendencies of which he is the object. His act may be nothing but an unconscious organic response to a stimulus consciously and intentionally initiated by others, and would never have occurred if these others had not been socially interested in him: This is true of an infant or an unconscious adult.

In most cases, however, the individual is aware of what others are doing, and his consumption of the values given, or his use of the services offered, is a social reaction to a social action, an act of acceptance of what somebody else does for his benefit. This act of acceptance is essential for the achievement of the original action, and indispensable for the final realization of the tendency of the original agent to have the needs of his social object satisfied. It may require supplementary changes of the value given to make it fit for consumption, or additional activity completing the service offered, to make its effects fully satisfactory from the point of view of the receiver's needs. But it is the giver's action that produces this reaction and enables the receiver to satisfy his need, as defined by the giver, merely by completing the giver's action.

These cases furnish a key to the solution of the second basic problem: What does the individual do to satisfy his own needs? In general, we might say that he does for himself what others leave undone for him. Specifically, this depends on who judges what this individual's needs are and what his share in satisfying them ought to be. A child's needs are defined by adults, and adults decide what they will do for a male or female child of a certain age, and what a child of this sex and age ought to do for himself. If the child wants something he does not need, according to adults, he may be allowed to satisfy his want by his own action only if this does not interfere with his own or anybody else's needs. On the contrary, an individual belonging to a dominant leisure class defines his own needs and decides which of these needs are to be satisfied by the actions of others and which he will satisfy by his own actions.

But how about individuals who depend on their own activities for the satisfaction of their needs? Consider a woman hoe gardener in an African community, who produces nearly all her food, her clothes, and even most of the implements she needs for their production. Is not this a typical instance of making a living by one's own efforts? However, a close investigation of this woman's social interaction with others shows that these activities of hers are also supplementary to the activities of others.

First, she had to be fed, clothed, protected, educated for years before being left to her own devices. Second, there are still many periods of her life—during illness or on visits—when her needs are attended to by others. And some of what are considered her basic needs must at all times be taken care of by others, such as her protection against physical, social, and magico-religious dangers, as well as her sexual needs. Even her activities of production and consumption could not be carried on unless an area was reserved for cultivation and another area was allotted to her for her home within the total territory made safe for her by the men of the community. Moreover, often her horticultural activities begin only after a part of the forest has been cleared by men, and her domestic activities only after her hut has been built by men. Finally, she is given some raw products of man's hunting or pastoral activities to prepare for final consumption, in which she shares; and some of her instruments are usually made by men.

In short, if we view her life from infancy to old age, we find that those actions by which she satisfies her own needs constitute merely the residual portion of the total complex of actions by which her needs, as socially defined, are being satisfied: She is expected to do for herself only whatever others leave undone. It is a residuum steadily increasing as she grows from childhood to maturity; and in her mature age, it is large, indeed, as compared with the activities of her father or husband, with those of an honored guest, or with those of a leisure woman in an aristocratic class society. But its part in her total life proves relatively small when we subtract from those activities which are socially assigned to her everything she does to satisfy not her own needs, but the *needs of others*—husband, children, relatives, and friends.

This brings us to our third problem: What does a particular individual do to satisfy the needs of others? Any visiting investigator is bound to infer from his experience and that of other investigators, as well as from his observation of interaction between the people within his field of research, that there is no general correlation between the activities of an individual on behalf of others and the activities of others on his behalf. The relationship between what a guest gives and what he receives varies, depending on the relation between his prestige and his host's. A small child, an invalid, and a sacred king receive from others almost all they need; but, while the child and the invalid do nothing for others, the sacred king is supposed to do very much for others by magico-religious powers.

Many individuals give much to others and receive much from others, but they give to different persons than those from whom they receive. A Trobriand Islander gives the best products of his garden to his sister's family, but receives nothing from them, only from his wife's brother. A college teacher is supported partly by the living owners of economic values, partly by the dead who left endowments to his college; but he contributes nothing to the satisfaction of the biological needs of those who support him. His teaching, indeed, is supposed to prove eventually useful to his students, when they apply it later on in their own activities; but, in turn, most of their activities will serve to satisfy not their own needs, but those of others.

Of course, some individuals exchange their values and services for values and services of others, and each such exchange tends to comply with certain standards of valuation. These standards vary widely. Originally, they were conceived personally, in terms of the relationship between the needs of the particular individual receiver, as socially defined, and the ability of the particular giver, as socially estimated. They have evolved toward an impersonal conception, in terms of abstract economic relationships between demand and supply, which are not manifestations of normatively regulated needs, but of presumably unregulated actual wants. Demand is an expression of wants for the goods or services demanded; supply, an expression of wants for goods which can be obtained in exchange for goods or services supplied. But the very existence of such relationships depends on certain social conditions—availability of markets, social organization of production and trade, gradation of wants in importance, according to custom, or fashion, etc.

These impersonal economic relationships, however, are beyond the range of direct observation of the visiting investigator. If he applies knowledge derived from his own interactions with the inhabitants of his field to his study of interactions between the inhabitants themselves, he will discover that, even when direct exchange is used between them, it is impossible to determine any general correlation between what a particular individual receives from others and what he gives to others. For much of what he receives from some people he gives to somebody else; much of what he gives to them, they give to somebody else, though some of it may come back to him.

A merchant receives money from his customers in exchange for the values which he gives them, but he must give most of this money to those who supply him with more goods, which he again will give to customers in exchange for more money. Part of what he does not give to producers or wholesalers he gives to other merchants or producers for goods or services he needs for himself; part of it to his wife, who gives it to other merchants and producers for goods which, after being prepared for final consumption, she will partly use for her own sustenance, but mostly give to others—back to her husband, to their children, and to guests. Another part of what the merchant receives from his customers will go to the community or city from which he obtains the right to use some agglomerated products of the activities of several generations— roads, public buildings, street lights, perhaps gas and electricity for domestic usage, maybe a public library or museum—and such important services as protection against criminal actions and fire, medical protection against contagious diseases, and the education of his children. Of course, he on his side may also give services to the community or city as a whole or to some associations within the area in which he lives.

He may be able to calculate what he gives and what he receives in terms of money as the standard of measurement of marketable values; in other terms, to make an income-and-expense account. But this will substitute an artificial construct of himself as an abstract center of inflowing and outflowing monetary symbols, instead of himself as a social agent, giving values to others and performing services for others, and as a social object, having values given to him and services performed for him by other agents, many of which are not marketable at all.

6. Humanistic Redefinition of Material Techniques

Whatever may be the difference between the naturalistic and the humanistic approach to the territory of a collectivity, its population, the needs of the people, and the means and ways of satisfying those needs, it would seem that the naturalistic and the humanistic approach ought to coincide when students come to investigate the techniques by which material values are produced for human use. The cultural scientist must admit that every technical process is a sequence of natural changes occurring in natural objects, while the natural scientist must admit that every technical process is a culturally patterned performance of conscious human agents. The term "material culture," in the sense of the totality of techniques productive of material values, implies the theoretic coincidence of the two approaches.

And yet, as a matter of fact, two distinct ways are followed in studies of material cultures. The predominant method consists in observing materials and instruments used in technical performances, physical movements of the performers, changes occurring in instruments and materials in consequence of these movements, and the final products of these performances, taking these phenomena as they appear in the observer's own experience. This method predominates not only because it is simpler and easier than other methods, provided the investigator is allowed to carry on his observations undisturbed, but mainly because an investigator is usually inclined to think about the technical performances of people in other areas in terms of the cultural patterns with which he has become familiar in his own area.

Most investigators come from modern industrialized cities or regions, where many technical activities are rationally planned on the basis of scientific knowledge of natural objects and processes; consequently, they have been trained to think of technical performances in general as organized teleologically with ends fully defined and means carefully selected in advance. Such is implicitly assumed to be the universal cultural pattern of all technical performances, be they individual and relatively simple—like cooking a dish, plowing a field, or repairing a piece of furniture—or collective and highly complex, like building a skyscraper or producing an automobile. And since the means (materials, instruments, ways of handling instruments, and natural changes in materials while used) and the end (the final product when attained) can be observed and compared by the same methods as those applied by natural scientists, the investigator presumes that from observation he can deduce everything essential about the tendencies and valuations of the performers, provided, of course, that the latter actually follow the teleological pattern.

By this method, the material techniques used in particular collectivities have been abstracted and investigated in themselves, without reference to other components of the culture of those communities. Many anthropologists specialize in the study of material culture as a separate branch of anthropology; and every year hundreds of monographs are published dealing exclusively with the material techniques found in tribal and folk communities. Similarly, many students of modern industrial fields, especially economists, describe the objects and processes included in industrial production, and measure statistically their products, leaving out of consideration the cultural lives of the people who participate in this production.

Now, we do not mean to question the existence of a technical order founded upon the order of nature. Every object used in material techniques is a natural system or element; every process included in material techniques is a natural process, functionally connected with other processes. Technical agents are aware of this, as well as the outside observer. But there are many different technical purposes for which natural objects and processes can be used, and many different ways of selecting and using them. Technical actions are indeed organized; they constitute a distinctive category of dynamic cultural systems, irreducible to any other category, just like religious, aesthetic, linguistic, or social systems. But an investigator cannot know what these dynamic cultural systems really are, unless he learns what all the natural objects and processes included in a technical performance are to the human agents who use them in their actions, just as he cannot know what a religious ceremony really is, unless he learns what all the objects and processes included in it are to the agents who participate in it.

Investigators who, as visitors, are offered material objects for their own use have frequently been led to realize the necessity of learning what their hosts consider essential in the content of these objects, what the latter mean to their hosts in relation to other objects, and how they are supposed to be used. Of course, if the culture of the community or city is similar to that of the community or city from which the visitor came, the latter, being familiar with the ways in which specific objects are supposed to be used, is apt to take these ways for granted. But if the culture is unfamiliar to him, he will be unable to use specific objects without provoking sooner or later some reactions from his hosts. Such reactions may range from friendly guidance, through obviously purposive inattention, ridicule, contempt, or indignation, to exclusion from social relations with his hosts. His way of entering a tent, a room, a temple; of eating and drinking various kinds of food and beverages; of handling knives, forks, chopsticks, plates, or goblets; of using furniture, rugs, bedding, washbasins, bathtubs, or water closets: in short, any contact of his with products of material culture of the people within his field of research is apt to have consequences which prove to him that these do not always mean to his hosts what his own sensory observation indicates.

On the other hand, a visitor who brings with him technical products of his own culture, and offers them as gifts, is apt to find that these products are experienced, evaluated, and used by his hosts in ways which deviate from what he considers right and proper. Consequently, similar technical products brought by visitors are differently evaluated and used in areas with different cultures.

Thus, from the observations made by visitors, certain hypothetical conclusions can be drawn concerning the material techniques of the collectivities they investigate and concerning those of the collectivities from which they come. How any permanent or temporary participant in a collectivity defines and evaluates objects of material technique, and what he does with them, are questions of interest to other participants. For a technical object, as given at a certain moment, usually embodies the combined results of the past technical actions of several human agents; it has a cultural history. It has acquired a content and a meaning, and become subjected to certain cultural standards; every individual participant learns to experience and evaluate it in accordance with those standards, just as every participant who is taught a language learns to experience the sensory content of each word and to understand its meaning as shared by other individuals in the course of its history. As every technical object is expected to be used in the future by others, its present active usage by an individual is supposed to conform with certain norms, just as the active usage of words by every individual is supposed to follow definite norms of phonetics and semantics to prevent others from mishearing and misunderstanding these words.

Generally speaking, whatever material values have been produced by men are destined to be used in a definite way, and no other; whatever men do to a material value significant to other men is expected to be done in a definite way, and no other. At most, a choice of several well-defined ways is allowed, to the exclusion of all other ways.

Grain raised by a farmer has to be either ground into flour, with the definite instruments and methods available at the time, or used as seed, also with definite instruments and methods. Other usages may be possible, such as feeding it to domestic animals or producing alcohol; but each of these implies the existence of a specifically patterned cultural system in which the grain can be included as material for technical actions, probably by other agents. If grain has been ground into flour, the flour is destined to be used as a component of one of several other technical systems, to produce by definite instruments and methods bread, cakes, dumplings, or certain other dishes, each of which in turn is destined to be eaten in a culturally patterned way.

And if we go back to what preceded the farmer's activity, we find that the grain he produced was also a final component of a system of values that included: (a) a piece of land, probably prepared for cultivation by others and transmitted to him by others, and in any case (in accordance with some social pattern of ownership) recognized by others as "his own," at least while he uses it for this particular technical action; (b) seeds raised by himself or somebody else by an earlier action similar to the one he is performing; (c) agricultural implements designed for the purpose of cultivation and produced by some agents, probably someone else rather than himself; (d) a definite method of using these agricultural implements, which has been taught to him by others. Those agricultural implements were also produced in conformity with established cultural patterns, by a methodical use of other instruments, which in turn have a cultural history leading still further back.

Individuals can, and occasionally do, perform culturally unpatterned actions dealing with natural objects which have no reference to the actions of others, e.g., picking and eating wild fruit or hiding from rain under a tree. But whenever an individual performs a patterned technical action, it may be presumed that this action includes values that were, are, or will be, also included in technical actions of other individuals, and uses methods which have been communicated to him by others.

Technical interdependence of material performances implies

social interdependence of performers. Technical actions going on within a collectivity presuppose social interaction between its participants. And this interaction must conform with definite standards and norms; otherwise the purposes of technical actions could not be realized. This is clear when we find individuals regularly specializing in certain technical actions on which specific actions of others are regularly dependent, as when men specialize in hunting, and women in utilizing the products of the hunt; or when smiths produce instruments which hunters use to kill animals, or farmers to cultivate plants; and, even more so, when technical actions of several individuals are cooperatively organized for the realization of a common purpose, e.g., making a boat, building a house, or producing automobiles.

7. SUMMARY AND CONCLUSION

When an investigator who approaches an inhabited area as a field of research wants to understand the material data which he finds within this field—the territory, the human organisms which compose its population, the natural resources on which the population subsists, the tools and techniques by which these resources are prepared for use—he must ask what they mean in the experience of its inhabitants, and try to discover, first of all, the facts of social interaction between the inhabitants and the ways in which this interaction is regulated and organized. For the data which he observes are to the inhabitants values, objects of their actions; and whatever any one of them does to these values is a matter of interest to others, who tend to make his actions conform with recognized cultural patterns. As we shall see later, this applies even more obviously to data which compose the so-called "nonmaterial" or "ideational" culture—language, religion, literature, knowledge, etc.

PART 2

[SOCIAL RELATIONS]

CHAPTER 4

THE STUDY OF SOCIAL RELATIONS IN COMMUNITIES

1. INTRODUCTION

In Chapter 1, we assumed that the main function of sociology is to reach generalizations about social interaction between human agents, and we found that sociologists have been investigating two types of interaction—social conflict and social cooperation. We came to the conclusion that the knowledge about social cooperation is of primary importance from the scientific point of view, for without it no generalizations about social conflict are possible. The common characteristic of social cooperation is that the actions of cooperating individuals are interdependent and organized, thus constituting what we call a *social system*. But the number of people who can cooperate ranges from two to many thousands. Therefore, we may first consider cooperation between two individuals, which is usually called a "social relation," and then proceed to investigate various kinds of social systems in which larger numbers of individuals participate, i.e., social roles, social groups, and societies.

In Chapter 2, we saw that sociologists obtain factual material concerning social interaction in general by carrying on research within areas which are occupied by collectivities of interacting people; and we called these areas "fields of research." Most of the material about interaction between two particular individuals has been obtained within areas inhabited by people who form more or less united "communities." Consequently, a comparative study of social relations should be based on discoveries which investigators of communities have made.

In Chapter 3, we surveyed examples of sociological research in various fields, and came to the conclusion that the sociologist should use the humanistic approach to everything he observes within his field of research, that is, try to ascertain what it means to the people concerned as conscious agents. Thus, when he studies interaction between individuals within a community, he must find, first of all, what these individuals and their actions mean to each other and to other participants in it. Only then will he be able to distinguish clearly between social conflict and social cooperation, and discover what kinds of cooperative social relations exist in this community.

This is not the end of his task. As a sociologist, he is supposed to contribute to scientific knowledge by drawing generalizations about social relations. In order to draw such generalizations, he must compare the results of his research with the results of similar research carried on in other communities, whether by himself or by other investigators.

At every step of this investigation, he will meet considerable difficulty. Let us survey some of the difficulties and see how investigators overcome them.

2. The Multiplicity and Diversity of Social Actions and Reactions in a Community

When social interaction between two individuals occurs, usually one of them, A, initiates it by performing a social action intended to influence another, B; then B "reacts," i.e., performs an action in consequence of A's action. Sometimes each of them independently starts a social action bearing upon the other, and each reacts to the other's action; for instance, two individuals may expect to meet, and both prepare in advance to perform certain actions as soon as they meet. In any case, the connection between a particular social action and the reaction to it is an elementary fact of social interaction, though it may also be a component of a more or less complex system. It is directly accessible to observation, provided the observer not only sees the movement of the particular bodies, but understands whatever symbolic communication occurs between the interacting individuals.

The task of observing social actions and reactions between

individuals in a community habitat is not a simple one, even in a small community with only a few hundred active participants. For each participant every day initiates a number of social actions, nearly every one of which provokes a reaction. Manifestly, no investigator can observe all of them. He must select for observation a rather small proportion of social facts, compare them, and (after an extended stay in the community, if possible) try to draw some conclusions. But how does he decide what facts to select?

First of all, although actions differ widely, they may be classified. The main, familiar difference is between *positive* and *negative* social actions. Positive actions are intended to have results which their objects will evaluate positively, as "pleasant," "useful," "good," etc. Negative actions are intended to have results which their objects will evaluate negatively, as "unpleasant," "painful," "harmful," "bad," etc. Actions of the first category range all the way from companionate greetings, praise, or small gifts, to saving another's life or even helping him strive for eternal salvation. Actions of the second category range from blame, insult, or deprivation of minor values, to homicide or even damning the other's soul to hell. There are also intermediary types, such as promises of positive actions or threats of negative actions, according to the future conduct of the other individual.

Now, the way in which an individual reacts to the social action of another depends not only on the intention of the other, but also on his own evaluation of the other and of what the other is doing or intending to do. Similar social actions may provoke different reactions of different individuals or even of the same individual under different conditions. Compare, e.g., the reactions of believers and unbelievers to the positive and negative actions of religious leaders, or the reactions of various women to sexual advances from men, or the reactions of children and adolescents to certain actions of adults, etc. Thus, the variety of facts of social interaction is even greater than the variety of social actions.

From among this vast multiplicity and diversity of social facts, the investigator who observes social action and interaction in a community has to select those which seem relevant to his problem. If for some reason he is interested in a specific variety of actions and interactions, he will concentrate on the study of these, as they occur in the community during a certain time. For instance, statisticians have listed the frequency of such specific varieties of social facts as the commission of actions which are legally defined as "crimes," marrying, divorcing, producing certain goods, buying or selling certain products, attending school or religious ceremonies, voting, being involved in automobile accidents, etc. Originally, the reasons for such statistical surveys were practical: The investigators who planned how to deal with certain facts had to know the frequency of their occurrence. Eventually, some of these studies began to be carried on for theoretic reasons: to draw from them comparative generalizations about communities as wholes.

Of course, such surveys cannot explain why an individual at a particular moment chooses as object of his action a particular one of the many individuals accessible to him; nor why, in dealing with this individual, he performs an action of a specific kind, instead of any of the other, very different kinds which he might perform; nor why the other individual reacts to his action in one way, rather than another. Therefore, in trying to solve such problems, most sociologists and social anthropologists resort to a different method. They select for study, not varieties of social actions and interactions occurring within the community at large, but more or less long-lasting *sequences* of social actions and reactions occurring between the same two individuals. In most of these sequences, positive actions and positive reactions predominate: The individuals who perform them *cooperate* for a definite period of time. In other words, during this period, their actions and reactions to each other constitute a *social relation*, in the sense in which we are using this term, i.e., a system of functionally interdependent social actions performed by two interacting individuals.

3. THE SEARCH FOR SPECIFIC SOCIAL RELATIONS IN A COMMUNITY

Every investigator who enters a community is aware that he can discover many long-lasting social relations by observing how individuals who share a common dwelling, popularly called a "home"—a hut, a cabin, a house, an apartment—act and react to each other. Some sociologists have coined the term "domestic institutions" to denote such relations.

The investigator usually finds in such a dwelling a woman, a man, and a child or several children, occasionally also some other adult. Each of these individuals interacts with the others, day after day, month after month, with interruptions. Although some conflicts do occur, yet cooperation prevails. Thus, within a home several social (or "interpersonal") relations exist between the woman and the man, the woman and each child, the man and each child, a particular child and every other child. Of course, these relations are in some way interconnected; but any one of them can be investigated separately by observing the social actions which one of the two individuals involved performs, when dealing with the other, and the reactions of the other. Opportunities for such observations may be rather limited, especially when the observer is a stranger to the community, as most investigators are; and it is always difficult to observe sexual interaction. But additional information can be obtained by verbal communication, and much documentary evidence about these relations in modern communities is available.

Every such relation between two individuals living in a home includes several varieties of action, each of which is more or less frequently repeated. For instance, a woman dealing with a child repeatedly performs many different actions, feeding it, dressing it, putting it to bed, teaching it how to speak, helping it to learn desirable kinds of physical behavior, etc.; whereas the actions which a child repeatedly performs in interacting with another child may be limited to some varieties of play.

Social relations between individuals who do not dwell together can be discovered by observing periodical meetings during which they interact cooperatively. Such relations may differ considerably. Investigators have observed periodical meetings, short or long, between two men, two women, a man and a woman, two children, a child and an adult. When these individuals meet, they cooperate in various ways. Sometimes they help each other in performing actions which neither could perform alone; or they offer various gifts to each other; or they exchange goods for other goods, or goods for services; or they perform jointly specific complex actions for common purposes—technical, religious, social, etc.; or they merely talk or perform several of these cooperative activities.

But, however different these social relations, whether within or outside of homes, they have certain basic characteristics in common. Investigators can discover these characteristics, partly by observing or inquiring how each relation started, partly by ascertaining through symbolic communication what it means to participants in the community.

Each of these relations begins to function when the two individuals involved accept each other as what we may call "partners" in active cooperation. Both of them evaluate each other positively; each of them intends to perform certain actions on behalf of the other, and expects the other to perform certain actions on his behalf. Moreover, in the great majority of cases, investigators discover that this mutual acceptance of two individuals as partners, the ways in which they evaluate each other, and the kinds of actions which each intends and is expected by the other to perform are not arbitrary manifestations of individual feelings or volitions. They are based on certain *standards of valuation* and *norms of conduct* recognized as binding by participants in the community. And in the judgment of the partners themselves, as well as in that of the other people who are interested in their relation, they *ought to conform* with these standards and norms. If they do, their relation is *culturally patterned*, like other relations based on the same standards and norms.

The mutual acceptance of two individuals as partners may be obligatory. Such is the basis of "kinship" relations. Individuals who are considered descendants of the same progenitor—parent, grandparent, or more distant ancestor—are obliged to become partners in cooperative relations during childhood and to remain partners as long as they live. When the formation of a husband-wife relation is determined by the parents, the mutual acceptance of the conjugal partners is also obligatory. Many other relations are initiated by one dominant individual, the other being obliged to follow his initiative. Such is the traditional relation between a father and his child, a mother and her child, a master and a slave or serf, a ruler and his subject, a military commander and a recruit.

However, in most relations in modern communities, mutual acceptance is *voluntary* on both sides. Many are based on a contract in which both partners explicitly agree what kinds of actions they will perform in the future on behalf of each other, and how long their cooperation will last. Somewhat different, of course, is the voluntary mutual acceptance of two friends, two lovers, or two acquaintances.

Once a social relation has started in accordance with definite cultural standards and norms which both partners recognize, each partner is aware that it is his *duty* to perform in the future specific actions for the benefit of the other. Consequently, it is possible to *predict* the future course of their relation, under the condition that both of them continue to fulfil their duties.

An investigator who inquires what a husband and a wife, a parent and a child, two brothers, two neighbors, an employer and his employee, a minister and a lay member of his congregation, a merchant and his customer, or two business partners will be doing for each other during a certain time finds that not only those individuals themselves, but other participants in their community who know what their relation is, can predict their interactions in the near and sometimes even in the distant future. Indeed, since in a community every individual during his life is a partner in various social relations with a number of other individuals, each of whom is also a partner in various other social relations, if the future course of these relations were unpredictable, nobody could make any plans for the future; in fact, under such conditions, no community could continue to exist.

However, when tested by observers, these predictions of future cooperative interaction are not always confirmed by later events. For in every community many social conflicts occur which interfere with the normatively regulated course of social relations. Such

conflicts have a disorganizing influence—to use a popular term—
on social relations as organized systems; and this influence has
attracted the attention of many social scientists. Indeed, a special
branch of sociology is devoted to the study of "disorganization" of
all kinds of social systems, especially of social groups and societies.
Right now, however, we are concerned only with the disorganization of social relations.

4. THE IMPACT OF SOCIAL CONFLICTS ON SOCIAL RELATIONS

How social conflicts affect social relations obviously depends on
the way in which these relations are organized.

Thus, within certain relations some conflicting interaction is not
only considered compatible with positive mutual valuation of
the individuals involved, but is required by the cultural pattern of
the relation, as in competitive companionate play—sports, games
of chance, and intellectual contests.

In most relations, however, social conflicts usually occur when
the conduct of one partner *deviates* from the norms with which it is
his duty to conform, and this deviation provokes a negative
reaction from the other partner. Such conflicts are well known to
sociologists, especially in contemporary relations between husbands
and wives, parents and children, employers and employees. Whenever the conduct of both partners frequently deviates from established norms, and each deviation provokes a negative reaction, the
relation becomes partly disorganized and may even become
completely dissolved.

Another source of social conflict is the participation of the same
individual in different social relations with partly incompatible
duties. Investigators of families find that conflicts occur when
husbands or wives or both are involved in social relations with
fathers, mothers, or siblings which interfere with their conjugal
duties or disturb their cooperation in rearing children. Most of the
conflicts between the older and the younger generation start when
the young begin to cooperate with each other in common revolt

against the domination of their elders, and their elders start to cooperate with each other in repressing this revolt.

A third type of conflict is found between individuals who have not accepted each other as partners in a social relation and who consequently have not assumed any duties toward each other. Of course, the mere fact that no social relation exists between two individuals does not indicate a conflict; there may be little or no interaction between them.

Thus, most of the participants in a tribal or rural community have no social relations whatever with "outsiders"; so long as they seldom, if ever, interact with them, this lack of relations does not affect their lives. Even within a community not every individual has social relations with every other; many an individual who lives in an American farming community or a town regularly cooperates with only a limited number of inhabitants, and seldom interacts with others. Moreover, individuals who were partners in certain social relations cease to interact after these relations become dissolved.

But if what one individual is doing directly or indirectly disturbs the actions or injures the values of somebody who is not his partner, this antagonizes the other, who evaluates him negatively and tries to counteract or reciprocate the harm which he has done. Such a reaction, in turn, antagonizes the first agent; their mutual antagonism grows, and their active conflict continues. Investigators have found many examples of such long-lasting conflicts between sorcerers in tribal communities, farmers in rural communities, competing craftsmen and merchants in towns, heads of large ambitious families struggling for power, faithful adherents of divergent religions, and natives and newcomers whose cultures differ. When the interaction between antagonists is not subjected to any common standards and norms, conflict can become quite ruthless. And if other participants in the community take sides in such conflicts, the community may be partially divided into sections struggling against each other; and this has a disorganizing influence on the community as a whole. Probably the best-known examples of such divisions are the violent interfamily struggles which sometimes continue for generations—e.g., the old Corsican "vendettas" and the family feuds among certain American mountaineers.

Social conflicts within communities do not, however, always result in disorganization. They are often anticipated by leading participants, who cooperate to check or counteract them. This may result in the development of new standards and norms regulating social interaction.

Conflicts due to deviations of one partner from established standards and norms can be avoided if the other partner, instead of reacting negatively to these deviations, reacts in such a way as to stimulate further cooperation. For instance, when parents, instead of punishing children for all manifestations of nonconformity, tolerate minor deviations, and use positive inducements to make the children cooperate, later conflicts are prevented or reduced. This is a well-known trend in modern education, but it is found also in some tribal communities.

When husband-wife relations are based on the ideal of voluntary mutual love, social conflicts are usually overcome without repressing deviations. Conflicts resulting from the incompatibility of different social relations in which individuals participate can be counteracted by integrating these relations into new social systems (see Chapter 9). And ruthless conflicts between antagonistic individuals who do not accept each other as partners can be, and are being, avoided more or less successfully by inducing or compelling both individuals to conform with certain restrictive norms. Such norms may become an integral part of the mores or laws recognized as binding by most participants.

In short, when social relations within a community tend to become disorganized under the impact of social conflicts, active leaders who are aware that the unity, or even the very existence, of this community is thus threatened, usually try to reorganize these relations in such a way as to eliminate further conflicts. As we shall see in later parts of this work, reorganization of the more complex kinds of social systems—social roles, social groups, and societies—in order to prevent disorganization is a very significant trend in social history.

5. SOCIOLOGICAL GENERALIZATIONS ABOUT SOCIAL RELATIONS

Since sociology is a generalizing science, the ultimate task of students of social relations is to develop a systematic general theory applicable to all social relations, whenever and wherever found. Such a theory requires, first of all, an adequate classification or taxonomy.

Now, in every community the people themselves generalize about the social relations which exist among its participants. Their generalizations are primarily based on a classification of the partners. This is clear when common nouns are used to designate individuals who are partners in specific social relations. The same noun may be applied to both partners or a different noun to each; but in either case, all relations between individuals designated by such nouns are considered alike by participants in this community. There are such nouns in every language. Take a few examples of those which are used in English-speaking communities.

When two individuals are close partners in kinship relations, they are called "brothers," if both are men; "sisters," if both are women; "brother" and "sister," if one is male and the other female. Each of these three kinds of relation is supposed to include distinct mutual duties. All relations between a man who is called "husband" and a woman who is called "wife" are supposed to be essentially similar, so far as their mutual duties are concerned. All relations between a "mother" and a "daughter" are considered alike; so are all relations between a "mother" and a "son." Although these two kinds of relations differ somewhat, a basic similarity exists between them, for sometimes the noun "child" is used instead of the two nouns "daughter" and "son." The same applies to relations between "father" and "son"; "father" and "daughter"; and "father" and "child." When one of two interacting individuals is called "officer" and the other "soldier," or one "teacher" and the other "pupil," or one "doctor" and the other "patient," this implies that the relation is like all other relations where the partners are called by the same names.

These popular classifications are, obviously, not based on objective, scientific research; but are practical, intended to guide the ideas and actions of participants in community life. Nonetheless, if, and in so far as, individuals to whom such classifications are applied define and evaluate each other in accordance with the same general conceptions of partnership, and interact as they are supposed to do, such classifications are scientifically significant for studies of those particular communities. Most cultural anthropologists take them fully into consideration when learning the spoken language of tribal communities.

Our main problem, however, is how to achieve a systematic classification of social relations, not within one community, but within all communities. Such classification requires, of course, an adequate definition of the general terms used in various languages and cultures to designate partnerships in specific categories of social relations and a thorough comparative study of the mutual duties of partners.

This is a problem which social thinkers have been trying to solve for thousands of years; but, unfortunately, until modern times their solutions were not based on scientific investigations, only on their own evaluative and normative judgments. They selected those social relations which in their opinion were most essential for the good of all mankind, and formulated universal principles with which participants in these relations *ought* to conform.

Most of these generalizations formed parts of religious doctrines—e.g., Brahmanism, Buddhism, Judaism, Zoroastrianism, Islam, or Christianity. Others became partly independent of religion, like those of Confucius and his followers. Secular Greek philosophers included them under the concept of *ethics*. For instance, Aristotle in his *Ethics* selected as the most important interindividual relations those between husband and wife, parent and child, master and serf, and male friends; and he formulated universal moral norms for these relations. Friendship attracted considerable attention from other Greek and Roman thinkers, because it was considered the main basis of cooperation between men; and men controlled social life in general.

In modern times, as the range of research expanded to many previously unknown fields, and an objective scientific approach was slowly substituted for the ethical approach, generalizations about social relations became increasingly difficult in view of the vast diversity of cultural patterns discovered in particular communities. Most investigators agree, indeed, that the so-called "family relations" are universal; and many comparative studies of conjugal relations and of parent-child relations have been published. Other investigators consider kinship relations as fundamental. But even these widely spread relations are by no means uniform, and most of the others differ widely.

Consequently, these generalizations have been subjected to considerable criticism by various psychologists, sociologists, and cultural anthropologists. Doubts have even been expressed about the possibility of investigating social relations as separate phenomena and of drawing valid scientific generalizations about them in abstraction from the psychological life of the individuals who participate in them, the social organization of the community within which they are formed, and the total culture of community. Such doubts are partially justified, for investigators of social relations frequently ignore facts which they should take into consideration, thus making their approach defective. But, if these defects are corrected, a comparative study of social relations leads to important generalizations which can be scientifically tested.

6. The Theory of the Dependence of Social Relations on Psychological Factors

Critics of the theories of social relations cannot deny that the latter are subjected to certain standards and norms; for the evidence is overwhelming. In nonliterate communities, investigators find orally expressed evaluative and normative judgments concerning relations between mother and child, husband and wife, brothers, sisters, etc. In communities dominated by religious groups, such judgments are promulgated by priests, usually in writing, and eventually accepted by laymen. In modern communities dominated by states, the written laws contain evaluative and normative judgments regulating various kinds of social relations—among them, numerous and diverse contractual relations—and these judgments are supposed to be applicable to every particular relation of the given class between any two individuals within the state borders.

Many investigators based their generalizations about social relations entirely on such evaluative and normative judgments, and did not study the actions of the individuals who were supposed to conform with these judgments. Sometimes this was inevitable. Historians had to rely primarily, if not exclusively, on documentary evidence contained in religious books and secular legal enactments. An anthropologist who spent only a few weeks or months in a community which he did not know from previous studies had barely enough time to ascertain the generally recognized mores, and did not have an opportunity to observe how these mores functioned in particular cases.

Most of the methodical studies of factual interaction between partners in social relations were, therefore, and many of them still are, carried on by investigators within their own communities or communities with similar mores or laws. The majority of these investigators were social advisers, social workers, psychiatrists, or psychologists, primarily interested for practical reasons in social conflicts which might either lead to eventual dissolution of a social relation (e.g., separation or divorce in conjugal relations) or have socially undesirable effects upon the psychology of the partners, especially the psychology of children in parent-child relations. The emphasis in these studies is predominantly on psychological factors, since in order to explain such conflicts and eventually to prevent future conflicts, in every particular case some knowledge of the psychological background of both partners is necessary.

Inasmuch as social conflicts occasionally occur in nearly every complex, long-lasting relation, this psychological approach was extended by some investigators to all social relations, typically by Freud and his followers. Moreover, their methods were in accordance with the old doctrine of individualistic social thinkers that all social systems must be explained by the psychology of individual participants. And since most psychologists assume that certain basic psychological traits are universal components of human nature, they have made quite a few attempts to apply sweeping psychological generalizations to social relations in all communities, however their cultures differ.

But, when investigators concentrate on a thorough comparative study of social relations in which few conflicts occur, they find that the psychological background of the partners includes their awareness and acceptance of the standards and norms of those specific social relations and a tendency to act in conformity with them. An individual cannot become an effective partner in a social relation unless and until he has been psychologically prepared for such partnership. This preparation constitutes a part of what is popularly called "education." When a relation functions normally, this implies that both partners have been educated so as to be able and willing to cooperate with each other according to the cultural pattern of the relation. Thus, instead of trying to explain the social relations in which individuals participate by their psychological nature, we must explain their psychological similarities and differences by ascertaining for what social relations they have been prepared by their education. In short, without sociological generalizations about culturally patterned social relations, no psychological generalizations about individual participants are possible.

7. The Theory of the Dependence of Interindividual Relations on the Social Environment

Another well-known objection to comparative generalizations about social relations in different communities is based on the assumption of many sociologists that it is impossible to study any individual activities which conform with cultural patterns in abstraction from the social structure of the collectivities—large or small—to which the agents belong, for all individual conformity is due to societal pressure.

This theory, originally expounded by the French sociological group of which Durkheim was the initial leader, has been developed in a somewhat different form by American theorists of "social control." When applied to social relations, it claims that every social relation—e.g., between husband and wife, parent and child, employer and employee, or landlord and tenant—whether regulated by mores, religious principles, or rules of civil law, is collectively controlled by the community or wider society; and that without the sanctions which the community applies to the conduct of each partner, no regular conformity with cultural patterns would be possible. Every such relation is, thus, an integral part of the social structure of the community or of the larger "society" of which this community forms a part.

Individual actions are, indeed, usually subjected to some kind of observation, evaluation, and practical influence, whether we call it "social control" or something else. The term social control has been given by sociologists various meanings, some too narrow, others too inclusive. It might, therefore, be advisable to discard the term social control altogether; but, since it is so widely used, perhaps it should be preserved, provided it is defined in such a way as to avoid the two extremes, making it thus heuristically useful.

First of all, in studying the phenomena which are included under this term, we find that the noun *control* denotes some kind of purposive activity. Next, the adjective *social*, when applied to human activity, implies that the activity, whoever performs it, is intended to influence somebody else. In other words, *social control* denotes actions of which human individuals or groups are the objects. Thirdly, according to the prevalent use of this term, it applies only to those social actions which are intended to make other human agents conform with certain cultural patterns.

Social control in this sense is obviously inapplicable when an individual performs culturally patterned actions without any active interference from others, e.g., when a believer prays to his god in private, a mathematician solves a problem, or an author composes a poem. He probably learned to do it when he was subjected to the social control of educators; but that is past and gone, and he may have learned it without anybody's active control, through voluntary imitation of a model or from reading books of his own choice. Some sociologists use the term "self-control" to denote individual conformity with recognized norms without outside pressure; but this simply means that the individual considers the norms as binding, even when he does not expect to be subjected to anybody else's control.

Usually the term control connotes the use of coercive methods supported by *negative sanctions* of disapproval or punishment. But, if by social control is meant all kinds of social activity intended to make others conform, we shall find that the use of *positive sanctions*—approval, rewards, etc.—though less conspicuous, are at least as general and probably more effective. Conformity, after all, consists primarily in performing actions which certain norms require and only secondarily in refraining from actions which transgress those norms. Negative sanctions are mostly used to repress transgressions. But when an individual, under somebody else's influence, regularly *performs* certain actions, this usually indicates that the results of these actions have been made valuable to him—in other words, that the controlling agent uses positive sanctions.

Finally, in studying social control, it is essential to ascertain who the controlling agent is. Sociologists who insist that all individual conformity is collectively determined investigate mostly the control exerted by collective agents, either organized groups—government, church, economic corporation, etc.—or unorganized masses— "crowds" or "publics." They usually neglect social control exerted by individual agents, unless the latter are powerful rulers or leaders of social groups or masses. Whereas, if we investigate social relations, we find that the primary, universal type of social control is that exerted by one partner on the other partner; and that it is not one-sided, but mutual.

Once two individuals have accepted the standards, according to which they should evaluate each other positively, and the norms, according to which each should regularly perform definite duties toward the other, each expects the other to conform with these standards and norms, and each knows that the other expects him to conform. The voluntary conformity of each is conditioned on the conformity of the other. A intends to do for B what A's duties require, provided B does for A what B's duties require. This means that A uses positive sanctions to make B conform, but B also uses them, in so far as A's benefits depend on B's actions. On the other hand, so long as they continue to interact, each knows that, if he does something harmful to the other's values or interferes with the realization of the other's purposes, the other may reciprocate; thus, both can use negative sanctions to prevent transgressions. In short, each is subjected to the social control of the other by both positive and negative sanctions.

This mutual control is often unequal, for A may be able to do more for B than B can do for A; and, consequently, A's positive sanctions are more influential than those of B. A parent can do more for a child than the child for the parent; a physician can usually do more for the patient than the patient for the physician. Also A may have more power to apply negative sanctions to the actions of B than B to the actions of A. A parent can spank a child, and a teacher flunk a student, but not the other way around.

Thus, a sociologist who wants to investigate fully social relations must take into consideration not only the standards and norms which both partners accept and tend to follow, but also the sanctions which one or both actually use in the course of their relation to promote conformity and prevent nonconformity with the commonly accepted standards and norms. There are two kinds of social relations which, when fully developed, are almost entirely self-sufficient and able to exist without any external control: erotic relations between men and women, and friendship relations. In most cases, however, mutual control of partners is seldom sufficient to maintain the relation; and, consequently, the conduct of one or both partners is also subjected to some social control of outsiders.

Frequently, this control, positive as well as negative, is exerted by certain individuals. Thus, the social relation between one parent and a child is in some measure controlled by the other parent, often also by the parent's kin. The social relation between a husband and a wife in most communities was, and still often is, subject to the control of the parents of one or both of them. Moreover, the individuals who try to control it are themselves involved in social relations with one or both partners. This means that a social relation between A and B is connected with relations between A and/or B and some outsiders—C, D, E, etc.

We noticed above that sometimes these relations are partly incompatible and result in conflicts. But they frequently become functionally integrated, and this raises important sociological problems. Do such combinations of interdependent social relations constitute distinct social systems? If so, are these systems culturally patterned in such a way as to make comparative generalizations about them possible? We shall find that they are, and that only by studying such combinations can a general theory of individual participation in social life and culture be developed.

8. The Theory of the Dependence of Social Relations on Total Cultures

The third main criticism of generalizations about social relations as separate phenomena has been voiced by cultural anthropologists, according to whom no social phenomena—and for that matter, no cultural phenomena whatsoever—should be investigated apart from the total culture of the community within which they occur. And no particular social relation, religious rite, technical performance, etc. should be abstracted from the culture of a community to compare with social relations, religious rites, technical performances, etc. abstracted from the total cultures of other communities, because every such culture constitutes an integral whole.

This methodical principle, if taken literally, would prohibit the progress of all cultural sciences—sociology, theory of religion, theory of material technique, economics, etc. Only total cultures could be compared; and the best that students of culture could achieve would be half-poetic, half-philosophic typologies, as exemplified by *Patterns of Culture* of Ruth Benedict.

Fortunately, many cultural anthropologists not only write monographs on specific cultural phenomena in particular communities abstracted from their total cultures, but draw comparative generalizations about them. For instance, Malinowski's generalizations concerning sexual relations, father-son relations, "crime and customs," and the connection between magic and horticulture, are based primarily on monographic studies of such phenomena among the Trobriand Islanders, but hypothetically extended to other "savage" communities.

The emphasis of cultural anthropologists on the need of studying particular cultures in their totality may be considered not as a dogmatic assertion that comparative generalizations about specific cultural phenomena are impossible, but as a methodical principle requiring that such generalizations be based on a thorough comparative analysis of those phenomena, not as they appear to a superficial observer, but to the people themselves who participate in them.

Take, for example, Margaret Mead's succinct statement of the methodical postulate of cultural anthropology: "No fact about the behavior of the members of the group who share a common culture, and are in greater or less degree members of a given society, is relevant out of its context." What are we to understand by the words "relevant" and "context"? The scientific relevance of a fact depends on its relation to the problem which scientists are trying to solve. Obviously, when their problem is to discover the integrated culture shared by a "society" as a whole, any social fact is viewed as if every other fact within this society might be a part of its context.

But if the problem is to discover whether within this society, as a field of research, there are such specific systems of social actions as father-child relations, kinship relations between brothers, husband-wife relations, or cooperative relations between fishermen, each relation itself, as experienced and enacted by the partners, provides the context within which facts concerning the behavior of the partners must be viewed. The father and the son, the husband and the wife, or the cooperating fishermen are well aware of those cultural standards and norms current in their community with which they are supposed to conform in interacting with each other. This is the part of the culture of their community or society which an investigator of their social relations has to study in order to understand their behavior. What is essential from the scientific point of view is that comparative generalizations be based on objective inductive research, and take fully into consideration differences, as well as similarities.

This, however, raises another problem which cultural anthropologists are rather neglecting. Why do similar social relations exist in many otherwise different communities, but not in all of them? Why are kinship relations in some communities based on bonds of common descent on the female side; in other communities, on the male side; and in still others, on both sides? Why are marital relations monogamous in many communities, but polygamous in others, regardless of differences in the total cultures of these communities? Why did social relations between sick individuals and individuals who assumed the duty of curing them require in many communities a century ago, and still do in some communities, the use of magic; in others, an appeal to divine beings; but now in most of them only natural techniques? Why are the merchant-customer relations, found in many rural communities, absent from various tribal communities? Why do children in many rural communities, upon reaching a certain age, become partners in social relations with teachers, whereas such relations did not exist in most rural communities two centuries ago and still do not exist in various tribal communities?

This, as we know, is a part of a more general problem which theorists of *social evolution* have tried to solve. The most systematic and thorough of their theories was developed by Herbert Spencer. According to him, every society at any moment represents a certain stage in the universal evolution which follows the same line throughout the world. Tribal societies represent earlier stages, with some of them more advanced than others. Rural communities are parts of larger, more highly developed societies. Social relations are *institutions* of societies, and evolve as these societies evolve. Matrilineal kinship is found in societies at an earlier stage of evolution, patrilineal kinship at a later stage. Monogamous marriage represents a more advanced stage of family or domestic institutions than polygamous marriage. Merchant-customer relations can exist only in societies in which industrial or economic institutions have reached a high evolutionary level. Teacher-pupil relations are relatively late products of the evolution of professional institutions within societies.

The Spencerian theory of the parallel evolution of societies as wholes has been invalidated; but, nonetheless, the evolutionary approach can be applied to *specific* cultural systems, including social systems. Historical evidence proves that many new varieties of heretofore nonexistent systems evolve in the course of time, and their cultural patterns spread more or less widely, with the result that some of the older varieties eventually disappear or survive only in relatively isolated areas.

Consequently, an investigator who wants to explain why specific social relations exist in some communities, but not in others, should learn something about their history. This is easy, of course, when these communities have already been investigated, and the results of the investigations recorded in writing. Even without such records, it is often possible to ascertain whether social relations with a certain cultural pattern existed or did not exist in a community a generation ago, or even further back. If they already existed then, the problem of their origin remains unsolved. But if they did not exist then, they must have been recently initiated by participants in the community or—what is more probable—have penetrated from the outside. In the latter case, the recent appearance of similar patterns in other communities may be explained by similar extraneous influences. This is how, for instance, the existence of teacher-pupil relations in most modern rural communities is explained by the influence of urban intellectual centers; whereas no such influence has yet penetrated into many tribal communities.

9. CONCLUSIONS

Summarizing the above discussion, we may say that investigators of social interaction between individuals within communities can reach valid sociological generalizations only if they concentrate on a comparative study of culturally patterned social relations between individuals who evaluate each other positively by definite standards, and accept norms, according to which it is the duty of each toward the other to perform specific actions for the benefit of the other. And, furthermore, they must study social conflicts between individuals, in so far as they affect their social relations.

This comparative scientific study of social relations is not an easy task, for social relations are dynamic systems of social actions. It is not enough to know what rules of conduct—mores, religious principles, and legal enactments—participants in a community recognize as binding. Every social relation must be studied in the course of its duration, so as to ascertain what the two partners are actually doing; the actions which each of them actually performs will depend on the actions which the other performs.

Moreover, social relations within a community are in continual flux. New relations emerge all the time, when newcomers—infants or adults—enter the community, and when particular individuals, in the course of their lives from childhood on, become partners in relations in which they did not participate before—companionate relations during childhood and adolescence, conjugal relations with adults of the other sex, contractual relations with adults of the same sex, etc. Former social relations reach the end of their duration: some, because they were intended to last only for a limited time; others, because one partner dies or leaves the community; and others are dissolved in consequence of social conflicts. And when one partner or both become involved in new social relations or cease to participate in a previous relation, this may affect the course of other relations in which they participate.

Finally, in comparing social relations in many communities, it is not enough to ascertain their similarities and differences at a particular time. For all communities have a history; and whenever historical evidence is available, investigators discover that in the course of time new varieties of culturally patterned social relations, which did not exist before, have been evolving in some communities and gradually expanding into other communities. A thorough study of such evolution and expansion is essential for a systematic sociological theory.

In the following chapters, we shall apply this dynamic conception of social relations to four different categories, and try to show how sociology can reach generalizations about social relations in many communities, without having to study the psychology of individual partners, or the whole social organization, or the total culture of the community in which these relations are found. But we shall not attempt to develop a general theory of *all kinds* of social relations which sociologists, ethnographers, cultural anthropologists, and historians have been investigating. That would be too great a task to undertake here. Moreover, the evolution of social relations, especially in modern times, is closely connected with the integration of numerous social relations into the more complex systems to which we shall devote the latter part of this work.

CHAPTER 5

MOTHER-CHILD RELATIONS

1. The Sociological Significance of Mother-Child Relations

There are several reasons why we consider a comparative study of relations between mothers and children highly instructive for the understanding of social relations in general.

In the first place, these relations are probably the most widely spread. Although they are not equally important everywhere, and their patterns are constantly changing, they have been found in some form or other in all lasting communities, past and present.

In the second place, they are usually the first social relations in which individuals begin actively to participate, and this participation is achieved gradually and slowly. Consequently, their study throws a significant light on the problem of how individuals become partners in social relations in general.

In the third place, each of these relations is expected to change, and actually changes, in the course of its duration. Its cultural pattern requires new kinds of actions to be performed by the partners, while other kinds of actions cease to be performed. This is significant for comparative purposes; for certain social relations seem rather static, almost changeless. Indeed, some sociologists have even assumed that every social relation is essentially static, and that whatever changes occur must be due either to individual deviations from cultural patterns or to external influences. Therefore, the difference between social relations which are expected to change and those which are not raises important problems.

The fourth reason is that, although many investigators have studied mother-child relations in numerous communities with different cultures, no general systematic theory concerning these relations has been published. Works about "the family" contain some generalizations about mother-child relations, but the latter are considered an integral part of the family as a whole, and much less space is devoted to them than to generalizations about conjugal, or marital, relations, which are supposed to be the most essential for the existence of the family. General works about the child obviously take into consideration the influence of the mothers on the lives of children, but only as one of many influences which affect their personalities.

Our fifth reason is that there is an enormous amount of factual material from which generalizations about these relations can be drawn. The most reliable material concerns the standards and norms with which a mother and a child are supposed to conform in interacting with each other. Some evaluative and normative judgments have been expressed by mothers, occasionally by children. In the great majority of cases, however, standards and norms are formulated for the guidance of mothers and/or children by various authoritative judges, guardians of customs and mores in the community, priests, educators, advisers, legislators, and moral philosophers. From such ideological statements, models of these relations can often be validly reconstructed.

Less rich is first-hand material about *actions* of mothers and children, collected by scientific observers. As we mentioned above, only recently did the ethnologists investigating tribal and folk communities begin methodical observation of such actions. Most of the factual evidence which has been gathered by students of particular mother-child relations in their own communities—sociologists, social workers, psychologists, and psychiatrists—was selected with reference to practical problems of family disorganization. However, observations of normal family life, including mother-child relations, have been lately increasing.

Voluminous material is contained in reminiscences of individuals about relations in which they were partners or which they observed as interested witnesses. The majority of autobiographies contain reminiscences of the authors concerning active relations with their mothers, and many biographers record such reminiscences of the biographees and their associates. Some autobiographies and biographies of women describe their interaction with their children. Letters record experiences and observations of the writers. Answers to interviews contain, besides manifestations of attitudes, fragmentary descriptions of conduct. Although such descriptions can seldom be uncritically accepted as true, there are ways of estimating their reliability and using them for scientific purposes.

Our present outline is based almost entirely on material collected and published by other investigators. However, we do use some unpublished autobiographical materials and occasionally refer to "common-sense knowledge," which the author shares with his readers, concerning mother-child relations in modern Western communities.

We shall limit our survey to the mother-child relations which are considered indispensable for newborn children to become participants in collective life. Even so, we shall meet many difficult problems.

2. VARIOUS CONCEPTIONS OF MOTHERHOOD

The first problem arises when we ask: "Who is a mother?" For the word "mother" and its equivalents in other languages have several different meanings. The most general meaning, the one which most investigators accept as self-evident, is that of a woman who has given birth to an infant. We shall call such women *biological* mothers. But the term *mother* is also applied to other women.

Thus, in some tribal communities (e.g., the Zuñi Indians), the sister of a biological mother is also called mother of the child born to her sister; and the child, as it grows up, is supposed to act toward her as if she were its biological mother.

Sometimes a child becomes separated for a time from its biological mother, and another woman takes care of it, as if it had been born to her. She is designated by the English term "foster-mother." Right now in the United States, foster-mothers take temporary charge of children whose biological mothers are for some reason unable to perform their motherly duties. In quite a few folk communities, it was customary for two biological mothers to exchange their children for several years.

The permanent *adoption* by women of children born of other women, living or dead, known or unknown, is a widely spread phenomenon; and the relation between such a woman and the child which she has adopted is supposed to be similar to what it would have been if the child had been born to her.

A "stepmother" is supposed to accept as her own her husband's child whose biological mother is dead or divorced, and assume toward it the duties which the latter originally performed.

In many Christian, especially Catholic, communities, a woman who acts as ceremonial sponsor during the christening of a child is called "godmother" or "baptismal mother." Between her and the child a sociomystical bond is established, and she has certain duties toward the child similar to those which the biological mother performs.

There is still another old meaning of the word *mother*. In many religions, we find myths of *divine* mothers, to whom minor gods, men, or living beings in general, owe their existence, and who guard them, protect them, and even keep them alive.

We suggest, therefore, that a distinction be made between *biological motherhood, social motherhood,* and *mythical motherhood*. The term *biological motherhood* refers exclusively to well-known natural phenomena; whereas the terms *social motherhood* and *mythical motherhood* refer to cultural phenomena. As sociologists, we are interested in the cultural patterns of social motherhood. By that we mean a certain category of social relations which a living woman initiates between her and a newborn infant or a small child which is presumably dependent upon adults for its survival and development. We leave the study of mythical motherhood to religionists, although we recognize that it has some social significance, since a divine mother often represents the ideal of perfect motherhood, and human mothers who believe in her existence frequently appeal to her for help in dealing with their own children.

As the examples mentioned above indicate, biological motherhood is not an indispensable condition of social motherhood, though social motherhood based on biological motherhood usually provides the model for all other varieties of social motherhood. Nor does biological motherhood necessarily lead to social motherhood. In many instances in various communities, past and present, a biological mother, even though known to have given birth to an infant, does not become a social mother, and does not initiate a social relation between her and the infant born of her. A brief survey of these instances will help us understand under what conditions social motherhood originates.

3. Rejection of Children by Their Biological Mothers

The first essential condition of every social relation (in the sense in which we define this term) is mutual acceptance of two individuals as active partners. A newborn infant is, of course, commonly experienced merely as a little living animal. Any social relation between it and its biological mother must be initiated by her. This implies that the mother conceive it from the very first as a human being, capable of developing into a valuable participant in social life.

However, such a conception is not universally applied to all infants, as is proved by the custom of *infanticide*. In some communities infanticide is permitted under certain conditions, while killing an adult, an adolescent, or a child who is already an active participant is prohibited as a crime. This means that under those conditions an infant is not yet considered a human being or classified together with other human beings.

Infanticide is permitted for various reasons. Thus, scarcity of the means of subsistence is frequently the main reason: raising too many infants might deprive some adults or older, already valuable children of the necessary means. In communities where women in general are considered much less valuable than men, female infants can be killed, if rearing them would interfere with the most important social function of their mothers—procreating and bringing up male descendants. For this reason female infanticide was permissible in China and India.

More significant is infanticide which is not merely permitted, but required by the mores. In many communities, elimination of some infants is, or was, considered necessary, if they seemed destined to become socially *negative* human beings, unfit to participate in community life. Biological mothers are, therefore, obliged to reject such children.

Numerous types of obligatory infanticide have been described by ethnologists. Many of them are connected with belief in a magico-religious evil inherent in the infant, which is not only ominous for its own future, but dangerous to the family or even to the whole community. Since any infant may have characteristics considered symptomatic of evil, in some communities "wise men"—magicians or priests—inspect all newborn infants. Frequently all twins are considered bearers of evil.

Even after a child has been accepted, his rejection may be obligatory, if after some months or even years his negative, socially dangerous potentialities, hidden at first, become manifest. During his physical growth, symptoms may appear showing that a dangerous magical force is inherent in his body; e.g., his upper teeth may grow before his lower teeth. He may also unexpectedly and irremediably change under a powerful external influence. Perhaps he is no longer the original child, only a substitute, a "changeling." In all such cases, whenever he must be eliminated lest sooner or later he bring harm upon others, the mother is bound to repudiate him and sever all relations with him.

In some militant societies—e.g., Sparta and early Rome—every infant was killed who was deformed or weak, and therefore judged to be physically unfit to grow into a strong and healthy warrior or a worthy wife and mother of warriors.

Another well-known reason for eliminating newborn infants was their illegitimacy. When extra-conjugal sexual intercourse was branded as impure or sinful, an illegitimate child was apt to be considered infected by the impurity of its mother. Consequently, both the child and its biological mother were rejected—sometimes killed, sometimes simply excluded from community life.

4. Acceptance of Children by Mothers

We know that the rejection of newborn infants as socially undesirable, whether voluntary or obligatory, was and is much less frequent than their acceptance. A biological mother accepts her infant as a valuable being whenever she is aware that other participants in the community expect her to do so, because they judge this infant to be a socially desirable future participant. Every lasting community needs new participants; and most of its women, during childhood and adolescence, have been trained to think of themselves as future mothers of desirable children. Consequently, by the time they reach adulthood, they usually want to bear children.

The acceptance of an infant by its biological mother is usually accompanied by a symbolic performance, her own or somebody else's, which shows that the infant is desirable. Thus, a symbolic recognition of the infant by its mother's husband, presumably its father, was found in many communities: for instance, the infant was put on the floor, and the father lifted it up. Or the infant may be ceremonially washed, or ceremoniously fed sacred food, or suckled for the first time by the mother in the presence of important witnesses. Or the infant's birth may be announced to relatives and neighbors; sometimes, competent authorities visit it, inspect it, and approve of it. Or the mother, after a few days, takes the infant to a temple, and subjects it to the judgment of a priest. The most explicit and final symbolic manifestation of the infant's acceptance is giving it a name. In certain communities, this is postponed for some years, during which the infant is watched in order to detect previously unnoticed symptoms of its undesirability.

Not all desirable infants, however, have to be accepted by their biological mothers. Sometimes the biological mother gave her newborn infant to another woman who would make it more valuable. Thus, children of lower-class women, if born of upper-class fathers, were adopted by upper-class wives who had no children of their own. And if the biological mother died or was unable to rear the child, some other woman was supposed to assume her task.

When the biological mother or some other [woman accepts] an infant, she is aware that for a long time to come he will be socially identified as "her child," and she will be identified as "his mother." In other words, in the opinion of others who recognize her maternity, as well as in her own, a definite long-lasting *social bond* connects her with the child she has accepted. The child, at first, has nothing to do with the formation of this bond; in fact, knows nothing about its existence.

And, as she has been socially trained to anticipate the future of her child as a valuable human being, she has also been socially trained to foresee her own future actions bearing on this being, long before she starts performing them. This foresight is associated with the consciousness that her future actions may be "right" or "wrong," according to definite norms. She has become acquainted with some of these norms, partly by remembering the actions of her own mother and her reactions to them, partly by observing the actions of other mothers and hearing how these actions were judged by witnesses.

Other norms are communicated to her in the form of advice given by more experienced women or men; and some have been abstractly formulated by authoritative thinkers—priests, moralists, legislators. In dealing with her child, she is conscious that she is expected by others regularly to perform "right" actions and to refrain from performing "wrong" actions; that she will be judged by others positively when she performs right actions, negatively when she performs wrong actions; and that, eventually, her child, as it grows up, may judge her, as perhaps she has judged her own mother. In so far as she believes these norms to be valid, as she usually does, she recognizes that, whenever she deals with her child, it will be her *duty* as its mother to conform with every norm which prescribes what she ought to do or ought not to do.

A survey of various cultures shows a wide range of variations in the conceptions of motherly duties; yet, in comparing them, we find certain similarities in the purposes which the *actions* of mothers are intended to achieve. Differences are mostly limited to the selection of instruments and techniques by which in different cultures similar purposes are supposed to be realized.

5. Mother's Duties Concerning Her Child's Body

(a) In many communities, we find that, whenever a child is wanted, some of the duties of its mother begin before it is born. They concern its safety and normal growth while still in the mother's womb. They presuppose, of course, that she can actively influence its body. This belief is especially prominent in those cultures in which magical or religious techniques are used. The fact that the infant in the womb is almost inaccessible to sensory observation and planful physical activity is not considered an obstacle to the effectiveness of magic, since gods, who are much more powerful magicians than men, if induced by prayer or sacrifice, have nearly unlimited ability to make the unborn child safe, healthy, and perfect, and to assure its normal delivery. Consequently, the mother has a duty to perform such magical and religious actions as are deemed effective for these purposes.

For instance, in ancient Rome, a pregnant woman had to make sacrifice and prayers to half a dozen gods and goddesses, some of them—like Uterina and Alemena—specially in charge of the child in its mother's womb. During the Middle Ages, St. Anne was the favorite patroness of pregnant women. The prospective mother should also carefully avoid any contact with dangerous magical forces which might injure the child, and refrain from doing everything which would be harmful to it. In most nonliterate communities, numerous taboos are laid on pregnant women. Thus, they must refrain from eating various foods, often because certain characteristics of edible animals or plants might communicate themselves by sympathetic magic to the child. As belief in the effectiveness of magical and religious methods decreases, these duties dwindle; until all the prospective mother has to do for the sake of the child she is bearing is to follow hygienic rules.

Another set of duties which partly antedate the child's birth consist in preparing in advance what is considered an adequate material environment for him. The most general and elementary requirement is that the child should have a safe place ready and waiting for him, as soon as born. Under simple and primitive conditions, any place near his mother's body will do, and little preparation is needed; in more complex cultures, a special portion within a room or even a special room within a house may have to be carefully prepared for his safety, health, and comfort. When the family home is a sacred portion of space separated from the outside world, preparations are needed to make it secure for him, and he will be ceremonially admitted into it. If the home has a sacred center—a hearth, a corner, or a room for the family gods (like the *Lares* and *Penates* in ancient Rome)—it is essential that the influence of beneficial religious forces radiating from this center be assured to him in advance, or at least immediately after his birth. When an unwanted infant is exposed, it is put outside the limits of the area where it would be safe, if wanted.

Still another duty of a mother which frequently begins before the child's birth is the preparation of clothes and covers in which the child will be wrapped. This duty is in some communities vicariously performed by other women, relatives or friends of the pregnant woman, who offer baby clothes as gifts. But in such a case, his mother either had or will have to perform vicariously the same kind of duty for other pregnant women.

(b) After the child's birth, the mother is aware that for years ahead it will be her duty to perform numerous actions intended to keep her child alive and healthy. She will have to feed it regularly, provide it with the necessary conditions for rest and sleep, keep it warm when the climate is too cold for survival, and safeguard it against all kinds of bodily harm. Variations in such duties of mothers depend mainly on what they believe children need to remain alive and healthy; and these beliefs are culturally conditioned.

Thus, suckling the infant is almost universally considered the best, if not the only way, of feeding it; but the length of the suckling period varies from several months to two years, or even more. There are considerable differences as to the kind of food which ought to be substituted for the mother's milk during the weaning period and for years thereafter. In some cultures, the mother must regularly wash the infant; in others, no such duty is required of her. And when washing is obligatory, the fluid used may be plain or salt water, with or without soap, oil, milk, or urine. Rubbing may take the place of washing; and the infant may be rubbed with dye, cloth, oil, salt, or snow.

As for providing the infant with a place to sleep, we find a considerable variety of patterns, e.g., laying it to rest in an immovable spot, putting it into a cradle which can be rocked, or carrying it in a basket on the mother's back. Some mothers wrap their infants carefully in swaddling clothes, so that they cannot move; while others entirely omit wrapping. Belief in the degree of warmth which the infant needs may also vary: Fuegian mothers have been seen carrying their infants almost naked, even when it snows.

(c) The greatest diversity, however, is found in the motherly duty of protecting children from dangers which threaten their bodies. Of course, some generally recognized dangers of bodily injury come from observable physical processes—impact of inorganic natural forces, behavior of wild animals, and careless or hostile humans. But some dangers cannot be so easily observed—dangers of sickness from unknown causes, and particularly dangers from destructive magical forces or supernatural beings.

It is astonishing how many dangers can threaten the defenseless child from powers of evil. Inanimate objects and plants may be possessed of destructive forces which can be communicated by mere touch. Maleficent animals, acting from a distance or through invisible presences; spirits of forests, mountains, caverns, and waters; ghosts, vampires, and devils from hell: any of them can injure or kill the child. Professional witches are known to exert their malevolent powers upon helpless children; seemingly ordinary women and men may bewitch a child intentionally by the evil eye, or unintentionally by ill-omened words or even mere praise.

Mothers must, thus, be continually on the watch to avert or counteract dangers, by keeping their children within magico-religiously secure areas, attaching to their bodies amulets, or making them wear clothes impermeable to magic, giving them sacred food, purifying them by immersion or aspersion with conse-crated fluids, pronouncing certain words, sentences, incantations, whenever danger threatens, and especially by appealing for help to benevolent guardian spirits. This protection is still one of the main duties of mothers throughout the world. Only when belief in magical and supernatural dangers decreases, do other forms of protective duties take their place.

(d) Although keeping the child alive by satisfying its biological needs and protecting its body against danger is obviously the primary and indispensable task of the mother, she is usually supposed to perform still another task concerning the child's body. Since the child is considered socially valuable by those participants in the community who are positively interested in him, not so much because of what he is during infancy and early childhood as because of what he is expected to be when he grows to maturity, his support and protection must be progressively supplemented by stimulation and control of his organic development, so that his puny, weak body may become as big, strong, handsome, healthy, efficient, and immune against dangers as the best bodies of adults. When his immediate survival has been assured, the mother—usu-ally in cooperation with others who share her responsibility—must give active attention to his biological future.

This is particularly clear where the belief prevails that the child's distant future can be determined by magical or religious forces. The mother's ideal of the kind of being which she wants her child to become will be realized if she, or other more influential mem-bers of the community, through magical rites can endow the child with an inner power to grow into a physically perfect adult, or can enlist the aid of gods who will guide his growth. However, these mystical methods are usually supplemented and eventually supplanted by more realistic techniques.

We mentioned above various customs of wrapping and swaddling infants. Many of them are based on the assumption that the infant's body, if properly swaddled, will grow to be straight and well-shaped; whereas, when swaddling is discouraged or prohibited, the infant is expected to grow normally only if left free to move. Well known to anthropologists and historians are the diverse customs of shaping certain parts of the body in early life according to some model of adult normalcy or perfection. Shaping skulls was a widely spread custom, not only in tribal communities, but in some pastoral folk communities. Other bodily changes were introduced during childhood or adolescence: changes in the shape of nose, ears, or lips. With the development of a class hierarchy, the bodies of high-class children were subjected to certain influences which were supposed to make them grow into adults different from and aesthetically superior to low-class persons. The famous "lily feet" of high-class Chinese girls illustrate this.

Selection of food for the child is also supposed to be guided by its presumed usefulness in promoting its normal and healthy growth. While other methods of determining the child's biological future are decreasing or disappearing, this method is being increasingly used in modern times, in consequence of the development of scientific hygiene and the growing influence exerted upon parents by physicians, nurses, and social workers. The same may be said of methods of promoting the child's organic development by providing him with adequate physical exercise.

Now, the very growth of the child, in turn, obliges the mother to change progressively the actions by which her duties of satisfying the child's biological needs and of protecting him against danger are fulfilled.

Some of the basic duties may last, indeed, so long as the child is still supposed to require the help which she can supply—as late as adolescence, sometimes even later. Thus, mothers usually prepare food for their adolescent boys, frequently make the clothes which these boys will wear, take care of the place where they sleep, and nurse them, as well as the girls, in sickness. But none of these actions are the same as they were during their infancy or early childhood.

Normally, as we know, the task of supporting the child, protecting him, and guiding his growth is not achieved entirely by the mother, but is shared by other people. This raises important problems which will be discussed later.

6. The Mother's Duty of Making the Child a Conscious Partner in Their Relation

When the mother is required to accept an infant as valuable, she is usually supposed to define it as already having a soul or mind. This is most clearly manifested in those religions in which the infant is regarded as an incarnation or reincarnation of a spirit which existed before its birth in the supernatural world, or as endowed after its conception with a new soul by a divine creator; or else the psychological entity inherent in him may have emerged from the psyche of his mother or father, or from the common psychological essence of his progenitors.

In any case, this belief in the innate psychological nature of the child is meant to influence his mother's conduct. Having invested her child in advance with the capacity of experiencing, feeling, acting, and thinking like other conscious human beings, she is supposed to promote the development of this capacity. Since the child is expected to become in the future an active participant in the adult community, it is in some measure the mother's task to prepare him for this participation. But she cannot perform this task adequately unless the child, as he grows (not only physically, but psychologically) and becomes increasingly active, learns to cooperate with her. In short, he must become a conscious and active partner in their long-lasting social relation.

Now, for a social relation to be cooperatively maintained by both partners, each must evaluate the other positively and be aware that he is positively evaluated by the other. In view of the fact that the mother is supposed to initiate a long-lasting social relation with her child, her duty is to have the child evaluate her positively, and make him aware that he is positively evaluated by her. But, inasmuch as a newborn infant is not yet conscious of her or of himself, she must help him acquire such consciousness. This is usually done by combining active performances with symbolic communication.

A mother normally begins to speak to her child very early. She refers to him most frequently by a name. Even if it is not a personal name, but a common name, like "baby," or an expression denoting the relationship between them, like "my child," if used as a symbol exclusively designating the child, it eventually makes him aware of his identity. When she teaches him to use a specific word, like "mama," to designate herself, his awareness of their mutual identification begins to emerge. Such symbolic communication, usually initiated by the mother, but later carried on also by other adults, makes the child gradually conscious of himself as an object of other people's valuations and actions, and as an agent whose actions provoke the reactions of others. This development of the child's consciousness of his own self has been thoroughly studied by many social psychologists, and its ultimate consequences are of primary importance for the subsequent life of every individual. But just now we are concerned with its significance for mother-child relations.

Obviously, the mere fact that the child learns to identify his mother does not imply that he evaluates her positively. He may also identify other human agents, yet fear or hate them. All depends on what they do to him. The mother's duty is to perform actions which should be satisfactory to her child, or—to use a popular expression—"to make her child happy." This implies that she should relieve it from painful experiences and give it pleasurable experiences.

The duty to relieve the child from pain is the most obvious and universal, starting right after its birth and continuing as long as the relation lasts. While originally limited to physical pain, it extends, as the child grows, to other unpleasant experiences—fright, deprivation of values, social humiliation, etc. In all such cases, if she cannot prevent the pain or suffering, it is the mother's task to comfort her child psychologically.

The duty to give the child pleasure begins with feeding him, making him physically comfortable, petting him, etc. As he grows, in many communities he receives new, often unexpected pleasures: tidbits for enjoyment rather than for nourishment, toys selected for amusement, special children's holidays and parties. Modern Christmas gifts and celebrations for the enjoyment of children are familiar instances; and, although mothers are not the only ones who perform such actions, their performance is considered an essential part of her duties.

As the child becomes conscious of himself as an agent whose actions provoke the reactions of others, the mother's duty is to make him aware that she evaluates him positively, by praising or rewarding him for some actions which he has performed and helping him perform desirable actions which he spontaneously begins to perform. Of course, there are various kinds of actions which a child is not supposed to perform, because they may be dangerous to himself or harmful to other people; and the mother should prevent their performance by actively interfering with them—explicitly prohibiting them, or even punishing the child, if he disobeys. Nonetheless, she is supposed to persuade the child that such prohibitions or even punishments do not imply that she evaluates him negatively; but that, on the contrary, she does it for his own good, because she wants him to remain valuable and to become even more valuable in the future.

The duties of making the child happy and aware of being positively evaluated as an agent are included under the popular concept of "motherly love," but various communities differ in the relative importance they ascribe to such duties in comparison with other fundamental duties of hers.

7. DUTIES OF EDUCATIONAL GUIDANCE

Every mother is expected to perform many actions intended to make her child psychologically fit for future active participation in the adult community. We use the term "educational guidance," rather than the simple term "education," for the latter as commonly used is too inclusive for our present meaning. Many theorists of education include under it all the influences which, intentionally or unintentionally, contribute to the development of an individual's personality. Whereas we shall survey here only a few of the actions which are explicitly intended to make specific contributions to this development.

Obviously, the process discussed above, in the course of which the mother makes the child conscious of her and of himself, is educational. Its purpose, however, is not to prepare the child for future participation *as an adult* in the adult community, but for immediate active partnership *as a child* in the cooperative relation between them. And this purpose sometimes conflicts with the former. Vice versa, when a mother has exacting duties toward her husband or other adults, these may interfere with her duties toward her child.

In communities with strict ethical standards, like the early Puritanical New England, the difficult task of guiding the child into the straight and narrow path of righteousness did not permit the mother to indulge in such apparently useless actions as giving a child pleasure which had no educational value, or praising him for his "goodness," when he should rather be taught to be continually aware of his sinfulness. Making life too pleasant for a child or making him feel that it was not difficult to be good was apt to spoil him. He had to learn that "life is real, life is earnest"; otherwise he would not be prepared to face it. Of course, this did not mean that the mother should not love her child during his early years, only that active manifestations of her love should not interfere with her duty of preparing him for his later years.

The mother is not the only one on whom the sociopsychological future of the child depends. In communities dominated by religious beliefs, the psychological growth of children is presumed to be controlled by divine powers, and mothers have to appeal to those powers; but the effectiveness of their appeal usually depends on the aid of priests, who also regulate the education of children in religious matters. In every community, the educational guidance of boys is, sooner or later, assumed by men; and, as we know, in most modern communities, the task of educating all children above a certain age is partially taken over by professional educators.

Nevertheless, the mother is usually the first adult to function as educational guide for her child; and she continues to function as such for a long time. The entire course of this educational guidance is normatively organized, so long as it lasts. It is a continuous, dynamic process. During every period of the child's psychological development, the mother has definite educational duties preparatory for later periods. She ceases to perform them whenever the purpose has been achieved; and meanwhile she has already assumed or subsequently assumes new duties. It is impossible to separate any specific educational duty of hers from other duties which preceded it or follow it. Her task is to guide the continuous *expansion* of the child's conscious life, provide it with new experiences, and aid it in performing new actions, while taking care that the new experiences be valuable to him and the new actions useful for his future.

The first educational duties of the mother consist in training the child to take care of himself, as he becomes physically capable of doing so, since he is destined to become eventually independent of her support and protection. He must learn to regulate his excretions, to eat, to walk, to handle various material objects, to dress himself, and to avoid physical and magical dangers—in short, to perform many of the actions which she originally performed for his benefit. Although, in consequence of this educational guidance, her own duties decrease, this is not its socially recognized purpose, except if and in so far as she must be relieved of some of her duties toward him in order to perform her duties toward somebody else in another social relation—for instance, if she gives birth to another child.

Otherwise, it is obvious that her teaching the child to substitute for her in taking care of himself is intended for the child's good, not for her own. She must not let the child take care of himself in any odd way which will relieve her of her task, but train him to behave in conformity with the customs which he will be expected to follow as he grows up. He must not simply eat anything available, whenever hungry, but eat specific food at appointed times in a customary manner; not merely walk and run anyhow anywhere, but do it properly at the right time in the right place and direction; not handle any material objects any way he wants, but only certain objects in certain ways; not use any odd thing to cover himself, but put on proper clothes properly.

Nor is the mother supposed to train the child to do things for himself which it is still her duty to do for him, or which he will not have to do when he grows up; for instance, usually she should not let a child cook its own food or make its own clothes, so long as it is her duty to do it; or teach a boy activities belonging to a woman's sphere, or a girl activities proper for a man. On the other hand, she must not prolong the period of her child's dependence on her services, merely because she still wishes to take care of him; for in every culture the pattern of the mother-child relation prescribes at what age the child must be trained to perform specific activities on his own behalf, and in many cultures boys at a certain age are taken away from their mothers and compelled to become independent of their care.

To these primary duties of educating the child for self-care, other educational duties are gradually added. The mother is expected to teach, or at least to begin teaching, the child such attitudes and activities as he will need in social relations with other people. Since symbolic communication is an essential condition of all social participation, the mother must prepare the child to communicate, not only with herself, but with everybody else within the range of his potential participation—in other words, she must teach him the common language of the people among whom he is expected to live. Since all social relations imply a positive valuation of partners, it is her task to develop in him positive attitudes toward those with whom he already is or will be socially connected: other family members, friends of the family, neighbors, members of the social groups of which he will eventually become a member—clan, tribe, religious group, class or occupational group, etc.—and toward individuals endowed with prestige or power. On the other hand, it may also be her duty to develop in him negative prejudice toward people whom he is expected later to avoid or toward whom he will have to act antagonistically: dangerous strangers, people of an "impure" race or an inferior class, worshipers of "false" gods, members of hostile tribes or nations, etc.

Inasmuch as social participation in the adult community requires some acquaintance with the dominant cultural systems of this community and their acceptance, the mother should start the child's initiation into these systems, give him information and appreciation of the religious beliefs and ceremonies, of the most generally accepted customs and mores, legends and traditions, and common-sense knowledge essential for practical orientation in nature and in society. She is not expected to give the child a complete cultural preparation, particularly if the child is a boy; and, in any case, the more complex the culture, the less adequate the preparation which she can give. But whoever will supplement her educational guidance, she must begin it while the child is under her care.

Finally, she is in duty bound to impart to her child the occupational skills which she possesses and which the child, when grown to adulthood, will be socially expected to possess. Since in every society considerable occupational differentiation exists between men and women, most of the occupational skills of mothers are imparted to daughters; few, if any, to sons.

This transmission of skills from mothers to daughters has been well studied by ethnologists and historians. The methods of educational guidance vary. The child may be simply allowed to follow and imitate the mother; or intentionally stimulated and encouraged to reproduce the mother's activities in imitative play, with no expectation of useful results; or made through invitation or coercion to help the mother in her functions, by subordinate activities of gradually increasing difficulty; or made to substitute for the mother in certain functions, beginning with housecleaning, dishwashing, and taking care of young children, and ending with more intricate and skillful operations. In communities with a complex and highly standardized domestic industry, these educational duties of a mother toward her daughter continue for a long time. Even a daughter who has grown up physically and mentally may still need occupational training from her mother to perfect such skills as cooking and preserving food, spinning, weaving, sewing, adorning the home, and entertaining guests.

8. Duties of the Child Toward the Mother

When the child gradually becomes conscious of himself as a social object and agent, he learns that in the judgment of his mother, and usually also of other adults, he has definite duties toward her. These duties differ considerably from his mother's duties toward him. The mother is in duty bound to perform actions bearing upon him which will be beneficial for him and to refrain from performing any actions which might be harmful to him. Whereas most of the actions which the child is in duty bound to perform or refrain from performing have no direct bearing on the mother; he is the main value involved.

When, under the mother's command or guidance, the child eats approved food, takes care of his body in conformity with the prevailing customs, acquires certain technical skills, learns to use the common language according to its rules, or prays to a deity for protection, what he does is supposed to benefit him. When he is in duty bound not to eat forbidden food, not to move into dangerous areas, to refrain from using profane words, and to avoid contacts with bad children, it is because such prohibited actions would be physically or psychologically injurious to him. It may be said, therefore, in the terms of social philosophers, that most of the child's duties are "toward himself."

But the child is a positive value to the mother *long before he becomes conscious of himself;* and, even after that, she presumably knows what he should do or should not do for his own good long before he learns it. She cannot wait until he becomes fully conscious of what is good or bad for him, especially for the more or less distant future. She has to make him conscious that, whenever she explicitly requires him to perform any action or refrain from performing any action, it is his duty *toward her* to conform with this requirement; and that praise or reward will depend on his conformity, blame or punishment on his nonconformity. His duty is not merely to do something or not to do something, but to do something *because* his mother wants him to do it or to refrain from doing something *because* his mother wants him to refrain from it.

This basic and general duty of the child, which corresponds to the mother's duties toward him and is a necessary condition of their successful performance, may be termed the duty of *trustful obedience*. He is supposed to do willingly whatever she tells him to do and to refrain from doing whatever she prohibits, trusting her judgment of right and wrong and her altruistic intentions on his behalf.

The qualifying adjective, "trustful," is essential to distinguish this duty from that of *unconditional obedience* exacted in some other relations. For the child's duty of obedience to his mother is not binding if she is not worthy of his trust. While mentally immature, he may be unable to judge whether she is trustworthy, but nonetheless this condition exists, as is proved in several ways. First, the mother is supposed to justify his trust by requiring obedience only when the actions and restrictions she demands are expected to have consequences beneficial for his development into a positively valuable adult. Secondly, she is supposed to make him conscious, as far as possible, of her trustworthiness by allaying his doubts and explaining the reasons for her orders and prohibitions, in so far as he can understand them. Thirdly, if he is not yet able to understand these reasons, she is supposed to anticipate his future understanding and keep in mind that, as he grows up, he will judge restrospectively not only what she did for him, but what she made him do or refrain from doing.

9. THE DUTY OF GRATITUDE

This is another general duty of the child toward the mother which is extolled in many tribal and rural communities as well as in modern ones. Some religions explicitly include it among their ethical principles. For instance, the commandment in the Decalog to "honor thy father and thy mother" implies gratitude for the past, as well as submission to guidance in the future. Recently, this duty has been explicitly recognized by the national celebration of "Mother's Day" as a festival of gratitude and an expression of indebtedness to "mother."

Now, gratitude, as part of the cultural pattern of the mother-child relation, is supposed to be a purely altruistic, disinterested duty, not intended to affect the mother's future behavior, but to show appreciation of benefits received. It becomes more active as the child becomes less dependent on the mother, for it implies the child's ability to do something by his own agency which will benefit the mother. It begins with thanks or other symbolic expressions intended to give the mother pleasure in reward for what she has done, for this is all a small child can do for his mother. It gradually comes to include services which are of some use to the mother, helping her in her activities and contributing to her comfort or safety.

Gratitude is a *supererogatory* duty, over and above those duties which the child is obliged to perform under his mother's guidance; if exacted by the mother under pressure, it loses its distinctive character and becomes just another special duty included within the general duty of obedience. All the mother can do in return is to express a positive valuation of her grateful child. Ingratitude does not mean mere lack of gratitude, but behavior injurious to the mother and therefore conflicting with the fundamental standard of positive valuation of the mother, which the pattern of the relation requires. According to the pattern, the mother should remain a positive social value to the child, even when he needs her less and less, as he grows up; only the basis of valuation shifts from the future to the past. If in the mother's old age, a son or daughter does more for the mother than she can do for him or her, their relation has become the reverse of what it originally was.

10. Entrusting Specific Motherly Duties to Others

The multiplicity and complexity of motherly duties makes it often difficult for women to perform adequately all of them. Of course, some of these duties are supplemented by duties performed by men; for a woman can seldom, if ever, fully and adequately support her child, protect it from dangers, control its growth and education (especially if it is a boy), without the cooperation of her husband, perhaps of some male relative, a medicine man, a priest, or a guardian of order in the community.

But even for her specific motherly duties, she often needs help. In many old tribal and peasant communities, where mothers are frequently engaged in hard technical activities outside the home, they have to entrust the physical care of young children in their absence to older children, sometimes to old women, especially grandmothers. More significant, however, is the help which many women in modern communities need when they assume new functions.

Thus, for many centuries upper-class women in Europe, whenever their main duties were to participate in companionate intercourse with other upper-class people, had to entrust their supporting and protective duties toward their children to nurses and other servants, and their educational duties to governesses or teachers in exclusive schools. When in the course of the Industrial Revolution an increasing number of women began to work in factories, this obviously interfered with their motherly duties. The problem was solved slowly and gradually by organizing nurseries, kindergartens, and other social centers where mothers could leave their children while they worked. And during the last hundred years, as more and more women started to perform diverse professional functions previously monopolized by men, they found it at first very difficult to combine their new functions with the old, complex motherly duties.

In our section on social roles, we shall discuss the various functions of women. What is important from the point of view of mother-child relations is that in modern communities certain specific motherly duties—guarding the health of children, promoting their physical and psychological development, and educating them—have been, at least partially, taken over by specialists. The result is that new varieties of social relations between children and adults have evolved from mother-child relations.

CHAPTER 6

FRATERNAL RELATIONS

1. Social Bonds Between Siblings

The second category of social relations which we have selected for comparative study is that between men who are considered brothers. We call this relation *fraternal*, rather than *brotherly*, because fraternal is the more commonly and widely used term. Investigation of these relations is scientifically important for two reasons. In the first place, in their original form they are universal, found in all communities. In the second place, they have been considered for thousands of years a perfect example, an ideal type, which many other social relations are supposed to follow.

In tribal communities, relations between brothers constitute a specific variety of so-called "kinship relations." As we noticed in Chapter 4, a kinship relation is one to which two individuals are born; they become partners because they are presumably united by bonds of common descent. The closest of such bonds are between siblings, in the sense of children of the same parents. The term *brothers*, or its equivalent, is universally applied to male siblings; *sisters*, to female siblings.

Conceptions of parenthood, however, differ considerably. In some tribal communities, children born of the same woman are siblings, innately bound together; whereas biological paternity is either ignored or considered unimportant. In other communities, the father is judged to be the real progenitor; thus, when a man has several wives, all their children are his, and consequently siblings. But if a woman bears children to two or more men, these children are not considered real siblings (unless their fathers are brothers). However, whether having a common mother be a stronger bond

133

than having a common father, or vice versa, children who have the same father *and* mother are the most closely united.

Another fundamental difference is based on the sex of the siblings. Whether they are bound by common maternal, paternal, or bilateral descent, the relations between a brother and a sister, between two sisters, and between two brothers differ, so far as their duties are concerned.

Viewed in historical perspective, brother-sister relations are relatively the least important. First of all, in many communities direct cooperation between them is limited, sometimes almost entirely precluded, lest it lead to sexual interaction, which is almost universally prohibited as incestuous. Secondly, even when within a family a brother and a sister cooperate in certain respects, because of division of labor between the sexes, this cooperation usually stops as soon as either gets married. There are, indeed, some exceptions. Thus, in matrilineal communities, an elder brother often assumes the tasks of a father toward his sister's sons. In patrilineal communities, if the father dies, a brother sometimes takes the place of the father in relation to his sister. And when a married sister loses her husband, and needs masculine help, her brother usually provides it. However, relations in which the brother dominates are getting relatively scarce.

The relation between two sisters is normally closer than that between a brother and a sister, for it is based on mutual assistance, rather than one-sided domination. We mentioned how, in some tribal communities, sisters share motherly duties toward each other's children. They also cooperate in various technical activities reserved for women, and sometimes also in religious activities. If a woman needs help because of sickness, deficiency of food, too much work, or during childbirth, her sister provides it, if she can; and she will be helped, in her turn, in time of need.

The performance of such duties, however, depends upon spatial proximity, since—according to the predominant mores—a woman cannot leave her home for a lengthy period of time. Although in some communities, especially where descent counts on the mother's side, a husband moves into the locality where his wife's parents live, in most communities, especially where paternal descent predominates, the wife moves into the locality of her husband. Thus, sisters frequently become separated after marriage— the more so, the wider the community habitat. Such separations increase when migrations between communities multiply. Even within the community, men cooperate in more activities performed outside of their homes than women can. Thus, brothers usually have more opportunity to interact during their lives than sisters; and, consequently, their relations have proved much more influential throughout the course of history. This is why we single them out for study.

2. The Formation and Extension of Relations Between Brothers

When two male children have been born of the same parents, each of them is unconditionally obliged to accept the other as a brother, and neither has anything to say about it. Of course, the older boy is the first to accept the other boy as his brother; but eventually both of them, as they learn the standards and norms of their community, are made fully aware that they are innately and inseparably united as brothers, and will remain so, as long as they live—perhaps even in the next world, according to the religious beliefs of some communities. Their mutual acceptance implies a mutual positive valuation; for, if one of them evaluated the other negatively, he should also evaluate negatively himself, since they share the same hereditary nature. For instance, among the Dakota Indians, "The relationship most depended upon . . . is that between brothers. . . . As they phrase it, 'He is a part of me,' and the verb used to express love between brothers is different from that used between a man and his wife, or a man and his children."

So far as their mutual duties are concerned, it is a minor matter whether male siblings are considered brothers because they are of the same father, or the same mother, or the same father as well as the same mother. These differences, however, are significant in view of the fact that relations similar to them are usually extended beyond the immediate family to other male descendants of certain more distant ancestors on the mother's, or the father's side, or on both sides; so that these are considered innately bound together like brothers, and are obliged to accept each other as lifelong partners.

Thus, when descent counts mainly on the *maternal* side, every son of a particular mother is considered hereditarily connected with all the sons born of all the mothers of the same generation as his own mother who are considered descendants of the same female ancestress. In other words, the bonds of common descent unite him, first, with every grandson of the same maternal grandmother; next, with every great-grandson of the same maternal great-grandmother; and so on, as far back as common descent, real or mythical, is supposed to be traced. This is manifested by maternal clans found in many tribal communities, where every clansman has lifelong duties toward every other clansman of the same generation.

On the other hand, when descent counts mainly on the *paternal* side, every son of a particular father is hereditarily connected with all the sons of all the fathers of the same generation who are common descendants of the same male ancestor, however distant. This is exemplified in the Greek *phratria* and the Roman *gens*, which included the totality of such male descendants. In China, bonds based on presumed descent from the same real or mythical ancestor were recognized throughout centuries, and symbolized by the common family name, which was shared by many thousands of men.

And when descent counts on both sides, a man is considered hereditarily connected with all the sons of mothers and fathers of the same generation as his own mother and father, and with all who are descendants of the same female or male ancestors as his father and mother are. This conception predominates in medieval and modern European communities.

Obviously, although all the relations between men who have common progenitors are often conceived as similar to relations between brothers, and sometimes even designated by the same terms, they are not equally influential, so far as social interaction is concerned. Naturally, the mutual duties of sons of the same parents have priority over duties based on more distant hereditary bonds. And the latter are frequently graded in importance: the further back the common ancestor, the less exacting the duties. For instance, in European communities with bilateral descent, where "brothers" are distinguished from "cousins," the "cousins" are often classified into "first cousins," "second cousins," "third cousins," and "fourth cousins." Duties toward first cousins, though less exacting than duties toward sibling brothers, are more exacting than duties toward second cousins, and so on.

The concept of brotherhood is sometimes applied to relations between men who share, not the same ancestors, but the same descendants. Thus, a woman's brother and her husband are often considered like brothers, because the woman's children are direct descendants of her husband and also of her brother's father: They share the "blood" of their father and that of their maternal uncle. In some communities, when a husband offered his wife for sexual intercourse to another man, and a child was born as a result of the intercourse, the two men were thereafter united by permanent bonds. In certain Eskimo communities, men exchanged wives for a longer or shorter time, shared the paternity of their children, and became brothers to each other.

3. Voluntary Formation of Relations Similar to Brotherhood

Still more important from the historical point of view is the voluntary creation of interindividual fraternal bonds unconnected with biological heredity, by men who want to become *like brothers* for the rest of their lives. Such relations have spread beyond the range of tribal communities and develop best in culturally more advanced and complex collectivities.

These bonds were originally rooted in magical or religious beliefs. Thus, one of the earliest and most widely spread ways of creating them was the so-called "blood covenant": Two individuals drank or sucked each other's blood, and became thereafter forever united. Ceremonial sharing of food endowed with sacred characteristics could also create a mystical bond similar to that of brotherhood. Later, secular interindividual relations of lifelong solidarity were voluntarily formed through symbolic ceremonies, accompanied by permanently binding oaths. For instance, in Germany, when two men who evaluated each other positively wanted to become associated for life, they ceremonially drank wine—a symbolic substitute for blood—from each other's cup, kissed, and called each other by their given names, announcing that this created "Bruderschaft" between them.

Relations between neighbors in rural and small-town communities also frequently follow the example of brotherly relations, after some bonds of mutual solidarity have been voluntarily established. Indeed, we are commanded, "Love thy neighbor as thyself."

Perhaps the best-known voluntary, long-lasting relations between individual men, as intimate as fraternal relations, but independent of hereditary bonds, are those of *friendship*. They have emerged in various complex collectivities, but reached their full development only in ancient Greece and Rome—judging from the evidence contained in the works of Plato, Xenophon, Aristotle, the Epicureans, and Cicero. Friendship was seldom mentioned in medieval literature, where the basic cooperative relations between men were supposed to be religious; but it was revived during the Renaissance, and is now widely spread in the Western world.

Standards and norms similar to those of brotherhood eventually became applied to relations between all the participants in certain *exclusive associations* in which participation is based, not on descent, but on voluntary selection. This type of fraternal relation began with the spontaneous formation of new religious associations closely united by mystical bonds. When such an association grew in size and developed a complex organization, a priestly hierarchy usually emerged, and the relations between its members became subordinated to the patriarchal domination of the priesthood. This was well illustrated by the evolution of Christianity from the first to the fifth century. There are now considerable differences between the various religious denominations, e.g., the Quakers and Jehovah's Witnesses as compared with the Roman Catholic and Greek Orthodox Churches. Within the large churches, however, solidary fraternal associations exist, e.g., monastical orders, composed of members who are exclusively devoted to the religious life.

Secular fraternal associations are increasing in number and influence. The Free Masons are probably the oldest and most powerful of these. Many similar associations have been formed, especially in the United States: the Elks, the Knights of Columbus, the Knights of Pythias, the [. . .] Eagles, the Moose, the Kiwanis, the Lions Clubs, Rotary Clubs, etc. Social fraternities formed by college students in Europe and America have exerted great influence on college life and among alumni. In all these we usually find some hierarchical gradations of authority, especially among the Masons, but they are based partly on the length of individual participation and partly on ability for active leadership.

The broadest conception of fraternal relations was initiated by the religious thinkers who formulated the idea that *all men are brothers*, because they have a common Father, the God who created them. This idea has been accepted, without its theological implications, by secular thinkers, according to whose opinion the welfare and progress of mankind require that every man should treat every other as if he were his brother.

The fact that the concept of brotherhood has acquired such a wide significance shows that the fraternal relation is judged to be a model which most human relations should follow. We must, therefore, investigate the duties which brothers connected by lifelong bonds have toward each other. A comparative study of these duties indicates that they are not specialized, but include widely different actions, just as motherly duties do. Unlike motherly duties, however, they are reciprocal: When one partner does something valuable for the other, the other is expected to do something valuable for him, sooner or later. This does not mean, however, that their duties are necessarily equal: One partner may do more for the other than the other does for him. It depends on how much each needs the aid of the other, and on how much each can actually do for the benefit of the other.

4. THE FRATERNAL DUTY OF SYMPATHETIC UNDERSTANDING

The primary duty on which the formation and duration of every fraternal relation depends may be called "sympathetic understanding." Brothers are supposed to communicate to each other their attitudes, experiences, feelings, desires, and ideas, and to respond sympathetically to such communications, so that each of them knows what kind of actions performed at any time will be satisfactory to the other, and expects the other to know what kind of actions will be satisfactory to him. Their individual attitudes may differ and change; but, in so far as they understand and sympathize with each other, each learns to adapt his actions and expectations to the experiences, feelings, desires, and ideas of the other.

Such sympathetic understanding often begins spontaneously in childhood during companionate play between boys. For instance, in Polynesian communities, where boys have considerable freedom until adolescence, mutual understanding between men of the same generation is highly developed. In most tribal communities, however, it is imparted to the young while they are being taught to participate in adult relations. Thus, according to one author: "The clan system of the Kafirs is . . . the seed-plot in which the altruistic sentiment develops. . . . The clan system could not exist without a strong sense of brotherhood of the members of a clan. . . . The spirit of unselfishness and *camaraderie* is very evident."

Similarly, when a relation analogous to brotherhood is voluntarily formed, it usually begins with a preparatory period, during which future partners learn to understand and appreciate each other's attitudes. This is how, according to classical thinkers, relations of friendship were supposed to be formed. Such preparation may be initiated by both, if they already share common values and are equally experienced and trained in social cooperation; or by one of them who is more experienced and better trained than the other. But, by whomever initiated, it is supposed to lead to mutual, not one-sided, understanding.

Thus, when we investigate the admission of newcomers into fraternal associations, religious or secular, we find that the task of preparing them for participation in brotherly relations is assumed by experienced members. Every newcomer learns to understand and appreciate both the member who initiates him and the other newcomers who are being initiated. After the initiation is completed, he becomes a brother of every other member, old and new, and is presumably able to understand and appreciate each of them.

5. MUTUAL AID BY GIFTS

This is a universal duty of brothers toward brothers, whether the relation is consanguineal or artificial, and whatever the degree of its closeness and intimacy.

The main purpose of offering gifts is to help the other partner satisfy his needs, whenever he lacks the means necessary for their satisfaction. But even if the other partner does not need any particular gift at a particular moment, when one offers the other a share in the values which he owns or in the pleasures which he enjoys, this is an active manifestation of their fraternal solidarity.

Gifts of food are the most general in tribal and rural communities. When a man has less food than he needs for himself and his family, be it because of sickness, a natural calamity which destroyed his domestic animals or crops, or failure in hunting or fishing, every brother of his who can afford it is supposed to offer him food. On the other hand, when a man has acquired more food than he needs, he is expected to share it with his kin. This is the predominant principle among hunters and fishermen. A man who kills a large animal or catches a big fish takes only a part of it and divides the rest among his kinsmen. Similarly, when a herdsman kills a steer, he offers to his kinsmen most of the meat. Some products of successful gardening are shared with relatives, the most extreme example being that of the Trobriand Islands, where every man delivers the products of his garden to his sister's husband living in another village, mainly to feed their children. In well-integrated agricultural communities, a farmer who has had a bountiful harvest shares some of it with his poor or unsuccessful kin. In many rural communities, this custom of offering gifts has been extended from kinsmen to neighbors.

Those who receive gifts are usually expected to reciprocate, sooner or later. The gifts they offer may be larger or smaller than those they received, depending on their ability and the needs of those who gave them the gifts. In some communities where fraternal relations are well developed, each partner strives to give the other as much as possible, regardless of needs. When a partner is unable to offer gifts of any value, he may still reciprocate by offering his services. But that is another matter.

An interesting example of the reciprocity of gifts is found during feasts to which kinsmen living in the community and sometimes even neighbors are invited. A feast, especially a ceremonial feast, celebrating a wedding, the birth of a child, or a funeral, often requires a much larger amount of food than the host can obtain by his own efforts. Consequently, the guests invited to the feast contribute minor gifts of food. Eventually, some of them will reciprocate by giving feasts on ceremonial occasions to which their former host will be invited; and he, in turn, will reciprocate the gifts he received by bringing to those feasts gifts of his own. We shall see later that such feasts, in which not only men but women participate, have influenced the evolution of a different kind of social relation.

Many other gifts apart from food may be offered by men to their brothers: gifts of domestic animals and gifts of technical materials or instruments to those who lack them or have lost them. In militant tribal communities, warriors who invade foreign communities and bring home bounty—cattle, material products, even human heads—usually offer most of it to their kinsmen.

When relations similar to brotherhood are voluntarily formed, the duty of offering gifts remains, especially when they are needed. It is a well-known duty of friends toward friends: "A friend in need is a friend indeed." But friends also frequently offer gifts to their friends simply to make them enjoy certain values—hedonistic, aesthetic, or intellectual. Within fraternal religious associations, one of the fundamental duties of all members toward every other member is to prevent or counteract "poverty," by helping him or his family, if he dies, satisfy what are considered basic needs. This may require various kinds of gifts, from food and clothes to money. In modern secular fraternities, whenever a member is involved in some economic difficulty, he expects the aid of other members who can afford it.

Historically significant are gifts of products made by individuals who specialize in one kind of production to those who specialize in another kind. The latter reciprocate; and the result is the exchange of products between specialists which occurs in many tribal and folk communities. It leads eventually to the development of *trade* between participants in different communities. Such trade was often preceded by the formation of artificial bonds analogous to brotherhood.

Even in larger and more complex societies, some bonds of friendship or companionship are frequently established between foreign merchants and local merchants.

6. Mutual Aid by Active Services

In tribal and folk communities, probably the most widely spread active services are actions intended to protect partners in brotherhood against various dangers to life, health, economic possessions, and personal prestige. Although children and women are supposed to need more protection than men, and protective duties are essential in relations between fathers and children, husbands and wives, and brothers and sisters, yet men are especially subjected to dangers in the course of some activities which they perform.

Thus, physical and magical dangers threaten their lives during big-game hunting or deep-sea fishing, and obviously during defensive or aggressive warfare with hostile communities. The duty of brothers and other kinsmen to defend each other against such dangers to life, even at the risk of their own lives, is universal and persists throughout history.

If a member of a clan has been killed by somebody of another clan, it is the brotherly duty of his kinsmen to avenge his death, and thus to protect other kinsmen from similar dangers in the future. If a man is sick, some of his brothers are supposed to do their best to help him recover, or obtain help from a presumably competent medicine man or doctor. If he dies, his kinsmen participate in his funeral, which often includes religious ceremonies that will protect his soul against evil powers in the other world.

Protecting the property of a brother against destructive natural forces and human thieves and robbers is also a fraternal duty. When a man is absent from home, one of his brothers or several of them assume the duty of protecting his wife and children. And if a man's brother is slandered or ridiculed by other community members, it is his duty to defend his brother's personal dignity and good name.

Such protective duties still persist in voluntary fraternal relations, even though many of them have been taken over by special organized groups. Thus, the protection against natural catastrophes or sickness is furnished collectively by various insurance companies; and yet individual friends, neighbors, and members of fraternal associations supplement those collective functions whenever necessary. Although violent conflicts between religious associations have decreased, many associations recently were, and still are, subjected to persecution; then their members are supposed to, and usually do, protect each other from hostile actions which endanger their welfare and even their lives. Within small, but long-lasting military groups, sometimes relations of mutual friendship or "comradeship" between members develop which imply that, in case of war, each assumes the duty of protecting the life of the other.

Many other varieties of active services are performed by brothers on behalf of brothers who need them. Thus, when a herdsman, a farmer, or a craftsman, because of sickness or some other obstacle, is unable to perform a technical activity, a kinsman or friendly neighbor substitutes for him. If a friend or a member of a fraternal association faces a problem which he is incompetent to solve, a more competent friend or brother should assume the task of solving it or at least advise him what to do. This is a well-known duty of more advanced and experienced members in fraternal associations toward their less advanced, inexperienced brothers, and also of specialists who have certain knowledge or skill which their friends or fellow members need, but lack. An interesting example of this duty is the aid which more capable members of college fraternities give their less capable brothers in preparing for examinations and even in passing the examinations. Many examples of the aid of specialists—scientists, scholars, lawyers, physicians, and technicians—are found in other kinds of fraternal relations.

Moreover, if a man tends to achieve a goal requiring a complex action which is difficult, or even impossible, for him to perform alone, his brothers or friends are supposed to give him active help. This is another, familiar type of fraternal duty.

7. COLLABORATION

Collaboration differs from mutual aid, for it means not only that one individual performs an action which the other needs and which the other later reciprocates when needed, but that two or more individuals act together for the realization of a common purpose, or—in other terms—perform a *collective action*.

In nearly every community, men collaborate from time to time in performing specific kinds of collective actions. For instance, in certain tribal communities, big-game hunting or deep-sea fishing requires the collaboration of several hunters or fishermen. In others, clearing the woods in preparation for female horticulture is a cooperative task of men. Houses for social centers are built by several technicians acting together. Magico-religious actions for the purpose of counteracting common mystical dangers or gaining common divine benefits are performed collectively by a number of men; and warriors collaborate in struggles against enemy warriors.

Counteracting or preventing conflicts among participants in the community also requires the collaboration of several men. Collaboration in rural communities has often been investigated by sociologists.

Now, in a tribal community the men who collaborate in any collective action are already partners in lifelong relations based either on common descent within a clan or on some bonds of solidarity between members of separate clans; and it is a duty of each of them toward the others to collaborate with them when his collaboration is needed. In rural communities, the duty of collaborating is based partly on kinship, partly on permanent neighborly relations.

Within exclusive fraternal associations, various kinds of collaboration occur. Every religious association periodically performs collective cultus; and if the religious association is settled in a limited area, some technical collaboration for common purposes is often carried on, as among the Mormons during the early days of their settlements in Utah, and now among the Amish and the Hutterites.

Members of secular fraternal associations usually collaborate economically in raising and maintaining a common dwelling or social center, in satisfying their common needs if they dwell together; and in organizing ceremonial or companionate meetings. Moreover, in some associations the members collaborate in performing activities intended to benefit not their fellow members, but other participants of the collectivity within which the association functions.

These duties of collaboration are not necessarily equal, any more than the duties of mutual aid. An individual's duty to contribute to the achievement of a common goal depends upon his presumed capacity. If he has more knowledge and/or ability than his partners, his duty is to assume the responsibility of leadership. The duty of his partners is to make his leadership successful by effective followship.

Long-lasting collaboration of individuals for a common purpose results in the formation of an organized social group. However, most of the social groups which have been organized in the course of history have been composed of individuals who were not previously united by any lifelong bonds analogous to brotherhood. Yet, as we shall see later, in many of them the duties of members are somewhat similar to fraternal duties.

CHAPTER 7

MARITAL AND EROTIC RELATIONS

1. Distinction Between Marital and Erotic Relations

The third well-known category of social relations to which we devote considerable attention is comprised of those relations between men and women who carry on sexual intercourse with each other. Sexual intercourse by itself, obviously, does not constitute a social relation in the sense in which we use the term; for a social relation exists only when a man and a woman accept each other as partners for a certain time and recognize the duty of evaluating each other positively. We shall omit, therefore, one-sided sexual action (e.g., rape) and brief sexual intercourse between a man and a woman who are not connected by any lasting bonds (e.g., between a prostitute and a stranger who pays her and leaves), as well as that between a man and a woman who are partners in a long-lasting relation, but whose sexual intercourse conflicts with the standards and norms of that relation (e.g., between a brother and a sister, or a parent and his child).

A comparative historical survey of this category of social relations indicates that there are two distinct types, which differ in standards of selection and valuation of partners, and in other mutual duties which they include in addition to those of sexual intercourse.

One of these types, which probably developed earlier and has always been more widely spread and more influential, is usually denoted by the term "marriage." Since, however, this term frequently refers not to the relation in its total course, but to the process of forming the relation, "getting married," we prefer to call it "marital relation," or "conjugal relation." The other type, which developed fully only during the last twenty centuries in areas with advanced secular literary cultures, we shall call "erotic relation," or relation of mutual sexual love.

In the past, these types were frequently separated and often conflicting. Many individuals had only a marital, but no erotic relation; a few only erotic, but no marital relation. Of course, the same individual can have simultaneously a marital relation with one partner and an erotic relation with another. Often he has first one or several erotic relations with other partners before becoming a partner in a marital relation. Sometimes he has first an erotic relation and later a marital relation with the same partner. In the latter case, the erotic relation either disappears or continues to exist as an integral component of the more inclusive marital relation. Occasionally, after a marital relation has been formed, an erotic relation between the partners develops later as a new component. In recent times, the mutual duties of partners in marital relations have been decreasing, the mutual duties of partners in erotic relations increasing. Indeed, if this trend continues, erotic relations may gradually absorb marital relations.

No other social relations have been studied so widely or systematically as those between the sexes, but the vast majority of studies have been limited to marital relations. Every monographic study of a community contains a survey of these relations; every generalized ethnological work about tribal communities and every sociological work on "society" in general or on "social institutions" has a section devoted to a theory of these relations. In all books on the family, these relations form the central part; and some well-known larger works specialize entirely in comparative studies of marriage.

This predominant interest in marital relations is fully justified; however, there is no justification on scientific grounds for ignoring erotic relations. Of course, it is difficult to obtain factual material about sexual intercourse. But the difficulty is the same, or even greater, in studying sexual intercourse between a husband and his wife. And when such material is obtained, it is not easy—sometimes impossible—to have it published.

The main reason why most social anthropologists and sociologists leave out erotic relations is that they conceive sexual intercourse between individuals who are not married as mere manifestations of psychological "impulses," "drives," "desires," etc. which are not subjected to cultural standards or norms. This conception is based on ideological systems, religious or secular, which prohibit all kinds of nonmarital sexual interaction. Whereas the fact that a certain kind of conduct is prohibited by adherents of one ideological system does not preclude it from conforming with the standards and norms of another ideological system. For instance, religious conduct of "heretics," which from the point of view of the dominant church seems sinful, perhaps even instigated by evil powers, may be right, virtuous, divinely inspired from the point of view of the heretics themselves.

Actually, an investigation of erotic relations throws a significant light on the problem of social relations in general, especially on the modern trends in their evolution. However, let us first consider marital relations. We can add nothing new to the vast amount of knowledge about them which has been agglomerated by historians, ethnologists, and sociologists. But we can try to ascertain the common characteristics of all of them which enable scientists to treat them as social systems of a distinct category.

2. The Common Purpose of Marital Relations

In our preliminary survey of social relations, we came to the conclusion that they must be studied in the course of their formation, and that every relation when fully formed involves the mutual acceptance of two individuals as partners. True, in mother-child relations, the acceptance is at first one-sided: for the mother accepts the child before he is aware of it. But in sibling relations and their extension to kinship relations, individuals who are presumably descendants of the same progenitors are obliged to become partners as they grow up; both must accept each other, and neither has a choice.

Now, partnership in marital relations, unlike that in mother-child relations, implies from the very first the conscious mutual acceptance of both partners; but, unlike kinship relations, it is not based on the idea of common descent. On the contrary, if (according to the conception of hereditary bonds prevailing in the community) a male and a female are closely connected by such bonds, any sexual intercourse between them is usually prohibited. Various explanations of this almost universal prohibition have been attempted. The most probable of these explanations is that such a relation, if permitted, would interfere with existing relations, would disrupt the solidarity of brotherly relations on the one hand, and of sisterly relations on the other hand. Secondly, and this is more important from the point of view of our present problem, the main function of marriage is to create new connections between individuals who were not connected before. When the individuals are already connected by bonds of common descent, their marriage would not fulfil this function.

Marital relations, as we know, differ considerably in various cultures. Monogamy, polygamy, and polyandry are terms denoting important differences. Endogamy and exogamy connote variations in the standards of selection of partners. Matriarchy and patriarchy connote two types of marital relations—those in which the woman as mother and those in which the man as father is the domininant partner. Other distinctions have been observed and described by social anthropologists, historians, and ethnologists.

Such differences are culturally conditioned, depending on the diverse standards and norms with which marital relations in various communities are expected to conform. They obviously invalidate all attempts to explain marital relations by biopsychological "instincts" inherent in the *genus homo*—sexual, parental, or gregarious instincts—as well as all efforts to trace them back to relations found among various genera and species of higher animals. What is common to all of them and what distinguishes them from seemingly analogous animal relations is that their formation and duration is socially regulated in every community, because they are considered important *for the community*.

The importance ascribed to them is clearly manifested in the active interest shown by other participants in every marital relation, in the selection of partners, the process during which the relations is being formed, and its later course. This interest is more active in certain communities (e.g., early Roman, Chinese until recently, European, and Latin American) than in others (e.g., Eskimo, and Amerindian in the Western Plains or California); and in the same community (e.g., where class or caste divisions exist), some marital relations are considered more important than others.

But, whatever the variations in the relative importance ascribed to marital relations, in most communities every individual who reaches the age of sexual maturity is expected to marry, unless he or she is a supernormal person devoted to the performance of some highly important functions, especially religious functions, with which (according to the beliefs prevalent in the community) marriage would interfere.

Otherwise, the only individuals who are not expected to marry are those considered subnormal or inferior, that is, unworthy of becoming marital partners of normal, valuable individuals of the opposite sex. For instance, in many communities, an unmarried girl who has had sexual intercourse with a man is considered inferior to one who has not, and sometimes entirely unfit to become a marital partner. In communities where slavery exists, a slave is unfit to marry a free person, sometimes even unfit to marry anybody. A foreigner is often unfit to marry a participant in the community, until he or she has been adopted by a fully active participant in it.

Furthermore, in most communities every marital relation, once formed, is expected to be long-lasting, usually lifelong, unless unexpected factors interfere with its duration. It is not supposed to be dissolved by the partners without the sanction of other participants in the community.

Why are participants in a community positively interested in the formation of a long-lasting relation between a particular man and a particular woman? Why do they require that the man and the woman should be valuable persons, according to definite standards, and that any person who is valuable by these standards should marry a valuable person of the other sex?

Certainly, this is not because the relation involves sexual intercourse. Sexual intercourse is in most communities carried on in secrecy and not subjected to the observation or control of witnesses. This has been true in historical Europe, China, Japan, India, most of Africa, and in Amerindian societies. Thus, it should be secret, whether required or prohibited. Only when it is allowed and considered socially unimportant, as between youngsters in some Malayan, Polynesian, and Melanesian communities, can it be carried on openly.

Moreover, sexual intercourse has never been considered a sufficient foundation for a lasting social relation. According to social standards, the mere fact that a man and a woman have had sexual intercourse does not make them permanent partners—obviously never when the intercourse was forbidden, frequently not when it was allowed, and sometimes not even when it was required. Permitted premarital intercourse has never been enough to make the relation lasting. Sexual intercourse between a master and a slave by itself involved no permanent duties. Lending one's wife to a guest strengthened the relation between the guest and the husband, but established no lasting connection between the guest and the wife. In many communities the required sexual intercourse between a married couple is not enough to make their relation permanent: If the bride does not become pregnant, the relation can be dissolved. Finally, a marital relation lasts even after the married couple have become old and ceased to indulge in sexual intercourse.

Nor can the importance ascribed to marriage be explained by the economic cooperation it initiates between a man and a woman. Of course, in every known community, except some modern urban communities, we find a technical division of labor between the sexes; and, therefore, any lasting relation between a man and a woman must involve some mutual aid and cooperation. But this does not require that the man and the woman be married. Economic mutual aid and cooperation, based on a division of labor, can be and often is carried on between mother and son, father and daughter, brother and sister, as well as between men and women unconnected either by descent or by sexual intercourse—a master and a female slave or servant, a mistress and a male slave or servant, and slaves, servants, or employees of the two sexes. When a man and a woman get married, they simply continue to perform activities in which they have been specializing, and instead of or in addition to cooperating with other individuals start to cooperate with each other.

We believe that only one hypothesis can explain the universal importance ascribed to marital relations in all communities where such relations are lasting and where their axionormative order follows explicit ideological patterns. This hypothesis is not new; it has already been formulated, though in somewhat different form, by several sociologists.

The marital relation is considered positively important, nay, essential in every community because its purpose, on which the continued duration of an orderly community depends, is to provide valuable *new participants*. The common task of partners in a marital relation is procreation of socially desirable children and their preparation for future participation in conformity with definite ideological patterns. Such was the task which the parents of the young man and those of the young woman performed in the past; and now that the young man and the young woman have reached the proper age, it is their turn to become parents, to procreate and bring up a new generation of valuable children.

Thus, every socially valuable individual is supposed to have begun his life-cycle as a joint product of socially valuable predecessors, to continue his life-cycle as a joint producer of socially valuable successors, and to end his life-cycle as a valuable ancestor of valuable descendants.

3. SELECTION OF MARITAL PARTNERS

Since the parents of the boy and those of the girl assumed the responsibility for his or her birth, growth, and preparation, they are considered and consider themselves responsible for his or her becoming a partner in a new marital relation, which will result in the birth, growth, and preparation of a desirable new generation.

This makes it the parents' task to select as conjugal mate for their son or daughter a girl or boy who will prove valuable as future mother or father.

Since, in most communities, a girl or boy before marriage is not yet a fully active participant in community life, the almost universal standards which guide parents in the selection of conjugal mates for their children are those by which *the parents of prospective mates* are evaluated. These standards are recognized and maintained by the community; the parents simply apply them in choosing future wives for their sons and future husbands for their daughters. This obviously presupposes that the parents be known and their worth ascertained. No person of unknown parenthood is considered acceptable as a mate of their child by parents who are themselves positively valued in the community. An illegitimate child of a known mother, but unknown father, cannot be accepted, although an illegitimate child whose father is known to belong to a superior class might be accepted by parents of an inferior class.

Now, when stating that the parents choose conjugal mates for their children, we remember that conceptions of parenthood differ, depending on the relative importance ascribed to male and female descent. When descent counts on the mother's side, as in tribal communities with matrilineal clans, conjugal mates are chosen by the mothers and their brothers or the maternal uncles. When descent counts on the father's side, and especially when hereditary bonds extend to distant ancestors, the father, usually with some aid and advice from the mother, assumes complete responsibility for the selection of his sons' wives, so as to be sure that every wife will bear progeny worthy of his ancestors.

And, on the other hand, a girl's father aims to give her in marriage only to a man of valuable ancestry; for it would be humiliating to the dignity of his own ancestral family, if the girl whom he begat bore children to a descendant of inferior or unknown ancestors.

This is how conjugal mates were selected in China, in patrician families of ancient Rome, and among the royalty and nobility of Europe up to the end of the last century.

In polygynous patriarchal families, where fathers controlled family property, and a wife could be obtained only by offering economic compensation to her parents, the choice of mates also depended primarily on the fathers. It was the young man's father who selected a young woman for his son, since it was he who gave compensation to her father; it was the woman's father who gave his daughter to the man whose father offered him adequate compensation.

In bilineal families, where descent counts on both sides (though not always equally), the selection of mates is often made jointly by fathers and mothers. Such was frequently the case among European peasants and bourgeoisie; and then an important factor in the selection was economic. The parents of both expected to make economic contributions, not merely for the benefit of the married couple, but for their future children.

Inasmuch as both the young man's parents and the young woman's parents usually had quite a few possible choices of a future marital partner for their child, an agreement had to be reached, sometimes with the help of mediators. And in many communities, the young—especially the young men—were granted some freedom of choice, but within the rather narrow limits determined by their parents. If the agreement was made some time before marriage—often even when the young couple were not yet sexually mature—a formal betrothal was arranged by both families, implying a binding promise that the marriage would take place when both were ready.

But, no matter whether mothers, fathers, or both selected their children's mates, in nearly every community the range of possible selection usually was, and still is, limited. As a rule, parents are supposed to limit the choice of mates for their children to the young who belong to their own community or another community with which positive interaction exists and a common culture is shared. The great majority of marital relations are, consequently, endogamous.

Thus, in tribal communities regular marriages usually occur only within the tribe. Intertribal marriages are precluded, if and in so far as members of one tribe, or of both, consider members of the other tribe inferior, and their children unacceptable mates for their own children. This does not, of course, preclude sexual intercourse with women taken in a war raid as slaves or concubines, or certain exceptions which cannot be discussed here.

Such endogamy is clearly manifested in areas with culturally mixed populations. Thus, Germans, Rumanians, and Magyars in Transylvania; Germans in the Sudeten Mountains, in Polish rural areas, in the Baltic States, and in Tsarist Russia; Italians and Germans in the Tyrol: all have for centuries avoided intermarriage. In the United States, rural immigrant communities of different ethnic orgin have also maintained their social separatism for several generations.

We are also familiar with religious endogamy. Faithful parents of one religion are not supposed to let their child marry a child of parents who have transmitted to him "wrong" religious beliefs and practices, lest the children of the married couple become subjected to bad influences. Of course, the other mate might become converted; but, obviously, that child's parents, if faithful to their religion, do not want their child and its descendants to become unbelievers.

While in tribal, ethnic, and religious endogamy, this avoidance of mixed marriages is mutual, in caste endogamy it is one-sided. Parents belonging to a certain caste do not permit their children to marry children of lower-caste parents; and though they might wish their children to marry into a higher caste, the resistance of parents belonging to the latter prevents such marriages. For, by marrying a lower-caste partner, not only would the child itself lose status, but its children and even grandchildren would belong to the lower caste—typically the children, grandchildren, and even great-grandchildren of a White-Negro couple in the Southern States.

4. THE WEDDING

After both mates have been definitely selected and an informal agreement or formal betrothal reached, sooner or later comes the *wedding,* i.e., the establishment of a lasting social bond between them and the acceptance by each of definite duties.

The wedding is usually accompanied by a ritual—magical, religious, or legal. According to Westermarck, the most general purpose of marriage rites, as he calls them, "is to give publicity to the union. 'Publicity,' says Miss Bu[—] 'is everywhere the element which distinguishes a recognized marriage from an illicit connection.' " In other words, it not only announces the newly formed marital relation to participants in the community, but also secures the positive sanction of those who function as guardians of the mores. This is obvious when the wedding is performed with the approval or in the presence of an official—chief, priest, or lay head of the local community. It is also clear when older members of the two families, eventually neighbors, witness the ceremony. Usually they not only witness it, but actively share in some parts of the ritual.

Most marriages include some symbolization of the union: joining hands, being tied together, giving a ring or exchanging rings, verbal expressions of mutual acceptance, oaths, sharing food or drink, sometimes even sharing blood, just as in blood covenants between males. All these rites are meaningful, for they indicate that the relation is expected to be permanent.

Other rites, magical or religious, are meant to bring benefits to the couple—health and economic welfare—and to protect them against evil. And whenever magical or religious ritual plays a leading part in the wedding ceremony, some rites are explicitly intended to insure that the married couple will have desirable children, male children being especially mentioned in many cases. Furthermore, the marriage ceremonies usually include entrance of the bride and/or the groom into a common home, be it a separate house, hut, tent, or merely a section of a multifamily home. This is often accompanied by a magico-religious rite or social symbolism indicating that the partners will share this as a lasting spatial center of close personal contact.

Finally, when premarital sexual relations have been prohibited, the formation of a conjugal relation is usually not considered complete until the married couple has had sexual intercourse. Therefore, in some communities, the final stage of the wedding ceremony consists in preparing the couple for cohabitation, and later informing participants in the ceremony that they have actually had sexual intercourse.

5. MUTUAL DUTIES OF HUSBAND AND WIFE

Hereafter the husband and the wife assume numerous duties toward each other. Their chief task is to cooperate for a common goal: procreating and bringing up children. We find many proofs that this is, indeed, the ultimate purpose of their relation, and that all their duties are subordinate to it.

Thus, both the husband and the wife have the duty of maintaining sexual intercourse; but, according to the religious tenets of several Christian churches and sects, bearing children is the only justification for such sexual intercourse. And in many tribal communities, as well as in those controlled by the priests of certain religions, if marriage does not result in the birth of a child, the marital relation becomes dissolved. If its persistence is nonetheless considered desirable, various ways may be found to provide the couple with children. For instance, the husband may take a concubine and, if she bears a child, his wife adopts it. Or, if it is the husband who seems to be sterile, he may lend his wife to a sibling, a friend, a prominent guest, or hire a cicisbeo, and accept as his own the child born to her. Or if the marital relation is supposed to be strictly monogamous, the couple may adopt children of other parents.

On the other hand, in communities where sexual intercourse between the young is permitted (e.g., among the Masai and the Nandi in Africa), sexual intercourse may lead to a marriage relation, if the woman bears a child.

Perhaps the most conclusive proof that the sexual duties of conjugal partners are subordinated to the duty of joint parenthood is that sexual intercourse between husband and wife is prohibited during the period when it is believed to interfere with the bearing or rearing of children. Thus, it is often prohibited in the later stages of pregnancy, when it is supposed to be injurious to the unborn child, and after a child's birth, during the period of lactancy, when the mother's milk is the main or only food which the child is given.

Condemnation of extramarital intercourse of the wife is found in all communities with patrilineal or bilineal descent (except in the cases mentioned above, when the husband favors such intercourse for the sake of having children). Although often due to the possessive domination of the husband over the wife as his exclusive property, and sometimes to sexual jealousy, it is nevertheless rationalized on the ground that, in consequence of such intercourse, the wife may bear a child which will not be her husband's descendant, as all his wife's children are presumed to be. This rationalization explains why no condemnation or only mild condemnation is applied to the husband's extramarital sexual relations, since they do not affect his and his wife's common progeny.

The economic duties of husband and wife require that both cooperate in satisfying not only each other's needs, but also the needs of their children. Such duties vary widely, depending on the culturally patterned division of labor between the sexes in communities with different economies. For instance, at one extreme, as in some Amerindian communities, almost all the husband does is to provide the wife with raw materials, mostly dead and skinned animals, while her task is to produce from them and from the vegetables she gathers all the food to be eaten, clothes to be worn, and domestic furnishings, as well as the instruments necessary for this production. At the other extreme, in a European upper-class marital relation, the husband, with or without the wife's dowry, provides the funds necessary to purchase everything needed for consumption, and even servants to prepare it for its final use. The wife has nothing to do but control the servants and buy any new ready products which are needed. This pattern is being gradually approached in American urban communities, even when the husband and wife have no servants, since nearly everything they and their children need can be bought ready made or almost ready for use. But, however diverse the economic activities of husband and wife, each of them is in duty bound to contribute what he or she is supposed to contribute to their common task of supporting and bringing up their children.

An important duty of the husband is to protect his wife and children against dangers—natural forces, human enemies, or evil supernatural beings—whenever she lacks the necessary power.

All these duties are subjected to the social control of those community members who want the married couple to become parents of valuable children—the parents of both, older members of the clan or gens, ruling members of a tribal, a political, or a religious collectivity who want it to be perpetuated and to increase in size.

But until recent times, explicit norms seldom required that the married couple should *love* each other as sexual partners. Indeed, manifestations of mutual sexual love are discouraged in many communities—e.g., in Africa and even in Puritanical New England. Of course, loyalty is usually required, sometimes mutual respect; mutual affection is considered desirable, but not indispensable.

6. Selection of Partners in Erotic Relations

Erotic relations, unlike marital relations, are not originally intended to contribute to the perpetuation of the clan, the gens, or the community as a whole. They are purely private, interindividual relations; their direct purpose is mutual satisfaction of the partners. The choice of partners does not depend on the decisions of parents or any other authorities: They select each other voluntarily, on their own initiation, and their relation is not subjected to the control of other people. In these respects, erotic relations resemble relations of personal friendship between two individuals of the same sex. Their development has, however, led to the formation of ideals which are affecting social relations between husband and wife and between parents and children.

The earliest, simplest, and least important type of erotic relation is found in those nonliterate communities where premarital sexual intercourse is permitted. For instance, among the Masai and the Nandi in Africa, where young men who function as warriors live apart from married people, young girls visit them at night for sexual intercourse; but, when a girl becomes pregnant, the young man with whom she has been having sexual relations, marries her, settles in the village, and ceases to be a warrior. In other African communities where polygamy predominates, and there is much competition for women, a girl with an illegitimate child is acceptable as a wife in preference to a barren girl. In some Polynesian, Melanesian, and Malayan communities, adolescents have sexual relations, sometimes under the guidance of adults, so as to acquire enough skill for their future marital relation.

However, in the majority of communities on all cultural levels, no woman destined to become a wife and the mother of legitimate children is permitted to carry on sexual intercourse and become an active partner in an erotic relation before marriage—even with her future husband. Only a preliminary, tentative approach to such a relation is permitted in communities where young men and women are allowed to select their mates from among candidates approved by their parents. This implies that young men and young women be given the opportunity to meet several individuals of the opposite sex and to become more or less acquainted with those who appear personally attractive, until two of them accept each other as potential partners in a marital relation which will include voluntary sexual intercourse, besides the other conjugal duties which we discussed above.

We are familiar with this process of mutual choice in modern premarital courtship, as carried on, for instance, between college students; but it goes much further back into history. The period of personal acquaintance which ends with mutual acceptance is, of course, nothing but an introduction to the fully developed relation; nonetheless, it deserves attention, for it indicates the general standards by which partners in erotic relations are selected.

The primary standards are aesthetic, however different and changing. This is clearly manifested in the universal custom of making the body aesthetically attractive to the other sex. Even children's bodies, as we noticed before, are often subjected to influences which will presumably make them grow into aesthetically admirable adults. More universal and better known is the custom of adorning the body, whenever young men and women have the opportunity to meet and enjoy each other's company. Such opportunities for a selection of partners, based on beautification, occur during various kinds of holidays, festivals, rest periods, parties, etc., when no work spoils bodily adornments, distracts attention from sexual interest, or interferes with interpersonal communication and contact. On such occasions, individuals of the same sex compete among themselves; for the more attractive an individual appears, the greater his or her chances to select an attractive individual of the other sex.

In most communities, men are supposed to initiate social interaction with women, as denoted by the term "courtship." Consequently, it is at first more important for a woman than for a man to appear beautiful, sexually attractive, in order to induce men to court her. But, inasmuch as she also has a choice, her response to a man's initiative will depend upon her aesthetic valuation of him; therefore, men also try to make themselves aesthetically attractive, according to the established standards of masculine beauty, so as to gain a positive response from attractive women.

After preliminary social interaction has started, other standards of personal valuation are introduced. If bodily contacts between men and women are permitted—e.g., dancing together—harmonious cooperation in various movements and the resulting sensory pleasure are significant. Much more general are the psychological standards applied in the course of symbolic communication. Positive response of one to the other's attempt to initiate symbolic communication; manifestations of recognition by one of the other's self as valuable; and agreement with one's verbally expressed attitudes: all contribute to raise the personal valuation of the other. So, eventually, does any action which one performs for the other's benefit.

Such standards, however, are by no means limited to premarital courtship. Indeed, they were most fully developed, as we shall see in our survey of polite acquaintance, in princely courts and upper-class sets, where companionate intercourse between individuals of both sexes was regularly carried on without resulting either in marriage or in erotic relations. Indeed, if mutual acceptance of a man and a woman as potentially valuable partners in a future long-lasting personal relation leads to a marital or erotic relation, one or both partners may become disappointed. This, as we know, frequently occurs after a couple who fall in love with each other get married and find it difficult to remain in love, when faced with the complex, often boresome or unpleasant, everyday duties of a marital relation or with conflicts between their mutual duties and those toward other people. This is nothing new; according to an old French statement, "Le mariage est le tombeau de l'amour."

Even an erotic relation without marriage does not always prove as satisfactory to the partners as they expected when they started it. Many such relations are soon broken off by one of the partners; others are voluntarily dissolved by both partners; but some last indefinitely, unless external factors make their maintenance impossible.

To understand such differences, we must investigate the standards and norms with which partners in erotic relations are supposed to conform. These standards and norms have been gradually developed by various thinkers, especially by poets and moral philosophers who disagreed with the traditional antithesis between regulated marital relations and irregular sexual intercourse. Although much of the literature on this subject, especially lyric poetry, is a symbolic expression of one-sided individual "love," and thus provides material for the psychology of sex, yet even this can be used in sociological studies of erotic relations; for it often represents a model of perfection which lovers are supposed to follow.

The basic principle of these relations is their *exclusiveness*. No individual should have an erotic relation simultaneously with two partners. Each partner should be the "one and only love" of the other, so long as their relation lasts. If either of them starts an erotic relation with somebody else, his conduct conflicts with this principle. Sometimes, of course, partners agree in advance that their exclusive relation will last only for a certain period of time, and that thereafter both will be free to initiate new relations. When the same man or the same woman carries on sexual intercourse with several individuals of the opposite sex who know about it, but do not oppose it, for each of them also carries on sexual intercourse with other individuals, this is not a true erotic relation, as here defined. For partners in a true erotic relation are supposed to accept a common, very exacting altruistic ideal.

There is considerable biographical and autobiographical evidence that such exclusive, exacting erotic relations, though at first relatively rare, have been multiplying in modern times, especially during the last hundred years, in Europe and America.

7. MUTUAL DUTIES OF LOVERS

The obvious, universal duty of each partner in an erotic relation is to give a maximum of sensory pleasure to the other in sexual intercourse. Since the man is the more active partner and can satisfy his sexual impulse, when the woman passively submits, without giving her much pleasure, it is of primary importance that he should assume the duty of making her reach full enjoyment. As her cooperation can increase his pleasure, and her lack of cooperation decrease it, she also has an active duty toward him. Furthermore, awareness by each of the other's pleasure enhances the pleasure; therefore, it is a secondary duty of each toward the other to try to enjoy the intercourse and make the other conscious that he or she enjoys it.

The fulfilment of these duties, however, depends on the technical skill of the partners. In the course of history, many different ways have been invented for carrying on sexual intercourse and stimulating enjoyment. Nearly a hundred techniques have been described by various authors—Hindu, Arabic, and European. In certain historical cultures (e.g., in Japan, Greece, Rome, Italy after the Renaissance, and France), women who specialized in extramarital sexual intercourse—whose function will be discussed in our survey of social roles—have transmitted the skill or art of this intercourse to younger women, by the method of apprenticeship, and trained the young men, unmarried or married, with whom they had sexual interaction. And those men who are relatively free to make such contacts with women communicate the results of their experience, orally or in writing, to less experienced men.

The majority of young men, however, especially in Western communities, have very little sexual training; and the majority of women have none. Under these conditions, the pleasure derived from sexual intercourse depends, at first, upon innate biological drives, the emotional disposition of the couple, and their relative compatibility. However, if both are aware that their relation requires the performance by each of actions which will be satisfactory to the other, in so far as both tend to conform with these requirements, they learn gradually by companionate *self-education* to make their sexual intercourse, just as other kinds of interaction, mutually enjoyable. Recently, medical and psychological specialists who have studied and compared sexual behavior have been giving advice, not to partners in erotic relations, but to unexperienced married couples, and some of this advice has been published.

As we mentioned above, according to the principle of exclusiveness, neither partner should have sexual intercourse with anybody else, so long as their relation lasts. But this principle is difficult, often impossible to maintain, when the relation is extramarital, and one of the partners, or both, married to somebody else, since a marital relation requires sexual intercourse between husband and wife. The conflict is expected to be solved by not initiating sexual intercourse with one's spouse, unless necessary. The wife who loves somebody else is supposed to submit passively to her husband, when obliged to do so; the husband who loves another woman, when obliged to have intercourse with his wife, is not supposed to give her the kind of enjoyment which he gives his beloved.

Sexual duties, however, are not the only duties of lovers. Mutual love, just as brotherhood or friendship, involves sympathetic understanding of one's partner's experiences, attitudes, and volitions, as well as active cooperation, whenever needed. In the course of history, cultural patterns of erotic relations have become increasingly complex, and included more and more of the personal lives of the partners. Mutual understanding and cooperation gradually extended beyond the range of sexual intercourse to other values and activities which the lovers began to share—social, economic, aesthetic, religious, and intellectual.

The main obstacle to this development has been the traditional division of functions between the sexes. Until modern times, men were not supposed to share most of the interests or to participate in most of the actions of women at home; women engaged in domestic duties were not expected to share the interests of men outside the home, could not participate in their actions, and often were not even allowed to know what the men were doing. Only as the range of cultural participation of women expanded could erotic relations become more inclusive, and this expansion implied the partial liberation of women from domestic duties and family control.

In ancient Greece, almost the only erotic relations which were not limited to sexual intercourse were those between prominent men and unmarried *hetairai*. A *hetaira* was an educated woman who understood and shared with her lover his intellectual, artistic, and political interests, offered him response, encouragement, even advice, and participated in his companionate meetings with other men, while he gave her recognition, protection, and economic support. In Rome, when women of prominent families began increasingly to participate in political, intellectual, and aesthetic life, their erotic relations included more than sexual intercourse.

During the Middle Ages, upper-class women who were well educated participated in companionate meetings, public ceremonies, aesthetic, sometimes even political activities; and their erotic relations, mostly extramarital, became exalted. Though at first the pattern of romantic love, as formulated by poets—troubadours and minnesingers—was supposed to be purely idealistic, platonic, involving no sexual intercourse, many romantic relations actually became realistic. This was obscured by the fact that they had to be kept secret; and, consequently, most of those recorded and exalted in history and legend had a tragic ending, since the husband who discovered them was expected to take revenge, and often did.

There was no secrecy, however, about the extramarital erotic relations maintained by kings from the sixteenth century on, e.g., Louis XIV and Mme. de Montespan, Louis XV and Mme. de Pompadour, Napoleon and Mme. Walewska. During the same period, such relations between upper-class people, though disapproved of, were often tolerated, as long as they were not too conspicuous. Later, in the nineteenth century, they developed quite openly among the rebellious intellectual bohemians.

From the recorded histories of such erotic relations, it is clear that, although each partner remains to the other a sexual value, yet the content of their personalities which they are supposed to share harmoniously, and with which their altruistic duties are concerned, is often so rich and significant that an erotic relation can be maintained for some time without sexual intercourse. This explains how erotic relations may continue to exist during long intervals between sexual intercourse, and often persist even after sexual intercourse has ceased to be possible.

Still another duty is included in erotic relations: the duty of protecting partners from the harmful influences of other people. This is primarily a masculine duty, for, inasmuch as men have more sexual freedom, women need more protection. Thus, in the Middle Ages and later, men who had erotic relations with other men's wives defended them against their husbands, if the husbands were vengeful; and many duels were fought for this reason. Sometimes a lover took his beloved away from her husband's home into another community or a foreign country, where she would be safer, not only from her husband's revenge, but from any penalties of religious or civil authorities.

When a man starts an erotic relation with an unmarried girl, it is his duty to protect her from the danger of losing status or being treated by the community as immoral, sinful, or inferior to normal girls. This is usually done by preventing community members from learning about their relation. If this proves impossible, it is his duty to restore her status by marrying her. If he is already married, he should not have started an erotic relation with her, unless she had nothing to lose, either because he belonged to a superior class, and her partnership with him would not impair or would even raise her status among lower-class people, or because she lived in a community where unmarried women could participate in erotic relations without being condemned by public opinion, as in some bohemian communities.

8. The Extension of Erotic Ideals to Marital Relations

The incompatibility of erotic relations and marital relations was inevitable, so long as the latter followed the traditional patterns. Whereas the formation of a marital relation depended on the parents of the couple, who accepted them as future mates, an erotic relation was independently formed by the partners, who selected and accepted each other. Whereas the duties of partners in a marital relation were subjected to the social control of the parents and other community members, who made both conform with the norms imposed on them, so as to have the relation last as long as it was supposed to last, usually for a lifetime, the duties of partners in an erotic relation were spontaneously performed by each of them; neither could use external sanctions to make the other conform, for love cannot be enforced; and the relation lasted only so long as the partners were willing to maintain it. Moreover, whereas the traditional pattern of marital relations in most communities presupposes the domination of the husband and the submission of the wife, the erotic relation is essentially a relation of equality; it does not preclude leadership, but either the man or the woman, or alternatively both, can function as leader.

Of course, a marital relation did not always preclude mutual love between husband and wife; indeed, considerable evidence indicates that many marital relations did include it. But this means that the particular marriage in question did not follow the traditional pattern or else that mutual love was limited, subordinated to conjugal duties. However, during the last hundred years, the principles of erotic relations have been increasingly applied to marital relations, especially in Western Europe and America. This was partly due to changing patterns of marital relations, and partly to a redefinition of the ideal of erotic relations.

The ancestral family system has lost its power and even disappeared in most modern communities. Consequently, young people have not only more freedom in the choice of conjugal mates than they had before, but their activities as partners in marital relations are less dependent on parental control. Since the perpetuation of the family is no longer considered sufficiently important to make the marital relation permanent, conflicts between partners can be solved, not by extraneous coercion, but by divorce. Mutual understanding between husbands and wives has increased, and their common interests have widened. This is a result of the spread of education among women and their growing participation in the social life and culture of their communities, which was previously limited to the upper classes, but has now been made possible for most women by technical inventions of labor-saving domestic appliances. Finally, recognition of the equality of the sexes has made the duties of husbands and wives reciprocal.

On the other hand, the opportunity of maintaining an extramarital erotic relation for a lengthy period of time has remained limited to a small minority. Unless two partners permanently live together—and not many of them do—regular sexual intercourse is rather difficult to carry on. Nor is regular communication and mutual understanding concerning nonsexual values and activities easy to maintain. As a matter of fact, most of the erotic relations in the Western world were relatively short-lasting. Consequently, among the intellectual classes of Europe and America, the ideal of the marital relation as a *permanent erotic relation* began to be explicitly formulated and more or less widely accepted and applied.

This new ideal implies, first of all, that the freedom of partners to dissolve their relation be voluntarily limited or resigned when their relation is formed, by agreeing to make it last as long as they live. To be effective, this agreement requires not only that each should be ready to forgive and forget all deviations of the other, but also that both should be willing and able to keep their relation dynamic and harmonious by developing their personalities and expanding the range of their common values and activities, so as to make them more and more valuable to each other.

This means that the old duties of husband and wife have to be reinterpreted as the voluntary duties of mutual love. Thus, economic cooperation ceases to be an obligation enforced in the interest of the family, and becomes a free service of love. Children are not future continuators of the family, but new bonds of love; their lives become parts of the personal lives of both parents, to be harmoniously shared, like other personal values.

And this involves another very important consequence of the extension of the erotic ideal: a deep change in parent-child relations. For the mutual love of parents presupposes a common love for their children; one of the tasks of their cooperation is to make their children love both of them. Comparative studies of the attitudes of children toward their parents show that, when parents love each other and are happy, their children are happy and love both parents. While the fundamental parental duty of preparing children for active participation in community life remains, the methods of fulfilling this duty differs considerably from the old authoritarian methods required within the old family system. In short, when the ideal of the erotic relation becomes extended to the marital relation, the mutual duties of husband and wife and their duties toward their children remain, but are performed much more altruistically and with greater satisfaction than they ever were in the past.

CHAPTER **8**

RELATIONS OF POLITE COMPANIONSHIP

1. COMMON ENJOYMENT AS THE PURPOSE OF POLITE COM-
   PANIONSHIP

The fourth category of social relations which we survey here is composed of culturally patterned relations between individuals who carry on social intercourse regularly for the purpose of common enjoyment.

In every community, people frequently meet during leisure time for this purpose. Even in tribal and rural communities, they visit periodically their neighbors or kin, invite them to enjoy good food or drink, participate in various kinds of games, etc. And when they congregate for a ceremonial occasion, religious or secular, after the purpose of the meeting has been achieved, they often stay and continue to interact just for pleasure. In small communities, the people who participate in such intercourse usually are also partners in other relations in which the duty of contributing to each other's enjoyment is subordinated to more important mutual duties.

With the growth of cities and large regions, where many people come into contact who previously were not socially connected, perhaps did not even know each other, special social relations have developed in which contribution to mutual enjoyment is the main duty of each partner. The standards by which partners are selected, as well as the norms of conduct with which they are supposed to conform, differ from those which regulate other kinds of social relations. In the course of history, such standards and norms have been promulgated in writing; they are now called "rules of etiquette." During the last five centuries, hundreds of books, letters, and articles on etiquette have been written by Western authors; but some of these rules can be traced back to ancient Greece and

Rome. Similar rules, based on the same principles, though varying in details, are found also in Arabic, Chinese, and Japanese literature.

We use the term "relation of polite companionship" to denote this category, because the only universal condition for the formation of such a relation is that, after the partners have accepted each other as companions in social intercourse, they must be "polite" to each other, whenever they interact; that is, each should manifest a tendency to do something which will please the other and show appreciation of what the other is doing. Unlike partners in such relations as parenthood or kinship, in order to accept each other as companions in social intercourse, they need not be connected by any previous bonds; and their duties are limited to companionate play or amusement. The principle of politeness does not imply that either partner should perform on behalf of the other such important duties as those of parents, children, brothers, friends, husbands, wives, or lovers.

We have selected these relations for study mainly for two reasons. First, because they are the most extensive, as they extend to individuals of both sexes, at all age levels above childhood, and to individuals living in more or less distant areas, belonging to different specialized associations—political parties, professional or economic groups—and even to different states, churches, and nationalities.

Second, they are explicitly integrated. Every individual is a partner in a number of such relations. Whenever he carries on companionate intercourse with several partners, he can expect that each of them will perform some polite duty toward him and refrain from doing everything which conflicts with the principle of politeness; if not, the others will interfere on his behalf. On the other hand, he is aware that those others expect him to perform polite duties toward each of them and to refrain from being impolite; if he does not, they will exert some active influence to make him conform with the rules of etiquette. In short, his relations with those people with whom he carries on companionate intercourse are functionally interdependent and integrated in such a way as to make this intercourse satisfactory to him and to all of them. This may provide a key for the study of integration of other kinds of social relations.

We shall survey now the historical evolution of relations of polite companionship in Europe and America. It would take too long to make such a survey of their evolution in Asia.

2. POLITE COMPANIONSHIP IN PRINCELY COURTS

The beginning of relations of polite companionship in the Western world can be traced back to the Middle Ages. Feudal lords entertained guests in their castles and sometimes arranged festivals, with the help of their ladies. But only guests of noble origin participated fully at banquets, stayed within the castle, sat together, and were amused by jugglers, musicians, and declaimers. When inferior people were admitted as guests to a festival, they were sheltered and fed in outbuildings, courtyards, or the open areas outside the castle walls. The host and his guests often had serious affairs to discuss, but the discussions were carried on at other times, not during companionate gatherings for common pleasure.

More influential in the long run than such temporary gatherings were the permanent princely courts. The nucleus of such a court was composed of the courtiers and the court ladies who were lastingly connected by a relation of subordination with the ruler or his wife. As part of this relation, each of them had definite duties—military, civil, religious, or personal service in the technical or economic organization of the court.

Such a circle surrounding the ruler included only a selected minority of all the people living in or around the royal or ducal residence and serving the ruler and his family. Although their positions within the court were unequal, depending on the relative importance of their functions, all the members of the inner circle were separated from the rest by a sharp dividing line. They were essentially people of noble descent, hereditarily entitled to associate with other nobles. Outside their official duties, during their leisure time, they maintained personal intercourse with each other—sat at the same table during meals, conversed on unofficial matters, engaged in various kinds of sport or games, etc.

A commoner whom the ruler took into his service was admitted to this inner circle only if the nobles considered him fit for participation, and were willing to accept him. A ruler who tried to impose the company of such a parvenu upon other courtiers against their will offended their feeling of class dignity and risked alienating their loyalty, as well as lowering the reputation of his court among other courts and incurring ridicule. This happened, for instance, when King Louis XI of France included efficient, but low-class, commoners in his court; he lost in prestige, although he gained in power.

On the other hand, since all the men belonging to a ruler's court were dependent on him, and the competition among them for his favor was very strong, even in periods of leisure and relaxation from their specific duties, it was often difficult for them to maintain playful companionate intercourse, and anything said or done between courtiers could stimulate positive or negative attitudes toward each other, which might affect indirectly their careers. Of course, anything said or done between a ruler and a courtier during a convivial repast, a congenial discussion, a game or sport could affect directly their relation.

The progressive separation of the companionate and playful aspects of court life from its important practical aspects was due to two influences: first, the participation of women in companionate intercourse; second, admission into courts of prominent men of letters, thinkers, artists, and musicians.

Court ladies had no recognized share in the serious affairs of the ruler and his assistants. But they could participate in companionate leisure activities, either vicariously, by observing men's sports and games, or actively. And their participation not only banished from those activities all preoccupation with serious practical affairs, but modified the range and organization of the activities. It led to a new type of social relation between men and women, a kind of half-fictitious erotic play, which could be carried on indefinitely without leading to real sexual intercourse. Its active manifestation was often confined to symbolic expressions of aesthetic approval of a person of the other sex. The essential point is that it culminated in definite standards of physical appearance and definite norms of outward conduct—*manners*—with which every participant in companionate intercourse was expected to conform.

It was also the pressure of women which introduced into communication between men the norm of politeness, based on the idea that periods of playful companionate interaction were not only times of rest from serious affairs, but times of truce from all personal antagonisms that existed between participants, since any manifestation of such antagonisms disturbed the peace of others and spoiled their enjoyment. Men reciprocated by expecting similar politeness in communications between women.

When the ruler patronized literature, art, and music, his courtiers and guests could devote considerable leisure time to aesthetic enjoyment which had nothing to do with their political, military, or economic functions, as, e.g., at the "courts of love" in Provence, where visiting troubadours declaimed their poems, and the main topic of conversation was the ideal of altruistic love.

As a consequence of such patronage, courts became cultural centers. Thus, most Italian courts during the Renaissance were centers of Italian culture. Castiglione left a record of the small, but culturally influential court of Urbino. The courts of the Medici in Florence and of the Sforza in Milan were famous. From the end of the sixteenth century on, the French royal court became a center of French culture. Similar functions of patronage were assumed, sooner or later, by dukes, kings, queens, and emperors all over Europe. Therefore, courtiers and court ladies had to be sufficiently educated to understand and appreciate the culture which their rulers patronized; and, though noble descent remained the most important condition for being a court member, it could be waived in favor of superior personal achievements. Rulers admitted to their courts great men of letters, philosophers, artists, and musicians of plebeian descent.

This did not apply to women, however. A plebeian wife of a

great man was not admitted to the court to which her husband belonged. The only women who were sometimes introduced into courts without regard to their descent were the mistresses of the ruler. And, since the ruler could not compel his wife and her court ladies to maintain regular companionate intercourse with a mistress of inferior descent, he gathered a small circle of boon companions in which his mistress participated, and spent most of his leisure time with this circle.

3. RELATIONS BETWEEN STATESMEN AND VISITORS

With the growing size and complexity of monarchical states and the increasing interaction between governments, the residences of rulers became also social centers entertaining numerous visitors. Periodic ceremonial receptions were held, during which the monarch and his wife could meet prominent subjects and their wives, while courtiers and court ladies arranged musical, theatrical, and other performances which the visitors were expected to enjoy. Foreign guests, especially members of royal families, were entertained for some time in the palaces; and foreign envoys were invited to participate in special receptions. Such functions became extended to the presidents of republics and important governmental officials, and were reciprocated by the representatives of foreign governments.

As a result, the rules of etiquette regulating these functions became formalized in every detail. This is well exemplified by the so-called "diplomatic protocol," a system of rules in accordance with which gatherings of governmental officials and foreign diplomats in a capital are planned and arranged. But the essential principle of all these rules remains the same: It is the principle of politeness.

The task of such gatherings is to enable individuals whose official functions differ considerably in degree of importance, and are not connected or even conflicting, to meet together, become acquainted, and carry on companionate intercourse, with the expectation that personal relations, once started, may help them to initiate cooperation in serious affairs, or at least to avoid conflict. This is successful only if each participant in the gathering, when interacting with somebody else, behaves as if he evaluated the other positively, does or says something intended to please the other, and refrains from manifesting antagonistic attitudes toward anybody else. The presence of wives, interacting socially with men who are not their husbands, is the best way of making the principle of politeness effective. And this is why most of these gatherings are carried on in the residences of married couples; and all the wives of male guests are invited. Indeed, it is generally considered a disadvantage for a statesman or diplomat to be unmarried.

Nevertheless, those who plan such a gathering must be very careful to prevent any disturbance, to make every participant aware that he or she is welcome as a valuable person, and at the same time to maintain strictly the standards of hierarchy according to which all officials are graded in importance, manifesting this gradation symbolically whenever necessary, as, e.g., in the order in which they and their wives are seated during a banquet.

But, however influential the courts of rulers and the capitals of modern states have been in maintaining and regulating polite companionate intercourse, the opportunities they provide for such intercourse are limited. Only courtiers and visitors whom the monarch accepts and only people invited either by the president of a republic or by an important governmental official can participate in such companionate gatherings. The selection of partners is authoritarian and not mutual; it is one-sided.

4. FREE RELATIONS OF POLITE COMPANIONSHIP AMONG THE NOBILITY

A different pattern of polite companionate intercourse developed outside of courts and governmental residences. When feudal wars stopped, political and military power became centralized and cities grew in size; then the nobility within each kingdom became what has been called a "leisure class." Though a few gentlemen and ladies were members of royal courts, and some nobles performed the functions of military commanders and administrators, most of them had no governmental function; and in any case, their families had plenty of leisure time. They had a considerable income—mostly, if not exclusively—from rural estates; and even when the owners resided on their estates and managed them, their assistants did most of the managerial work. The wealthier nobles also had residences in the capitals and other large cities, where—unlike merchants, bankers, industrialists, physicians, and lawyers—they had little to do; for such occupations were beneath their dignity. And, of course, they had servants to take care of the necessary physical work.

Consequently, cooperation for common enjoyment became a socially important activity of members of the noble class. We say "socially important," because it contributed to the maintenance of class solidarity. As in medieval castles and royal courts, the initiative was taken by a host and hostess, who selected and invited guests, and offered them something for their enjoyment—food, drink, aesthetic pleasure, opportunities to participate in sports, games, dancing, etc. Other noble couples, in turn, assumed a similar initiative as hosts, and invited guests. Thus, the members of noble families living within a rural or urban area near enough to each other's residences by such means of transportation as were available—mostly horse-drawn carriages—were acquainted with one another, met from time to time in different homes, and had companionate intercourse in accordance with the rules of etiquette.

These relations of polite companionship might last indefinitely, since it was the task of every individual to maintain such relations by periodical meetings, either visiting or receiving the others, and to make every meeting pleasant for everybody. Of course, not all individuals performed this task regularly, but nonperformance had to be justified. An important function which left no leisure time, be it religious, military, administrative, or judicial, was sufficient excuse for a man, but not for his wife. Sickness was a justification, though many true-to-form "society people" would not let even bad health interfere with their duties. Poverty was, indeed, an obstacle, but it should be concealed; an impoverished person did not need to entertain often or luxuriously, but he ought to borrow the money for the minimum reception required by etiquette, rather than withdraw from upper-class society life.

With increasing travel, relations of polite companionship might be extended beyond the limits of a particular area. Traveling members of noble families came into contact with noble families in distant areas, were entertained as guests, and reciprocated, thus establishing a relation which continued through correspondence or later meetings. Nobles from distant areas, even from various nationalities, often congregated temporarily in recreational centers—summer resorts, gambling casinos (like Monte Carlo), or in capitals during special celebrations—became acquainted, and carried on some companionate intercourse.

Obviously only wealthy nobles with plenty of leisure could afford such travels and enjoy opportunities to establish relations with members of distant families. This resulted in a widening separation between the upper nobility, or aristocracy, and the lower, or petty nobility. Of course, the inequality of noble families went back to feudal gradations, but did not prevent companionate intercourse, so long as the number of families living within reach of one another was not too large. But when an aristocratic family, with a residence in both the country and the city, and opportunities to travel, could have contacts with numerous families, its members usually preferred to select those on their own class level.

5. THE EXTENSION OF POLITE COMPANIONSHIP AMONG CAPITALISTS AND PROFESSIONALS

On the other hand, with the development of class stratification in cities, the pattern of companionate intercourse was adopted by the wealthy bourgeoisie and, eventually, by professionals. Later, it spread into countries which, like the United States, have no old hereditary nobility. But the use of class standards in selecting partners still remains. No persons belonging to an inferior class are admitted to participation. This is well exemplified in such American cities as Boston, New York, and Chicago, where members of families listed in the *Social Register* regularly maintain companionate intercourse as hosts, and invite only guests whose families are included in the *Register*. Professional people—university professors, lawyers, physicians—and their wives carry on companionate intercourse with other professionals, but not with physical workers or salesmen. Commissioned officers and their wives exclude from companionate intercourse privates, corporals, and sergeants. Even in Soviet Russia, the higher bureaucracy and prominent intellectuals do not associate with workers or peasants. And, as we know, where caste stratification or racial discrimination exists, people of a higher caste or race do not allow lower-class people to participate in companionate intercourse.

There are several reasons for this maintenance of class standards. First, companionate intercourse is not supposed to be disturbed by conflicts between participants. While a particular individual is free to maintain a cooperative relation or even a long-lasting friendship with a lower-class person, he cannot impose the company of this person upon his host or guests who want companionate intercourse only with people of their own class. It would be an unpardonable breach of etiquette to introduce into a companionate gathering of people who are class-conscious a person whom they consider inferior—unless, indeed, the "inferior" person is known to be admitted, not as a participant in the companionate relations in which the others participate, but merely as somebody whose task is to serve the others or provide amusement (e.g., music or song).

The other reason why class standards still persist in polite relations is that active participation in this kind of companionate intercourse, which has been developed and maintained by the upper classes, requires not merely knowledge of the rules of etiquette and ability to conform with them, but also understanding and appreciation of the cultural values which are used for common enjoyment: hedonistic values, like food and drink; aesthetic values, like clothes, adornments, and artistic decorations of the home; music and literature, as subjects of conversation; as well as skill in such activities as dancing, games, sports, etc. All this obviously requires considerable education. Such an education was partly acquired at home, proving that the parents had been properly educated and actively shared in upper-class relations; partly in schools. And most of the schools where such an education was given were originally reserved for children of upper-class parents. Quite a few still are. Even in schools without class discrimination, we find associations of students—clubs, sororities, and fraternities —which limit their membership to sons or daughters of presumably upper-class families, and supplement their home education by enforcing conformity with the rules of etiquette.

Finally, in order to participate actively in polite companionate intercourse, the members of a family must have enough economic possessions and leisure time to act as hosts and to reciprocate in some degree the enjoyment which they received when they were guests. Families whose economic level is too far below that of a certain class cannot participate in companionate intercourse with families of that class.

Thus, limitation of relations of polite companionship to people on a relatively high level contributes to the preservation of class gradations and class solidarity, even where hereditary nobility does not exist.

This does not mean that companionate intercourse for common enjoyment does not occur on lower-class levels. It has always been carried on, as we mentioned at the beginning of this chapter, in rural communities, and has been growing in cities, among industrial workers. The economic limitations which make entertainment at home difficult have been partly overcome by the cooperative organization of large companionate gatherings. The spread of education among the masses enables them to enjoy aesthetic values, and some rules of etiquette are being taught to children in most schools.

Nevertheless, the cultural patterns of polite companionate intercourse are more complex, the relations are more clearly regulated, and their content is still much wider on upper-class levels. This is generally recognized by public opinion, as manifested in the

newspapers, which devote special sections to reports on companionate intercourse among people of the upper classes.

6. PERSONAL WORTH AS A STANDARD IN THE CHOICE OF PART-NERS FOR POLITE COMPANIONSHIP

Of course, in modern societies, especially where the democratic
ideal is generally recognized, the standards on which class gradation
is based are now not so strong or uniform as they were in the past;
personal worth often counts more than heredity or wealth. We
must remember, however, that in long-lasting relations of polite
companionship all members of the *family* are involved: husbands
and wives, as well as parents and their children, as they reach
maturity. For instance, an aristocrat or a millionaire feels quite free
to choose, when arranging a "party" for only prominent men; but is
restricted in arranging a "party" *with his wife,* and inviting men
and their wives, since he must later visit these men and their wives
in their homes.

The need for some standard of selection is obvious, when within
a certain area—a big city or a smaller urban center with all its
suburbs—there are too many people of the same class for each to
identify personally all the others and interact regularly with them.
Furthermore, in the course of time, newcomers enter such an area:
strange families, who settle more or less permanently; outsiders,
marrying into local families; and children of local families, who
become candidates for partnership in companionate intercourse
when they grow up. Finally, particular individuals who know each
other may evaluate each other negatively, and tend to interact
antagonistically whenever they meet.

Undoubtedly, personal worth is becoming an increasingly important standard of selection of partners in companionate intercourse;
and this has led to changes in the books of etiquette. But the
personal standards by which partners in polite companionship are
evaluated still differ from those by which individuals are judged in
other kinds of social relations.

The modern rules of etiquette allow considerable freedom to individuals in selecting partners and maintaining active social relations. This is manifested by the custom of "introduction." Introduction means the mutual identification by name of hitherto unacquainted individuals, and their presentation to each other as potential partners in companionate intercourse. It may be initiated by one of them, who introduces himself to the other; or, preferably, by a third individual, who introduces both to each other. In the first case, the individual who initiates it should be sure that the other is willing to accept him as a partner: if not, the other may not reciprocate by introducing himself. In the second case, the individual who introduces them should be sure that they are willing to accept each other. If they do, they are supposed to express their acceptance by some polite symbolic communication. Refraining from such symbolic communication is a sign of nonacceptance.

After two individuals have accepted each other as potential partners, they may limit their later intercourse to a minimum compatible with the principle of politeness. Only if they find each other congenial, is their companionate intercourse apt to become relatively frequent and intimate. Thus, when a number of acquaintances regularly take turns in entertaining and visiting one another, this implies considerable congeniality among them. But if two acquaintances meet only outside of their homes, though they recognize and accept each other, their relationship remains rather distant. Nonetheless, they are supposed to follow basic rules of etiquette, greet each other, ask questions manifesting positive interest in each other, and answer all inquiries politely. However, there are culturally patterned ways of tactfully changing an intimate relation into a more distant one, and vice versa.

But even among people of the same class we find a gradation of what is called "prestige"; an individual with high prestige has more freedom in selecting partners and making their relations more intimate or more distant than an individual with lower prestige. Prestige in a set of polite acquaintances is generally based on the contributions which the individual has been making as a leader in companionate intercourse. Older men and women who have made such contributions for many years obviously have higher prestige than the young who are only beginning to participate. Members of "old families" who have functioned as hosts for generations have more prestige than newcomers. Wealth is a source of prestige only if used to give pleasant, interesting, and original entertainments to numerous guests. Superior wisdom and competence in matters of etiquette may be a basis for prestige, independently of wealth or descent, e.g., Beau Brummel or Emily Post. The ladies who functioned as hostesses in French salons owed their prestige to their ability as leaders in organizing interesting gatherings of people on a high cultural level. Famous poets, artists, philosophers, scientists, and statesmen may be introduced into companionate sets and "lionized," but they do not gain prestige as leaders unless they stimulate polite conversation and cooperate with the other participants in their companionate gatherings.

7. The Active Duties of Polite Companions

As we have already mentioned, after two individuals become acquainted and accept each other, the principle of politeness requires that each of them should from time to time perform actions manifestly intended to give enjoyment to the other, and show appreciation of such actions which the other has performed. This principle applies to every relation, irrespective of age, sex, heredity, wealth, prestige, and power. The character and range of suitable actions, however, is determined by rules of etiquette.

They include, primarily and universally, *conversation*, during which experiences presumably interesting to both are discussed, positive attitudes toward the other's values are expressed, and his person tactfully praised. This is a duty equally incumbent on both partners, whenever they are brought face-to-face long enough to perform it, either accidentally or on the initiative of a third person. Naturally, it must also be undertaken occasionally on the initiative of each partner, either by writing the other or inviting him for a visit.

Another familiar duty is to offer *gifts*. Gifts of food (especially if prepared in the giver's home), ceremonial gifts on certain occasions (e.g., a wedding or celebration of the birth of a child), gifts symbolic of personal remembrance after a long separation, and gifts expressing good wishes are offered at intervals, and should eventually be reciprocated.

Aesthetic enjoyment is procured in various forms: artistic arrangement of the reception room and the dining room; music, song, or poetry, by either hosts or guests; sometimes even theatrical representations. *Intellectual* enjoyment is offered by the loan of books and opportunities to listen to intellectual discussions or to meet prominent leaders.

Companionship partners are also asked to participate in various interesting *activities*, especially games, sports, and amateur art; sometimes also in meritorious performances—charitable undertakings or cooperative church meetings.

And, last but not least, chances are given to a partner of *forming* relations of polite companionship with other desirable people.

This wide range of altruistic actions which relations of polite companionship involve has definite limitations. No action should seriously affect important values or active tendencies of the other partner. Conversations, while interesting, should never be too stirring emotionally: Each partner must not only avoid topics which bore the other partner, but even more carefully steer around topics which might arouse strong emotional reactions, and carefully conceal any signs of deep emotion on his own part.

When food is offered by a host to guests, it is a luxury, unconnected with real organic necessity. Everybody takes for granted that a host does not give up for the sake of his guests any of the food he needs for his normal nourishment; nor are the guests to any degree dependent on his food for their normal nourishment: He merely tries to provide them with "pleasures of the palate" over and above the satisfaction of hunger.

No gifts between polite companions should be so valuable as to affect their economic status. It is presumed that the gift involves no real economic sacrifice on the part of the giver, and is of no real economic benefit to the receiver: It is just a pleasant "token of good will." Aesthetic or intellectual entertainment, when offered to companions, should not require serious efforts of understanding on their part; especially must all suggestion be avoided that such entertainment has an educational value for them. Group activities in which companionship partners are invited to cooperate should always be "amateur" activities, without any professional standards of perfection or any long-term mutual obligations. They do not aim to produce objectively important cultural values, nor to satisfy future needs of the partners; their significance lies in the very pleasure of performing them and the opportunity of winning social appreciation.

If these limits are transgressed, and the actions of the partners become really important to them, involve exclusive communication of personal experiences or intimate sharing of emotions, personal sacrifices and valuable benefits, serious efforts for the future realization of common goals, the relation is no longer mere companionship, but changes into some other kind of relation—e.g., close friendship, love, economic partnership, common pursuit of a political goal, or collaboration in promoting creative innovations, to which the rules of etiquette are no longer applicable.

Etiquette shows how a relation of polite companionship can be made to change or be prevented from changing into a more exclusive or practically important social relation. If one partner manifests a tendency to greater intimacy, offers or asks real aid in need, or tries to convert playful cooperation into a utilitarian or culturally productive cooperation, and the other partner voluntarily responds, a new relation begins to be formed. But if the other partner wishes to keep their relation within the culturally patterned limits and to check this tendency, he has definite methods at his disposal for doing so, not by an explicitly negative reaction, but by a tactful evasion of the issue and an especially punctilious observation of the rules of etiquette, which imposes upon the first partner the duty to refrain from further initiative and to revert to the pattern of politeness.

CHAPTER 9

INTEGRATION OF SOCIAL RELATIONS

1. CONNECTIONS AMONG SOCIAL RELATIONS

In our survey of social relations between mothers and children, between brothers, between husbands and wives, between lovers, and between polite companions, we found that it is possible to investigate each relation separately as a limited system of actions performed by the two partners, when dealing with each other, provided they follow certain cultural standards and norms.

But only a few relations, such as steadfast male friendship and lasting mutual love between a man and a woman, can be initiated and maintained by the two partners exclusively, without the aid of anybody else; and these, as we have seen, are relatively late cultural products requiring considerable education of the partners.

In the great majority of cases, a social relation is subjected to the influence of some other people, each of whom is a participant in a social relation with one of the partners, or with both of them. We found, for instance, that marital relations are usually subjected to such influences from the parents of the husband, on the one hand, and from the parents of the wife, on the other hand.

This raises a significant problem. What is the connection between the various social relations in which the same individual simultaneously participates? Sometimes it is obvious that there is no connection between certain relations. For instance, a man's relation with his pastor usually is unconnected with his business relations. But when an individual is a partner in similar social relations with a number of others, they actively cooperate not only with him, but also with each other. This means that his relations with all these partners are functionally *integrated* in such a way as to facilitate the performance of their respective duties and to avoid conflicts between them.

Let us analyze a few typical examples of such integration.

2. INTEGRATION OF RELATIONS OF POLITE COMPANIONSHIP

We begin with relations of polite companionship, because integration is essential for their very existence. In surveying these relations, we found that most of the actions of two partners in companionate intercourse are performed in the presence of other companions with whom they also interact. The interaction between any two of them is inseparably connected with the interaction between each of them and the others—unless, indeed, their relation has ceased to be mere polite companionship, and become a different kind of relation in which their other companions do not participate.

Take, first of all, a host and a hostess who have invited guests to a dinner party, and are entertaining them. As a man and a woman, they are obviously different kinds of persons, but each of them is supposed to be evaluated positively by all the guests who have accepted their invitations. The host and the hostess have assumed on their own initiative somewhat different, but mutually supplementary, duties toward their guests: giving enjoyable food and drink, stimulating interesting conversation, perhaps offering aesthetic pleasure (e.g., music), or the opportunity for a game (e.g., bridge). They expect every guest to respond positively to their actions, in accordance with the rules of etiquette; and if a particular guest transgresses these rules, other guests are supposed to counteract such transgressions tactfully, so as to prevent the party from being spoiled.

On the other hand, every guest, male or female, is also supposed to be evaluated as a person by other participants, although his or her duties are more limited. The main duty of a guest is to help the host and hostess achieve the purpose for which the party was arranged, by carrying on polite intercourse with guests with whom he or she comes into contact during the gathering. Of course, some guests may assume the duty of assisting the hosts, by initiating specific activities—aesthetic, intellectual, or sportive.

In short, all the social relations between the host, the hostess, and each particular guest are integrated together. We might say that companionate intercourse during the party centers around the persons of the host and the hostess, who function as leaders in certain activities, and whose initiative all the guests are expected to follow.

Thus, in studying the relations between each individual and the others during a companionate gathering, it is possible to distinguish two main culturally patterned combinations of such relations, with secondary variations due to sex and to the specific function which each individual performs: relations between the host or the hostess and each of the guests; and relations between a particular guest, male or female, and the other guests with whom he or she interacts.

Now, as we know, *the same individual* can function as a host or a hostess during one companionate gathering, and as a guest during another gathering. Even more important is the fact that the same individual who participates in relations of polite companionship, as a host or a guest, participates also in other, very different kinds of social relations. Are some of those relations also integrated?

Suppose he is a married man, and he and his wife have several children. Thus, besides functioning as host and hostess, or as guests in companionate gatherings, both he and she are partners in social relations with their children. We have investigated mother-child relations, but not father-child relations. Let us look for a moment at the relations between a particular father and several of his children, and see whether they are integrated. We shall take into consideration only patriarchal families.

3. INTEGRATION OF SOCIAL RELATIONS BETWEEN A FATHER AND HIS DESCENDANTS

The duties of a man as father obviously begin only after he has been married. From the point of view of his father, who in patriarchal communities arranges the marriage, its purpose is to enable him to perpetuate the patrilineal family by procreating children. Since the children will be considered descendants of his ancestors, rather than of his wife's, he has considerable authority over his wife as a mother, whereas she has little authority, if any, over him as a father.

We have seen that in most communities, if his wife does not become pregnant, he can reject her. He can reject her, or even kill her, if she has sexual intercourse with another man without his permission, lest the child born of her be not his own progeny. On the other hand, in some communities, he can compel her to have sexual intercourse with some man of his choice, and yet consider the child she bears as his own, since she is his property in a mystical sense.

After his wife becomes pregnant, he often controls her behavior directly or through somebody else's agency, lest the child be defective; or he may perform himself some magical activities which will insure that it will be a desirable descendant of his. After an infant is born in many communities, it is the husband who decides whether it should be accepted and brought up, or rejected as undesirable; and the wife must follow his decision.

But even when a husband is religiously, morally, or legally bound to accept as his the child born of his wife, in so doing he assumes the chief responsibility for its future. Since he is a descendant of valuable progenitors, it is his duty toward them to make this new descendant worthy of them. Furthermore, as an active participant in the adult community, he will have to *vouch* for his child, when it becomes a candidate for participation, so as to have it accepted by other participants as valuable—primarily when his child is a boy who will share in masculine activities, but secondarily also when it is a girl, a potential wife of some male participant.

Therefore, although it is the mother who during the child's early years performs most of the duties of protection, support, promotion of growth, and educational guidance, and, if the child is a girl, continues to educate her in later years, these duties are presumed to be delegated to her by the father, who retains the right to control her performance. The main reason why he delegates to her many of the parental duties is that, in a community dominated by men, he may have to participate in various collective masculine actions—magical, religious, juridical, military, technical, or economic—which require much time and energy; and the security, subsistence, and reputation of his wife and children depend in considerable measure on this participation.

In all patriarchal families, the father is supposed to have several children; often, indeed, the more children he has, the higher his prestige. With the birth of every child, the duties of the father increase, as a new relation is initiated in which he is the dominant partner. On the other hand, as his children grow, they become increasingly aware of their duties toward their father. Since his children owe to him and his wife their very existence, and to him adoption into his family as legitimate descendants, he can expect permanent gratitude on their part. Although he, together with his wife, supports them, they are in duty bound to cooperate economically to the best of their ability. He assumes the responsibility for their future as active participants in the community; but, in order to be prepared for this participation, they have to obey his commands, as well as those of his wife or of anybody else to whom he delegates some of his duties. In particular, they are unconditionally obliged to follow his authoritarian guidance in learning those actions which they will perform as adults. This is well exemplified in communities in which sons gradually learn under the guidance of their fathers hunting, fishing, pasturing cattle, and agriculture; also in urban communities in which sons of craftsmen become apprentices of their fathers or of other craftsmen to whom the fathers delegate their teaching duties. At the same time, fathers demand that their wives teach their daughters by similar methods how to perform feminine functions.

Even after the children grow up and are prepared for active participation in the community, the father still preserves some authority. It is he who "gives his daughter away," when she gets married; that is, he delegates his authority to her husband, but even then he may take her back, if the relation between her and her husband is unsatisfactory. He usually retains moral authority over his sons also, even after they are married. He is, obviously, interested in their children as his descendants, and tends to exert some control over their bringing up.

And if he is the owner of any durable property, whether inherited or acquired—a pasture, a garden, a farm, a herd of cattle, a forest, a residence, a mine, a store, a factory, or a large sum of money—he usually grants some of his possessions or a share in their use to his children, when they get married, but frequently retains supreme ownership until his death. Such maintenance of paternal authority and possessive rights existed in ancient Rome and in China up to the end of the nineteenth century. The Roman *paterfamilias* and the Chinese father could, to the end of his life, exert obedience from sons, daughters, daughters-in-law, as substitutes for daughters, and grandchildren; he also preserved control of his family property.

Moreover, in many communities an influential and wealthy man extended these paternal relations to the children of many women: children of several wives, if polygyny was legitimate; children of his concubines, if concubinage was allowed; and adopted children of other fathers, known or unknown. This is illustrated in the semi-mythical case of Solomon, with all his concubines; the case of the old African chief with nearly two thousand descendants; and the more moderate case of the Sultan of Zanzibar, as reported by one of his daughters.

Of course, such authoritarian powers of the father had to have some support, lest his children disobey him or fail to manifest their gratitude. They were supported, indeed, by his kin of the same generation; by the old men who were considered bearers of magico-religious wisdom and power; by professional priests; and by political governments. From early childhood on, the youth learned how essential their duties toward their fathers were, and how their fulfilment would be rewarded, their nonfulfilment punished, either by men or by gods.

4. INTEGRATION OF THE SOCIAL RELATIONS BETWEEN A CHILD AND VARIOUS ADULTS

It might seem that we should be able to learn everything essential about the social life of a young child, if we studied the relation between it and its mother and the relation between it and its father. But the matter is not so simple. For even when the mother and the father together, under the father's authority, regulate the life of their child, seldom is the child isolated from other adults, unless—very rarely—the parental families live separately, as some pioneer or vagrant families do. Usually, since the relations between a child and both its parents are culturally patterned, conformity with the patterns is a matter of concern to other community members who, like the parents, are positively interested in the particular child as a potentially valuable adult, and therefore try to influence its growth and development.

Thus, in well-developed clans and gentes, or in a bilineal family system, grandparents and brothers or sisters of mothers or fathers initiate definite relations with the children, by assuming certain duties which supplement the duties of the parents, especially when the parents do not fulfil them properly. Some of these relations have been well investigated, e.g., in matrilineal families, relations between the child and its mother's brother, who was at least as influential in controlling the child's future as its father. Other relations, however, have been rather neglected by investigators, especially those between grandparents and grandchildren. For instance, in many agricultural communities, where the parents are busy, much of the traditional culture is transmitted to children by grandparents.

However, not all the partners in child-adult relations are connected with the child by kinship bonds. The parents may delegate some duties to adults who are not their kin. Thus, when a child is baptized, an adult man and a woman are invited by the parents to assist in the ceremony, and thereafter become the child's godfather and godmother, assuming certain religious, moral, and even practical duties toward it, when needed. In feudal Europe, sons and even daughters of vassals were often sent to the courts of suzerains, who assumed toward them parental duties of support and educational guidance. With the development of craftsmen's guilds, masters accepted as apprentices the sons of other men; the apprentices lived in the home of their master and were not only trained in technical skill, but given some moral and religious education. As we mentioned before, in aristocratic European families during the seventeenth, eighteenth, and nineteenth centuries, mothers and fathers delegated most of their parental duties to nurses, domestic servants, governesses, and tutors.

Most numerous were the relations in which the firstborn son of a king participated. Besides relations with his father, his mother, and the adults of royal descent with whom he was connected by agnatic or cognatic bonds, he was subjected during childhood and youth to the protective and educational guidance of a wet nurse, a physician, a trained nurse, several ladies and gentlemen of the royal court, officers of the royal guards, teachers of language and literature, of music, gymnastics, fencing, horseback riding, and dancing; later, tutors of religion, law, administration, and military tactics. All of these relations were under the control of the boy's father, and were well integrated; for their ultimate purpose was to make him fit to become a king, the supreme authority and most important person in the kingdom.

Now let us examine the total combination of social relations in which a middle-class boy in an urbanized American community participates from infancy to adulthood. Unlike the king's son, he is not considered unique, but one of many. Nor are all his relations controlled by his father. Yet they are also numerous. If some of his father's or mother's kin live within the community, they are usually in contact with him and actively interested in him. He probably interacts from time to time with a physician and a dentist, who assume definite duties toward him, perhaps also with a clinical psychologist. While on the streets, he—like other children—is subjected to the protective care of policemen. Throughout his school years, from kindergarten through high school, he participates in well-standardized educational relations with a number of teachers. If his parents belong to a church, the priest or minister prepares him for participation in that church. He may also follow the guidance of a Boy Scout leader. Not all of these relations are integrated. There is little connection, if any, between his relations with his physician, his pastor, and the Boy Scout leader. But his relations with adult family members are certainly interconnected; and so are those with his teachers.

In any case, the child is considered a positive social value by those adults who at some time during his bringing up assume certain duties toward him; and each of these adults is expected to contribute something to his personal development. In so far as their respective contributions are mutually supplementary, some cooperation must exist among them. Each is concerned with what is going on in social relations between the child and several other adults; and each is aware that other adults are concerned with what occurs in his relations with the child. All of them together are supposed to see that everything is done for the child which ought to be done to have him become the kind of valuable person which he is intended to become, and also that the child does what he ought to do in order to develop into that kind of person.

5. OTHER EXAMPLES OF INTEGRATED RELATIONS

We shall now take a few more specialized examples.

A well-known type of social interaction (mentioned in Chapter 5) is the exchange of values intended to satisfy the respective needs of the partners. It may be only one of the many mutual duties between partners. Or it may be carried on periodically between particular individuals who have little else in common with each other, as when rural people bring their products to a town and exchange them for the products of townsmen. But if a merchant assumes the task of regularly purchasing the values produced by certain people and of selling them to other people who need them, he establishes specific, more or less lasting relations with the producers, on the one hand, and the users, on the other hand; and those relations become at least partially integrated.

Technical collaboration between individuals is also frequently only one of several mutual duties. It may be temporarily carried on by a number of people who perform more or less similar actions, e.g., big-game hunting; or continually, by two individual specialists, e.g., a craftsman and his assistant. But long-lasting industrial collaboration between a number of partners who specialize in various mutually supplementary technical activities requires individual leadership. It is the leader, organizer, or manager, however we call him, who is connected by social relations with all his followers and thus integrates their technical performances.

We spoke above about the integrated relations between a school pupil and the teachers who cooperate in educating him. In a similar way, a professor is connected by a specific social relation with every one of his students, so long as the student attends his classes; both professor and student have definite duties toward each other. But all the relations between the professor and the students in a particular class are integrated. He teaches them the same subject, tests the knowledge they acquire by the same criteria, and frequently promotes mutual understanding and intellectual cooperation among them by stimulating discussion. Without him, there could be no regular gathering of these students in a class for the common purpose of learning the subject he teaches, and thus gaining academic credit for it.

Very different from all of these are the integrated social relations among men participating together in warfare. An enormous amount of material has been gathered concerning war. Here we are concerned only with that type of tribal warfare which is carried on by relatively small groups of warriors, all of whom are personally acquainted with [each] other and connected by bonds of social solidarity. Every one of them has definite duties toward every other—duties to cooperate in common aggression and to defend each other against aggression. As a rule, effective cooperation of the participants depends on the function of the leader, who integrates their individual performances.

What do all these combinations of integrated social relations have in common? Is there a fundamental similarity underlying their differences? In the following chapter, we shall try to show that there is, and consequently that all of them, however they differ, must be treated as belonging to and constituting a universal category of *social systems*, obviously more complex and more difficult to investigate than social relations, but also much more important from the historical and sociological point of view.

CHAPTER 10

THE CONCEPT OF SOCIAL ROLE

1. COMMON CHARACTERISTICS OF INTEGRATED SOCIAL RELATIONS

In studying social relations, we found that, when the same individual is a partner in social relations with a number of others, these relations are usually integrated. Some social relations in which the individual participates have no connection whatsoever, while others even conflict. For a number of social relations to become integrated, there must be cooperation not only between the individual and each of his partners, but also cooperation among his partners. When such cooperation exists, and the social relations between him and certain of his partners are integrated, they constitute all together a *social system*.

Such a social system implies, first of all, that the individual himself—the host, the hostess, the guest, the father, the child, the pupil in school, the merchant, the industrial manager, the college professor, or the leader in warfare—be identified and positively evaluated by all the partners who are supposed to cooperate with him in this respect—the guests, the hosts and the other guests, his patrilineal descendants, the adult family members, the school teachers, the sellers and the buyers, the technical workers, the college students, or the warriors. All these cooperating partners compose together what we shall call the social circle of which he is the center; and he, in turn, is supposed to evaluate all of them positively.

Such a person has definite *duties* which participants in his social circle expect him to perform. But he cannot adequately perform his duties unless the participants perform theirs on his behalf. Such is manifestly the case when the person is a guest, a child, or a school pupil; but also when he is a host, a father, a merchant, an industrial manager, a college professor, or a war leader. Consequently, the people who compose his social circle assume together the task of having everything done for him which the social norms require. To use a term which we shall define more exactly later, they grant him definite *rights*, and support these rights by applying positive or negative sanctions to the conduct of each member of the circle.

2. PARTICIPATION OF THE SAME INDIVIDUAL IN DIVERSE SYSTEMS OF SOCIAL RELATIONS

If we survey life histories of particular individuals in various collectivities during various historical periods, we find that every individual in the course of his life is the center of different social circles and that, in each of these, the standards by which he is evaluated as a person, the kind of duties which he is expected to perform, and the rights which others grant him vary and change.

Thus, as a child grows up to adolescence, he usually becomes a participant in social relations with a number of other children and, later, other adolescents. These relations, even when subjected to adult control (which is not always the case), differ from those with adult family members. He is differently evaluated by the circle of his age-fellows; his duties toward them and their duties toward him are not of the same kind as those between him and his elders. When he goes to school, his relations with his teachers differ from those with his parents and from those with other pupils. If, after reaching maturity, he is recruited into the army, his relations with his fellow soldiers and those with commissioned and noncommissioned officers are obviously unlike all his previous relations.

An adult man, outside his family circle, participates in different kinds of relations with the circles of adult men with whom he cooperates for various common purposes. In a tribal community, he may be a fisherman and cooperate regularly with several other fishermen; he occasionally participates as a warrior in common aggression or defense against enemies, and shares periodically in certain magico-religious ceremonies. In these activities, his duties toward those with whom he cooperates, and their duties toward him, vary considerably; and so do the standards by which he is evaluated. Different personal characteristics are required of a fisherman, a warrior, and a magician.

In a modern urban region, the man who is a father and a partner in relations of polite companionship may be also an active church member, a businessman, an amateur sportsman, and a minor politician. The social circles in which he performs these functions are seldom composed of the same people; his duties manifestly differ, and his person is differently evaluated in each of them.

3. THE CONCEPT OF ROLE

The possibility for the same individual to participate in many different social relations with different people has attracted considerable attention from those sociologists and social psychologists who were critical of the old doctrine, according to which the explanation of an individual's social life had to be sought in "human nature," and interaction of human individuals with one another was supposed to depend on their real essence as biological, biopsychological, or psychological beings. Since conceptions of this essence varied, and none of them could be proved true, they were obviously metaphysical, rather than scientific.

Studies of actual social relations led some twentieth-century thinkers to the conclusion that interaction between human individuals depends not on what they "really are," but—popularly speaking—on what they *believe* themselves and others to be. This conclusion made metaphysical controversies as to the "true essence" of human beings scientifically irrelevant.

To indicate this new approach, the term "role," derived from the theater, came into use. In a theatrical role, the actor appears and behaves toward others, and other actors appear and behave toward him, as if he and they were the kind of persons imagined by the playwrights. Ever since Shakespeare, playwrights and actors have seen an analogy between the theater and the social world, not only in the obvious sense that theatrical art partly imitates social life, but also in the sense that social life itself has much make-believe in it. Individuals appear and act for the benefit of an audience, and pretend or imagine themselves to be certain kinds of persons; the audience as well as other actors accept the make-believe as a reality.

Sociologists and social psychologists who became aware of this analogy adopted the term *role* (eventually with the adjective *social*) and applied it to individual participation in social life. They concentrated, first of all, on the individual's representation of his own self. Baldwin, Cooley, and Mead proved that this representation is a product of social interaction and communication: The individual imagines and conceives himself to be the kind of person that he believes others judge him to be. Park and Burgess, in their *Introduction to Sociology*, defined the term *person* (following the old Latin meaning of the word *persona*) as "an individual's conception of his role," and showed that an individual tends to behave in accordance with this conception. A few years later, they and other investigators pointed out that the way in which a particular individual is conceived as a person and expected to act varies in various groups in which he participates: He can perform several different social roles, just as an actor can perform several different theatrical roles.

Ever since 1922, I have been trying to develop a common conceptual approach to human individuals (not as total personalities, but as participants in social life and culture) which could be applied to such widely different kinds of individuals as little girls and mature men, young boys and old women, medieval knights and modern capitalists, kings and serfs, priests and craftsmen, farmers and poets, painters and lawyers, scientists and politicians, ladies of leisure, and factory workers. After experimenting with several concepts, I found that the concept symbolized by the term *social role*, if adequately defined, is the most useful for that purpose, and that the analogy with the theatrical role is helpful in defining it.

4. Definition of Social Role by Comparison with Theatrical Role

First of all, every theatrical role involves interaction between the actor who plays the role and other actors. No individual can play the role of Hamlet alone. He must have a circle of other actors and actresses playing the roles of the Queen, the King, Horatio, Ophelia, Polonius, etc., all of whom accept him as the impersonator of Hamlet. And the same holds true of every other role performed by an actor or actress who participates in the play. Although Hamlet is the central, most important person, whose role is the main role of the drama, yet at some time in the course of the play each of those other, less important persons becomes a minor center of attention, even if only briefly, while he or she is on the stage.

If we take this aspect of theatrical roles into consideration when studying social roles, we shall find in every social role a social circle within which the individual performs it, that is, a set of agents who accept him and cooperate with him. If no such circle exists, the individual cannot actually perform a social role, though he may imagine that he does, like a daydreaming child who identifies himself with some person he wishes to be, or a pathological adult who believes that he is some great hero.

The second important point is that, since a drama is a literary product created by an author to be visually and orally recreated by players, every theatrical role is *culturally patterned*; every actor who later recreates it has to learn the pattern from the author's work, and is supposed to follow it. The person of the actor who plays Hamlet, his bodily appearance, some symbols of rank as Prince of Denmark, and his general character are meant to conform with certain standards. Everything he says and does as Hamlet is expected to conform with definite norms. Such conformity is his duty as an artist, for without it no aesthetically adequate presentation of the drama, as originally planned, would be possible. But he cannot perform effectively this duty, unless the other members of the cast who are acting with him have also learned to follow the definite cultural patterns represented by the other characters.

Here again the analogy between a theatrical role and a social role is significant. For social roles are also culturally patterned; individuals who perform them are supposed to learn the patterns and follow them. Every host interacting with his guests, every father interacting with his descendants, every child interacting with adults, every merchant, industrial organizer, college professor, or war leader is defined and evaluated according to certain standards, and it is his duty to act in accordance with definite norms. He cannot perform his role adequately, unless the participants in his circle have also learned to follow certain cultural patterns.

Obviously, there is a fundamental difference between the cultural patterns which theatrical actors and social agents are supposed to follow. The task of the theatrical actor is to recreate, together with other actors, the original *aesthetic* creation of the playwright, in accordance with the standards and norms of *dramatic art*. In this respect, it is similar to the task of a musician who, together with other musicians (often under the guidance of a conductor) recreates the original aesthetic creation of a composer, in accordance with the standards and norms of musical art. Whereas the task of a participant in collective life who performs a social role, together with those who cooperate with him, is to apply certain *moral* standards, according to which human individuals are supposed to be evaluated by others, and to conform with certain *moral* norms, according to which their actions are expected to be satisfactory to others. The cultural pattern followed by him and the others interacting with him is seldom the product of one creator, but usually a result of the contributions of many thinkers.

Nonetheless, we observe a third instructive similarity between theatrical roles and social roles. In surveying the history of theatrical representations of dramatic art, we find that seldom do particular actors play any role created by a dramatist in exactly the same manner. For instance, during the last two centuries the actors and actresses playing the most famous roles created by Shakespeare have introduced many innovations. Most of their variations were treated as minor manifestations of personal differences; some, however, were disapproved of, as aesthetically undesirable; whereas others were considered valuable. Moreover, the significance of these differences has sometimes been hotly disputed in discussions between critics, between actors and critics, and between actors and their audiences.

Likewise, when we study comparatively the ways in which particular individuals perform *social* roles which are supposed to follow the same cultural pattern, we find that their performances also vary. For instance, when one of my classes investigated the roles of students in an American university, and compared the performances of 400 individuals, they found that their parts in college life varied from case to case. Indeed, certain psychologists postulate that every conscious and active human individual differs personally from every other, partly from birth, partly in consequence of environmental influences.

But, whatever the explanation of individual variations, they cannot be ignored by sociologists, for they may be socially significant to other participants in social life, e.g., the authoritative judges who maintain established cultural patterns of specific social roles, the social circles within which these roles are performed, the other performers who are supposed to follow the same cultural patterns, and the community members who are concerned with the influence which such variations may have on their own lives. Just as with theatrical roles, while many variations are treated as minor manifestations of personal differences within the cultural pattern, some variations are judged to be undesirable transgressions which must be repressed; whereas certain other innovations, on the contrary, are considered desirable by thinkers who are critical of traditional patterns, and these can eventually lead to the emergence of new kinds of social roles.

In view of the striking analogies between the function of a theatrical actor and that of an individual who cooperates with a number of partners in social relations, we feel justified in preserving the term *social role*, and applying it in a comparative study of systems of social relations in which a particular individual is the central person.

But before proceeding with our study, we must clarify certain differences between this approach to these systems and approaches which have been used more recently by some social psychologists, anthropologists, and sociologists.

5. DIVERGENT CONCEPTIONS OF INDIVIDUAL PARTICIPATION IN SOCIAL LIFE

It seems to us that the four components mentioned above—person, social circle, duties, and rights—are to be found in every social role, and that no social role can be adequately investigated without taking all of them into consideration. Whereas quite a few theorists of social roles omit altogether the study of social circles. Some of them, especially social psychologists, concentrate entirely on the attitudes and actions of individual performers. They forget that an individual cannot perform a social role alone, since in the course of its performance his attitudes and actions depend on those of the participants in his circle, and vice versa. A survey of the vast diversity and changeability of the social circles on which individual performances of social roles depend, and which depend on individual performances, will show the inadequacy of this sociopsychological approach. Especially significant is the difference between cases where a social circle is formed before the individual enters it, or even (like the adult family circle of a child) before he is born, and those where the individual himself gradually selects a circle which he needs in order to perform a role which he intends to perform.

On the other hand, some sociologists go to the other extreme, and identify the social circle with an organized social group; they assume that every social role is an integral part of the "structure" of some group. It is true, indeed, that many social roles are components of organized groups; and when we investigate social groups, we shall discover what this means. But numerous and diverse social roles are performed within social circles whose participants, though positively interested in the same individual and cooperating with him, do not constitute an organized group. Sometimes, indeed, in the course of time, such a social circle, at the initiative of its central person or some other participant, does form an organized group; e.g., the circle of followers of a prophet forms a new sect, or the circle of a political leader becomes a new political party. However, the very fact that an unorganized circle precedes the organized group is enough to invalidate the doctrine that all social roles are parts of group organizations.

The second essential principle which we use in our study is that a social role, like a social relation, is a dynamic system of actions which changes as it goes on, and therefore must be investigated, so far as possible, in the course of its duration. This is obvious when we study the social role of a child from birth to adolescence, or that of the father of a growing family from marriage to old age. It is even more obvious, when a new variety of social role evolves, e.g., that of a social reformer or revolutionist, or that of an innovator in literature, art, music, religion, philosophy, science, or material technique. All generalizations about social roles require, therefore, an inductive, comparative study of particular roles, as actually performed by individuals in cooperation with their circles.

And here we encounter a doctrine, according to which such studies are unnecessary, since the basic concept of the theory of individual participation in social life is not that of social role, but of *status*. Various meanings are given to this term. I formerly used it to denote the totality of rights which an individual is granted by the social circle within which he performs a certain role; for this meaning corresponds most closely with what is commonly called "gradation of status," found wherever a class stratification exists. But the meaning which now predominates is based on the definition and classification of individuals as persons, symbolically expressed in common names.

Thus, the "status" of husband, father, wife, mother, physician, engineer, manager, worker, president, or secretary means the common standards by which all individuals who are designated by such a name are defined in relation to others, who are also designated by some common name. Every individual who has such a status is supposed to have also explicitly defined rights, privileges, duties, and obligations, similar to those of all individuals of the same status. Statuses are, thus, abstract conceptual schemes by which social interaction between human agents is supposed to be guided. A role is simply a factual application of such a scheme by a particular individual agent.

In short, this conception of status provides a way of classifying social roles without investigating what the particular individuals who perform them and those with whom they interact are doing. A status in this abstract sense may even exist, although nobody performs the kind of role which the conceptual scheme is supposed to regulate. For instance, the status of president of a university or mayor of a city still exists as a concept after the individual who performed the role has retired or died, and before another individual who will perform a similar role has been appointed or elected.

There can be no doubt that in every realm of culture—religion, technology, art, language, literature, etc.—human actions tend to conform with standards and norms conceptualized by thinkers, just as human actions [sic] do; and the study of these concepts is indispensable for scientific purposes. But it still leaves important problems to be solved.

Among the problems which this theory of statuses neglects or fails to solve, we may mention: changes in the valuation of the person, as his role evolves; the range of permissible variation which every role allows; the processes of widening and narrowing the circle within which a role is performed; dynamic relations between simultaneous and successive roles of the same individual and of several individuals; and, finally, the gradual creative emergence in the course of history of new roles, with new standards and norms. Therefore, we shall leave out all classifications of statuses and, to avoid misunderstandings, drop our own early use of the term *status*, substituting for it another term—*rank*.

Our final purpose is to develop a general theory of social roles which will, obviously, include the four basic components mentioned above: person, social circle, duties, and rights. But the cultural patterns of each of these components vary and change so much that we might as well begin by surveying the range of their variations and changes, before proceeding to investigate their connections within specific roles or trying to reach systematic generalizations about roles as social systems.

CHAPTER 11

PERSONS

1. STANDARDS OF PERSONAL FITNESS

An individual can perform a social role only if his social circle judges him to be the kind of person who is fit for this kind of role. Such judgments are not made arbitrarily; they follow well-established cultural standards. We discussed some of the standards for deciding whether a newborn infant should be accepted and reared by a circle of adults; whether a grown-up man is fit to become a father of children who will be legitimate descendants of his paternal ancestors; and whether a man or a woman is fit to participate in polite companionate life. The individual is expected either to know before he begins to perform a particular role or to learn after he begins to perform it, by what standards his circle judges him.

A human individual, however defined by philosophers or scientists, is conceived by the human agents who interact with him, and by himself reflectively, as a combination of a living body or organism and a psyche or mind. To be judged fit for a certain role, he must possess in the opinion of his social circle definite personal characteristics, some biological or physical, some psychological or mental, which are considered "good," "right," and "desirable" for this kind of role; and not possess definite characteristics which are considered "bad," "wrong," or "undesirable." Such standards of personal fitness differ widely in different kinds of roles, and vary in various cultures. Since they are very important for the comparative study of social roles, let us briefly examine this diversity.

2. SEX AND AGE STANDARDS

Personal fitness for specific roles is judged, first of all, according to sex and age standards. We find such standards in every culture and in all historical periods. Indeed, differentiation of social roles in general probably began with biological classifications of human individuals; and in nearly all the collectivities known to ethnologists and historians sex is the primary and decisive standard of fitness for most social roles. Of course, only women can perform roles in which biological maternity is the essential condition, and those roles limit their opportunity for performing other roles. Consequently, in the course of history, most of the roles which require considerable specialization, as well as those which are performed within large social circles, became gradually reserved for men. Only in recent times has this old evolutionary trend been partially reversed. Many roles previously monopolized by men are now accessible to women.

Age always was, and still remains, a basic standard. Social roles considered important for the collectivity are accessible only to individuals who are judged to be socially mature. To be considered mature in a modern civilized collectivity, an individual must be biologically older than a socially mature person is in a preliterate collectivity. And in all collectivities, mature individuals must cease to perform specific roles when they reach a certain age and become old men or old women.

3. HEREDITARY BIOLOGICAL CHARACTERISTICS

Cutting across the standards of sex and age are other biological standards by which individual fitness or unfitness for certain social roles is judged.

We are familiar with "racial" standards. They are found in many tribal communities which have some contacts with outsiders noticeably different in hereditary bodily traits from their own members. Such outsiders are usually presumed to be inferior or dangerous, and in either case unfit to perform any important roles within the community.

Similar contempt or fear of racially different foreigners has often developed in consequence of mass migrations, military conquests, or economic expansion. In territories with mixed populations, great significance is still ascribed to racial traits. By standards which predominate in many communities of the United States, especially in the South, only a white person is considered fit to perform a professional role, as physician, lawyer, teacher, minister, or industrial manager, in a circle which contains white people; and a colored person is admitted into a white circle only in some subordinate role. According to the racial doctrine of Nazi ideologists, only a true Aryan, i.e., an individual of Nordic race, was considered fit to perform any important role. Individuals of "Semitic race" were both inferior and dangerous, and should therefore be eliminated; whereas individuals of other European races (Alpine or Mediterranean), as products of miscegenation, were inferior but not dangerous, and should therefore serve the Nordics.

In view of the fact that the great majority of individuals are of mixed racial descent, their racial classification can be based only on stereotypes. A minor physical characteristic which is presumably inherited may be sufficient to apply a racial stereotype to any particular person. Thus, an individual who has a physical characteristic similar to that shared by most people of the "Negro race" may be classified as a Negro, even though his total physical appearance is much more like that of the "white race." The racial stereotype of a Jew, constructed by anti-Semitics, was applied to all individuals who had some Jewish ancestry, notwithstanding the fact that racial differences between Jews are greater than those between members of any other white ethnic group, and many Jews are physically undistinguishable from people of some other racial subgroups.

4. ARTIFICIAL BODILY TRAITS

When innate biological characteristics are not sufficiently marked to distinguish "our people" from "strangers," artificial traits are often introduced into human bodies to make the distinction obvious.

Thus, in some tribal communities, the heads of all members are shaped during infancy and childhood in accordance with certain standards. In others, teeth, lips, ears, or noses are artificially fixed in a specific way. Tatoos and other bodily marks serve the same purpose. Circumcision is another well-known technique for making group members different from outsiders.

With the development of class stratification, conformity with certain standards of bodily appearance became a requirement for the admission of individuals to superior-class roles. These standards were primarily aesthetic, although aesthetic valuations differ widely in different cultures, and change in the course of time.

The Greek conception of a true gentleman included "beauty," as well as "goodness," and innate bodily imperfections were, so far as possible, corrected by years of training.

In many other cultures, beauty, innate but perfected, was also considered desirable for upper-class men. Thus, to European noblemen, who were presumed to be hereditarily superior to lower-class men, a handsome body gave a definite advantage in the selection for important roles, such as courtiers, diplomats, and leaders in polite companionate intercourse. Moreover, every nobleman's bodily appearance was supposed to be aesthetically improved by clothes and decorations. In some communities, lower-class men were even prohibited from wearing clothes and decorations similar to those of noblemen.

Feminine beauty is, of course, indispensable for courtesans, but also important for upper-class ladies. Artificial improvement of bodily appearance is recognized as a criterion of class distinction in many collectivities, however the aesthetic standards may differ. For instance, the "lily feet" of Chinese upper-class women reduced to a minimum their ability to move, while the training which European upper-class women received in courtly dances and horseback riding developed strength and grace. The long necks of Burmese ladies, the slim waists, delicate hands, and aesthetically arranged hair of European ladies were all products of much physical care. Wearing clothes in the proper manner also requires some training. Even longer training is necessary to develop aesthetically harmonious movements in the handling of all kinds of objects which ladies are supposed to use in the presence of other upper-class people. The latter were perhaps most fully developed in Japan, where the seemingly simple art of serving tea had to be acquired under the guidance of professional specialists.

A good illustration of the use of various aesthetic standards of women's bodily appearance in judging their fitness for certain roles is found in American sororities. When authoritative sorority members—actives, sometimes with the advice of alumnae—select candidates for membership, they judge them first by their appearance. Their standards include personal beauty, artistic ways of painting the face, right shape and color of fingernails, approved methods of arranging the hair, fashionable clothes adapted to the occasion, proper ways of walking, standing, and sitting, as well as correct "table manners."

Very different from such aesthetic standards are the well-known standards used by military authorities in judging the physical fitness of future soldiers, sailors, and airmen. However, until recent times, especially in Europe, aesthetic standards were also taken into consideration in selecting future officers, particularly for high-class regiments—e.g., the Black Hussars in Prussia, and the imperial guards in Russia. Rather exacting, though certainly not aesthetic, are the physical standards applied by football coaches in selecting prospective players. Different from all of these are the standards used by factory managers and foremen in selecting workers: Here physical skill, previously acquired, is the primary consideration.

This kind of skill, however, like the ability to perform various bodily movements in accordance with aesthetic patterns, though mainly physical, is also partly a psychological characteristic, since it implies some conscious purpose.

5. HEREDITARY PSYCHOLOGICAL CHARACTERISTICS

There are numerous psychological traits or characteristics which, according to popular thinking, human individuals possess in various degrees. In every language, we find hundreds of adjectives and nouns which denote diverse traits, more or less general or specific.

Most of them, especially the general ones, are positively or negatively evaluative: e.g., "intelligent" or "stupid," "good" or "bad," "courageous" or "cowardly," "virtuous" or "vicious." Some of the positive characteristics are considered essential for certain roles, but not for others. A child is expected to be good and obedient, but not learned or wise; a woman in a family circle is supposed to be affectionate, but not a naval or military commander to his subordinates, especially not in wartime.

Some characteristics are considered desirable in certain roles, but undesirable in others. According to traditional patterns, it is right for a businessman to be aggressive, but wrong for a hired worker or a debutante. It would never do for a member of a gay country club to be as virtuous as a Presbyterian minister is supposed to be. A poet or musician in his role is expected to be emotional; but not a physical scientist. The qualities required of a bootlegger in prohibition times were very different from those of a woman professor at Smith or Vassar College.

How do the people who compose a social circle conclude that a particular person is endowed with the psychological characteristics which are required of him in his role?

Conclusions about an individual's psychological characteristics are frequently drawn from his conscious actions and/or his attitudes symbolically manifested. But not always. In discussing the acceptance of a child by its mother and other participants in a community, we found that in many nonliterate communities the psychological potentialities of a child as future participant are often defined and evaluated as soon as it is born, or even earlier; in any case, long before it begins to perform conscious actions and to communicate symbolically with adults. Often conclusions are based on certain symptoms which, according to the prevalent beliefs, indicate that the child has an inherent good or evil essence derived from mythical beings, or magical powers. More general is the assumption that the child must have inherited certain desirable or undesirable psychological characteristics from its mother or father, or both, perhaps even from more distant ancestors.

The belief that essential psychological traits are inherited became closely connected in the course of history with the development of hereditary social stratification. The best known and most consistent example of this connection is the old caste hierarchy of India, which still survives in most communities there, even though the original conception of four main castes (Brahmans, Kshatrias, Vayshias, Sudras) is not adequate to cover the growing multiplicity and specialization of castes. In any case, however, every caste is strictly hereditary. Only those individuals, and all those individuals, belong to it whose ancestors, on both paternal and maternal sides, belonged to it; and only those individuals who belong to it are considered psychologically fit to perform the specific roles which their ancestors performed.

The same belief obviously underlies racial discrimination in the selection of individuals for specific roles in the Western world. The innate physical characteristics of a race are supposed to be accompanied by hereditary psychological characteristics. Those who share this belief do not have to observe what a particular individual does in order to conclude what his psychological traits are, or whether he is fit or unfit for the performance of a certain role. All they have to do is to notice the physical traits supposed to be distinctive of his race, or find out to what race his ancestors belonged. Racial doctrinaires have classified mankind into several races and drawn sweeping generalizations about the distinctive psychological nature of each race. For instance, Gobineau's psychological descriptions of the three "pure" races, with the "Aryan race" supreme; and, later, his mostly derogatory generalizations about mixed races.

These psychological generalizations help racial doctrinaires overcome the main difficulty they face when they apply a physical racial stereotype to individuals whose appearance deviates considerably from the model of his presumed race. A person who has one Jewish grandparent, but looks like an Aryan, or a person who, having one Negro great-grandparent, looks like a Caucasian may still be classified as a Jew or a Negro, because his heredity is supposed to make him psychologically inferior to pure Aryans or pure Caucasians. Although neither Hitler nor Goebbels, nor even Goering, looked like a perfect Nordic (compared, e.g., with Baldur von Schirach), yet they all were considered psychologically perfect, true Aryans; and their psychological perfection was proof that their blood must have been pure, uncontaminated by impure admixtures. On the other hand, an individual who *psychologically* deviates from the racial type to which he is supposed to belong must be of mixed descent, even if he physically conforms and his ancestry is unknown.

Another instance of the assumption that individuals inherit psychological fitness for certain roles is hereditary kingship. This idea goes back thousands of years, and has survived to this day. According to it, only sons of kings are fit for the roles of kings; and only daughters of kings are fit for the roles of mothers of kings. In some cultures—as in ancient Egypt—fitness for a king's role was directly inherited from the mother. Usually, however, a future king had to be a descendant of kings on both sides, although on the mother's side he could be a descendant of some sovereign family which was considered endowed with hereditary traits equal to those of the royal families. If the wife of a king was not of birth equal to her husband's (*ebenbürtig*), the blood of their son was contaminated, and he was psychologically unfit to become a king.

Similar standards were applied in Europe to the other important social roles which, though subordinated to the roles of king, included domination over large circles of subjects—feudal vassals, courtiers, military commanders, civil administrators, and owners of manorial estates. Individuals were supposed to inherit personal fitness for such roles from their progenitors who had effectively performed similarly patterned social roles. This principle underlies the perpetuation of *hereditary nobility*. It is expressed in the use of exclusive family names transmitted through generations from fathers to sons, along with honorific additions indicating their rank in the class hierarchy, and in coats-of-arms symbolizing their descent from prominent ancestors.

The belief that the bearers of such names are endowed with psychological characteristics which make them inherently superior to the masses of commoners is indicated by the dual meaning of some of the words which in various languages designate persons belonging to this hereditary class. Thus, in French *noblesse* and in English *nobility* denote a social class; but the adjective *noble* also connotes a morally valuable character. In Polish *szlachta* designated the total class of hereditary nobility, but the adjective *szlachetny*, like *noble*, has a purely moral connotation.

This assumption that individuals of a socially high class inherit psychological superiority is usually accompanied by the assumption that people of a socially low class are by heredity psychologically inferior. This sometimes finds expression in the meaning of certain words. For instance, *vilain* in French originally meant inhabitant of a village, a peasant; but it later acquired the connotation of a physically ugly and psychologically contemptible person. In English *villain*, with the same derivation, became the psychological antithesis of the noble, morally good person, and eventually in novels and dramas the evil opponent of the hero. In medieval Poland, the nobility believed that peasants were descendants of Cham, the inferior third son of Noah; the word *cham* still survives and means a bad-mannered, aggressive egoist.

The doctrine that heredity makes individuals psychologically fit by birth for superior roles or destined by birth for inferior roles has been, at least partially, accepted by several social thinkers. This is exemplified in Lombroso's conception of criminals who inherit from their ancestors subhuman biological traits; in Galton's theory of hereditary genius, approved by quite a few social psychologists; and in Nicefero's attempt to prove that the poor are hereditarily inferior. In America, studies of several generations of socially superior families—the Edwardses, the Adamses, the Lowells—and of socially inferior families—the Jukes and the Kallikaks—explicitly or implicitly assume that their superiority or inferiority was inherited. Ammon, who took into consideration the fact that in the course of two or three generations the descendants of lower-class families often rise to a higher class level, while descendants of higher-class families often drop into a lower class-level, concluded that the existing class structure provides the best framework for "natural selection," not for the survival of the fittest, but in the sense that class superiority or inferiority results from natural superiority or inferiority.

Here we shall not attempt to criticize these theories. None of them can be scientifically validated, since they all neglect the fundamental influence of cultural factors, especially education, in making individuals fit or unfit for specific roles. However, they have some significance from the practical point of view. For such theories give a pseudoscientific support to the belief of upper-class people in their own superiority, justifying in their own eyes their class prejudices, and influencing them in the selection and education of individuals for certain roles.

Nonetheless, in judging the fitness of individuals for various roles, more definite and specific standards have to be used, in addition to, or instead of, standards concerned with their alleged heredity. Even individuals of the same family, clan, race, caste, or class perform different roles; and each may be considered fit for some of them, but not for others. This implies that every one must be judged on his own merits, as a particular person.

6. Estimate of Personal Ability Based on Observation of Previous Performances

To decide whether a particular individual is fit for a certain role seems relatively easy, when those on whom the decision depends have known him for a long time, as is usually the case in a small tribal or rural community, where everybody knows everybody else. As an individual passes from one age level to the next—from childhood to adolescence, from adolescence to maturity—his fitness for a new role is judged by his performance of the preceding role. Sometimes he is subjected to special tests and to additional preparation, as in initiation ceremonies. Sometimes the father or mother, or both, may vouch for his fitness.

Similar standards of valuation are used in adult groups, whenever social roles are graded in importance and individuals slowly advance from lower to higher roles. They already exist in tribal secret societies, but are most fully developed and systematically used in military groups with a hierarchy of officers and in modern industrial and commercial groups with complex managerial gradations. To be admitted into such a group, an individual must be known to have passed successfully through a period of preparation. He then begins at the bottom of the hierarchy, and slowly advances. After he has performed for some time a lower role in conformity with its cultural pattern, he may become a candidate for a higher role. Since higher roles are less numerous than lower roles, for every higher role there are always several candidates in lower roles. Two principles are used, separately or together, in selecting candidates. One is the principle of seniority: The longer an individual has been performing a certain role, the more fit he is supposed to be for a higher role. The other is the principle of achievement: The more successful an individual's past performance, the more desirable he is considered as candidate for a higher role.

However, for certain adult roles no previous preparation is considered necessary, if there is a manifestation of supernormal ability. Thus, if an individual claims to have communicated with a divine being who endowed him with mystical power, his claim may be accepted by others, especially if he acts in an unusual way. Hereafter, whenever others need supernatural help, they will appeal to him. He then becomes what Max Weber has called a "charismatic leader." He usually is not, and need not be, the unique leader. If a number of divine beings are recognized, as in some Indian tribes, any young man or even a young woman may at some time come into contact with one of them, and thereby gain special mystical powers to be used only in certain situations. On the other hand, in many tribal communities, to become a charismatic leader it is necessary, though not sufficient, for an individual to be capable of communicating with some divine being. He must also be taught how to act in order to influence this being, and how to gain his help for the benefit of those who need it. Only a charismatic leader who already possesses the necessary knowledge and skill can teach him. This is how, for example, an individual becomes admitted into the role of a shaman.

Not all the individuals, however, who are chosen for superior roles because of their presumed ability are considered endowed with powers derived from the supernatural world. As we know, individuals can be exalted as military heroes, athletic victors, political leaders, inventors, or artists, without having any mystic *charisma* ascribed to them.

It is more difficult to decide whether a particular individual is personally able to perform a certain role when this individual is a stranger, previously unknown to the participants of a community into which he enters. He must first overcome the widespread mistrust of strangers. Usually when strangers are admitted, they are allowed to perform only specific, rather short-lasting social roles; and their fitness for those roles is judged by their initial conduct, which must conform with definite norms. For instance, in many tribal communities, when foreigners were admitted as traveling merchants, they were supposed to begin by offering gifts to community leaders, who in return gave them food; after eating the food and thus establishing some magical bonds with the givers, they could start trading their goods, but had to leave after the trading was finished.

In Western folk communities, peddlers were admitted for a short time whenever they showed that they had useful goods to sell. In communities which share fully developed, widely spread religions—Christian, Mohammedan, Buddhist, etc.—pilgrims going to or coming from sacred centers were, and still are, admitted as guests, after they manifested by their conduct that they were true believers, striving for holiness. A modern tourist is temporarily admitted as such, if he shows that he is willing and able to pay for shelter and food, and is actually interested in whatever aesthetic, historical, religious values within the community are supposed to appeal to tourists.

It is a different matter, however, when the conduct of a newcomer does not follow any one of the patterns which regulate the specific roles of strangers. If participants in the community are unfamiliar with the kind of role which this newcomer begins to perform, they are apt to be suspicious of him. The history of religious missions shows how suspicious participants in many tribal communities were of the foreign missionaries whom they considered to be dangerous because of unknown, perhaps evil, magico-religious powers. In recent times, many cultural anthropologists, folklorists, and sociological students of rural or industrial communities have found it difficult to gain the confidence of participants, since the social role of the investigator is unknown in most communities, and an investigator appears as a "busybody," prying into other people's affairs for some unknown, perhaps malicious, purpose of his own.

When a newcomer tries to settle in the community for a longer period of time, even when he manifests the invention of performing a role which is familiar to local people, the latter may be unwilling to accept him without knowing more about him than they can observe at first. It may take several months of observation by "natives" before a craftsman, barber, or shopkeeper will be recognized as fit for his role; perhaps a year or more, before a strange farmer who has bought or rented a farm will be accepted as a desirable neighbor; several years, before a well-to-do newcomer and his wife who settle in a small city will be fully admitted into the set of "old families."

7. ACCEPTANCE OF NEWCOMERS BASED ON THEIR RECOMMENDATION BY AUTHORITATIVE JUDGES

In consequence of increasing social mobility between communities and their progressive integration into large and complex societies, another way of deciding whether a relatively unknown individual is personally fit to perform a certain role has come into use. Information about him is obtained from some presumably competent judges who recommend him for this role.

Thus, when a stranger enters a European or American community which has an upper class, he will be admitted to polite companionate intercourse with people of this class, if he has letters of introduction from some important persons who are known to participate in upper-class sets in other communities; or if he can prove that he belongs to a family listed as belonging [to] the higher classes according to competent specialists in heraldry and genealogy.

A recommendation from political authorities is indispensable for individuals to be admitted into the diplomatic sets of modern capitals. A delegate of a foreign government—an ambassador, a minister, or a special envoy—brings with him personal credentials signed by the official head of the government which he represents; he calls by appointment upon the head of the government to which he is delegated, presents to him these credentials, and on this basis becomes formally recognized by him. Hereafter, he is accepted by other diplomats who gather in the capital, and their acceptance is manifested in relations of polite companionship during formal receptions.

Much better known and more widely spread are personal recommendations by competent judges of particular individuals as fit for professional roles. When a Church has a theocratic hierarchy and priestly schools, no individual is supposed to be admitted into any community as a priest, unless he is explicitly recognized by his superiors as well prepared for this role and is personally recommended by them. The same principle applies to other professional roles in modern communities. A physician, a pharmacist, a lawyer, a civil engineer, and a college or high-school teacher has a diploma granted by competent members of a professional school or association who vouch for his personal knowledge, intellectual ability, and moral character. Thus, even if he is a stranger, unknown to the local people who will eventually form his social circle, they rely on the judgment of professional authorities, so far as his fitness for this specific role is concerned.

Another kind of social role which nowadays requires recommendation from competent judges is the role of college or university student. Since most students are unknown to the faculty members who will compose the social circles within which the roles of particular students will be performed, the administrative staff of the college or university must decide whether each particular young man or woman who wants to be admitted is fit for this role. The decision is based on a high-school certificate which contains the symbolically expressed judgment of teachers that this particular individual possesses in some degree that amount of learning in various subjects which is considered essential for a college fresh-man, and enough intelligence to acquire more learning. The fact that an individual completed a high-school course and was granted a diploma also implies that his moral character was considered satisfactory; he would otherwise have been dismissed from the school.

Finally, in consequence of the vast diversification and multiplica-tion of social roles during the last fifty years, a new method of judging the fitness of particular individuals for specific roles has been developed by psychologists. It is the method of ascertaining by experimental tests what kinds of psychological traits individuals possess, and measuring comparatively the degree of each of these traits, under the assumption that the possessor of a trait in a relatively high degree makes individuals fit for certain roles, while the possession of some other traits makes them unfit. We know that such tests have been widely applied in accepting and rejecting future soldiers, and in assigning those who have been accepted to specialized tasks. They have been used also in the realm of industry, so as to distribute individual workers in such a way as to have them all perform roles for which they are psychologically adapted; and in the realm of education, to advise high-school and college students what kinds of social roles they are psychologically most capable of performing.

8. Compulsory Acceptance of Persons Appointed by Power-ful Leaders

In surveying the standards by which the social circles within which individuals perform various roles judge their personal fitness, we omitted a well-known way in which individuals assumed certain roles independently of the judgment of their social circles, after they have been appointed for these roles by persons endowed with superior power and authority. The people among whom such a role is performed are compelled to accept the individual who has been appointed, because the person who appointed him can use negative sanctions against them if they do not. For instance, when a military officer is appointed by a superior general to command a camp of soldiers, the soldiers are compelled to accept him, even if they do not know him personally; and they must obey his commands under threat of punishment if they do not. When the President, the Premier, the Governor appoints an individual as bureaucratic head of an administrative group, the group must accept him and cooperate with him, for members who do not can be dismissed or demoted. A foreman or superintendent appointed by the industrial manager has to be accepted by workmen, for workmen who refuse to cooperate with him may be "fired," unless they belong to a labor union which has some voice in judging the fitness of such appointees. We shall discuss later, in Chapters 12 and 13, problems connected with the gradation of authority and power.

CHAPTER 12

SOCIAL CIRCLES

1. DIFFERENTIATION OF SOCIAL CIRCLES ACCORDING TO THE VALUES IN WHICH THEY ARE ACTIVELY INTERESTED

The social circle within which an individual performs his role includes those individuals who evaluate him positively as the kind of person who acts or is expected to act in a way which is desirable from their point of view. His actions affect certain values which are more or less significant to them; and their participation in his circle implies that they are sufficiently interested in the values with which his actions deal to cooperate with him. The composition of each circle differs from that of other circles whose participants are interested in different values.

The social circle of a shopkeeper who sells food is composed mainly of housewives who buy and prepare food for domestic consumption; and its composition obviously differs from that of a shopkeeper who sells only men's clothes. The social circle of a minister of religion is composed of members of his congregation who share certain religious beliefs, are actively interested in propitiating their deity, and recognize their minister as the leader in cultus by which this propitiation will be achieved. This circle does not overlap the circles of ministers of other denominations with different beliefs and rites. However, members of several denominations may participate in the social circle of the same merchant.

The social circle of a physician includes people who are interested in bodily health—their own, their relatives', and friends'; and they expect the physician to cure their sicknesses, or at least a specific kind of sickness. Such a circle would not include Christian Scientists, who have a different, mystical conception of sickness and its cure.

The social circles of particular university professors are composed of students interested in the subjects which these professors are teaching, and differ in composition according to the subjects they are teaching, unless all the subjects are obligatory for the same students. In the latter case, it is a secondary matter of individual psychology, whether the interest of a student in any of their subjects is spontaneous or merely due to the fact that learning this subject is a required part of the curriculum which prepares him for his future career.

The social circle of a painter or a poet or a musician includes people to whom paintings, poems, or musical compositions in general are important values, and who appreciate positively the specific actions of the particular person who produces or reproduces such values. These circles may partly overlap, for many individuals are, or at least pretend to be, interested in all kinds of creative art. Nevertheless, the most active participants in these circles are usually not the same; for few individuals act simultaneously as connoisseurs and supporters of the works of painters, poet, and musicians. And none of these circles is apt to overlap that of the party boss who is positively evaluated by his followers mainly because, and in so far as, he helps them obtain governmental jobs.

The interests of certain social circles, however, are not so specialized. The adult social circle of a child is interested in everything the child is doing; for when he grows up to be an active participant in the adult community, whatever he will do may have a bearing upon some of the many diverse values which adults consider important—the material values on which physical life depends, language, religion, art, and especially people themselves as social values. Nevertheless, even here we observe some differentiation, at least by sex: the social circle of a growing boy, a future man, comes to include mostly men; that of a growing girl, a future woman, mostly women; for there are certain values—especially in preliterate communities—in which only men, others in which only women are actively interested.

No specialization of interests is supposed to differentiate the social circles of ladies from those of gentlemen in "polite society," for the rules of etiquette preclude it. Any values or set of values can become for a time, on somebody's initiative, an object of apparent interest for all participants in companionate intercourse: food, drink, clothes, homes, furniture, gardens, sport paraphernalia, playing cards, works of art, literature, music, moral ideas, religion, politics (provided no conflicting issues are involved), children, men or women who are sufficiently interesting for nonmalicious gossip. But no interest in a specific value is supposed to be taken too seriously or shared for too long a period of time, lest the companionate set be permanently divided into circles centered around specialists or into organized groups with different, unconnected functions.

2. The Size of Social Circles Within Communities

In the second part of this work, we devoted our attention to individual participation in a local community that was small enough for every individual at some time or other to come into face-to-face contact with every other individual, to identify him personally, and to interact with him. In such a community, whatever the role any individual performs, the size of his social circle obviously cannot exceed the total number of its participants. But most of the roles which individuals in the community perform include only portions of its total population. Merely meeting and interacting does not imply a social role. No social role exists unless there is active cooperation between people with positive mutual valuation and mutual duties.

The smallest possible social circle includes two individuals and a third person who is the common object of their standardized valuations and normatively regulated actions. This is exemplified by the parents of an only child who are not socially connected with any relatives or community members actively interested in the child. Except among new settlers in an uninhabited land or migrant workers, such cases are rare. Usually, as we saw in surveying comparatively the social roles of children, the child's family circle includes relatives on one or both sides; and some parental duties are delegated to nurses, physicians, ministers or priests, and school teachers.

Other instances of social roles with very small circles are found when three or four individuals regularly carry on companionate intercourse to the exclusion of everybody else. Each of them is positively valued by the others, has certain duties toward them, and can expect them to perform certain actions on his behalf. Although in such a circle, one role is much like another, the role of one member may become more influential, the "leading" role. But these small, exclusive companionate circles are rare, for they imply that for some reason the individuals who compose them are isolated from the companionate life of their community. Most individuals who participate in companionate intercourse belong to much wider social circles.

Relatively large, though varying in size, are the social circles of individuals whose actions are intended to satisfy specific needs of community members. Thus, a physician has his circle of patients, a craftsman or merchant his circle of customers who buy the material values which he produces or imports, and a teacher her circle of pupils. Several individuals in the community may perform similar roles, and the circle of one of them may be larger or smaller than those of others. In any case, in a limited local community such a circle is always small enough for the individual to identify person- ally everybody who composes it and for the participants to subject his interaction to social control.

The largest social circle within the range of a community may include all or nearly all of its inhabitants. Such is the circle of an authoritarian head who is accepted as such and whose task is to regulate the conduct of community members in matters pertaining to important values of the community as a whole. This is exem- plified by the role of the chief of a tribal community, the lord of a manorial estate, a priest acting as theocratic head of a parochial community of the faithful, the mayor of a town, and the manager of a mine or factory which owns the whole territory in which its workers live.

If the community is rather numerous and widely spread, such an authoritarian head cannot maintain regular personal contact with all the people who participate in it. In order to perform his role adequately, he must have assistants with auxiliary roles, who usually act as intermediaries between him and the other individuals composing his total circle. These assistants constitute what we shall call his *inner circle*.

The lord of a manorial estate has an inner circle of servants and foremen, perhaps also his wife and her maids, who get into contact with the women and children of serfs and tenants. The parish priest usually has an inner circle consisting of a curate, a sexton, an organist, sometimes also chairmen of specific religious associations. The mayor of a town has a circle of aldermen and administrative officials. And an industrial manager has a circle of superintendents.

3. Expansion of Social Circles Beyond the Range of the Community

The existence of inner circles makes it possible for individuals to perform social roles in circles much wider than the population of any community. The expansion of such roles is one of the most important trends in social evolution, and will be discussed in a later part of this work. Here we shall merely give some examples showing how the social circle of an individual can expand.

This expansion is often attained when an individual, on his own initiative, attempts to perform a relatively new social role, begins by gaining a small circle of collaborators, and with their aid more or less rapidly and widely increases his circle.

Take, first, the social circle of a modern poet or novelist. Innumerable individuals, especially young men and women, write poems or novels, but usually nobody except their friends and acquaintances reads or appreciates their works. Only after a writer gains the sponsorship of publishers who print his works, of booksellers and librarians who make them accessible to the public, of advertisers and critics who induce the public to read and appreciate them, does he have a large circle of readers who evaluate positively his works and himself as the author. He cannot identify most members of his circle, for they are anonymous to him; and yet he has some influence on their attitudes, and they have considerable influence on his life. Moreover, usually several of them communicate with him by writing letters; and some of them come into face-to-face contact with him in daily life or when he is invited to speak at a meeting.

However, the size and composition of such social circles does not remain changeless. Many authors enjoy popularity for a while, but their circles of readers dwindle, while the circles of others may steadily increase and even expand beyond the range of the country where their language is used, if their works are translated into other languages.

In consequence of the development of "mass media of communication"—movies, radios, television, and newspapers—some social roles are evolving with ever wider social circles: for instance, the role of a syndicated newspaper columnist, whose columns are read by hundreds of thousands; that of a "movie star," whose social circle is composed of millions of movie fans; that of a radio or television speaker who entertains listeners throughout the whole country and even abroad. The social role of the columnist is possible only because of an inner circle of newspaper editors who publish his columns; the role of the movie star requires an inner circle of producers and technicians to film the play and also an intermediary circle of local theater owners to bring it before the public; the role of a radio speaker requires a circle of sponsors—commercial or governmental—as well as a circle of producers and sellers of radios.

Another significant example is the social circle of a religious prophet. Many prophets have gained small circles of followers, but their circles soon ceased to grow and eventually disappeared; whereas the circles of others increased rapidly and widely, for instance, those of Confucius, Buddha, Mohammed, Luther, and Calvin, partly because of the sponsorship given by rulers, and partly because of the collaboration of social leaders and organizers.

Well known are the rapidly expanding social circles of certain economic leaders. Innumerable small businessmen have attempted to expand their social circles; some succeeded on a small scale, but others failed completely and their circles disappeared. Survey, by way of contrast, such instances as John D. Rockefeller, Andrew Carnegie, and Henry Ford. Each of these gradually gained an inner circle of economic collaborators, technologists, and local managers who helped him organize a large circle of employees and reach a wide circle of customers scattered over vast territories.

Probably best known, because found already in early historical periods, is the expansion of the social circles of political leaders. We may mention a few recent examples. Hitler's case is perhaps the most instructive.

After World War I, many individuals in Germany tried to become political leaders. The social circles of some of them increased for a time, but then ceased to grow. However, one of them, a housepainter of partly foreign origin, who first started with a social circle of less than ten men, became the head of the Nazi party, and eventually supreme ruler of Germany. Moreover, his social circle was supposed to extend far beyond the borders of the German state and to include a vast number of people of German descent scattered throughout the world. He was considered by his followers the "Führer" of the German people toward world domination and the defender and promoter of German culture as the highest human culture.

Obviously, he could never have achieved this important role, with a social circle of such tremendous size, if he had not gradually gained by oral and written persuasion the collaboration of various kinds of influential inner circles: ideologists who promulgated and spread the racial and cultural doctrines which he formulated in *Mein Kampf*; followers who proclaimed him a great national hero; politicians, dominant bureaucrats, military commanders, capitalists, educators, prominent scientists, and technologists who cooperated in the realization of his ideal of German supremacy.

Somewhat different was the expansion of the social circles of communist leaders.

The social circle of Lenin remained relatively small, and grew only slowly, while he lived and acted outside of Russia; but after his return to Russia in 1918, it expanded with increasing rapidity until his death. On the other hand, the circle of his associate and collaborator, Trotsky, after expanding, suddenly and rapidly diminished. In the whole history of social roles, no social circle, not even Hitler's, ever expanded so rapidly or so widely as Stalin's, from the death of Lenin up to his own death. He had an inner circle of his own, even when Lenin was still active. Later, he became the supreme political ruler of the Soviet Union, and his widest circle included all the people within this vast territory who accepted him as their ruler and exalted him as their supreme hero. It included also the communist governments and their subjects in satellite states and all faithful members of the Communist Parties in other countries. His inner circle was composed of a few top members of the Communist Party, the highest bureaucrats, military commanders, some prominent intellectual leaders, propagandists, and those heads of communist groups outside of the Union who were personally known to him, with whom he occasionally interacted and who obeyed him. Each of the participants in his inner circle had, of course, a wide social circle or circles of his own, and an inner circle of collaborators and assistants.

Such a vast expansion of the social roles of individual leaders in various realms of culture raises difficult problems. It is manifestly impossible to explain it by the old theory that the prominent leaders who gain many followers are "great men" or "geniuses," innately superior to the rest of mankind. We must study the composition and cultural background of the growing social circle of each leader, so as to ascertain the values which its participants share and to know how his actions and those of his collaborators affect these values.

4. THE DURATION OF SOCIAL CIRCLES AND THEIR ORGANIZATION

A social role, like a social relation, lasts only so long as the individuals who participate in it actively cooperate. But it differs from a social relation in one important respect. The social relation includes only two partners; when either of them ceases to cooperate with the other, the relation dissolves. Whereas the social circle of an individual who is performing a social role is composed of a number of participants; even though some of them cease to cooperate with him, if others continue to do so, his role will last as long as he performs it. Only when he ceases to act as the central person of a circle, does his role no longer exist.

On the other hand, this does not mean that a social circle depends for its existence on a particular individual and lasts only so long as he performs his role. It does so in some of those cases which we surveyed above, where an individual initiated a certain role and gathered a social circle which followed him. The social circle of an individual poet, novelist, prophet, economic innovator, or political leader which was gradually formed after he started his role often becomes dissolved when he dies or for some reason ceases to act. Frequently, however, a social circle is already formed before a particular individual enters it and assumes the kind of role he is expected to perform; and it may continue to exist long after he has ceased to perform his role within this circle.

Thus, in surveying the role of a child in the family, we found that usually the adult family members have already formed a social circle and are waiting for the child to be born; after its birth, they start to cooperate for its benefit months or even years before it begins to fulfil its duties. Likewise, when the inhabitants of a rural community find that their agricultural production lags behind that of other communities, some of them may join together to induce a competent agriculturalist to enter the community as a technical adviser and leader to cooperate with them in raising their production. Similarly, the circle of instructors in a college within which any particular student performs his role is formed before he enters the college, and continues to exist after he has completed his role and left college. It is true that, with the rapid increase of student enrollment in American colleges after 1945, there was a sudden demand for more instructors to come in and perform specific roles within the circles of students already formed there.

This implies that the people who form in advance a circle of which a particular individual will become the center consider the role which this individual is expected to perform—that of a child, a technical leader, a student, or an instructor—as socially desirable for their community or some other collectivity.

Even more instructive for a comparative study of social roles are the numerous and diverse cases in which the people who compose the social circle of a particular individual cooperate in having another person perform the same kind of role, after he has for some reason ceased to perform his role. For instance, when the only physician in a community dies, the ready circle of potential patients tries to persuade another physician to settle in the community. When a priest or minister of religion leaves the community, his congregation cooperates with another priest or minister appointed by a higher authority or attempts to import one themselves.

Likewise, when the chief of a tribal community ceases to function, his inner circle accepts or selects another chief. The circle of faithful followers of an influential prophet seldom dissolves after his death, but strives to remain united, not by seeking for another prophet, but by accepting some authoritarian leader designated by the prophet as his successor, or selecting from among themselves a leader presumably endowed with superior charisma or organizing ability, and continuing to select such an authoritarian leader for generations.

These instances show that the role which a particular individual performs is often considered so valuable and important for the collectivity to which the participants in his social circle belong that they will always seek for somebody to perform it.

We call such a social role an *institutional role*, in the sense that it is supported and maintained by an organized, long-lasting collectivity—be it a small social group or a large and complex society. Let us survey briefly a few examples of institutional roles, each of which has a social circle coextensive with the entire membership of a long-lasting social group or a society at large.

The role of member of the French Academy of Letters—a very old group—illustrates this on a small scale. This group has forty members—no more, no less. When a member dies, another person must be elected to fill the vacancy. The remaining thirty-nine members who compose the social circle, after careful appraisal of many candidates, select by a majority vote one candidate who is admitted as the fortieth member.

In a modern, rather long-lasting university, when a dean or president dies, retires, or leaves, a social circle functioning on behalf of the university as a whole—a committee of faculty members, the board of trustees, or both together, sometimes with the assistance of other committees—elects another dean or president, who will perform the same kind of role as his predecessor.

When the industrial manager of a factory dies, leaves, or fails to perform his task, the circle of factory owners or, as in the Soviet Union, the bureaucratic circle of supermanagers selects another manager.

A well-known and instructive institutional role, with a social circle of millions of people, is that of the President of the United States. It is considered so important—indeed, indispensable—for the American political society that for more than a century and a half there has always been somebody to perform it, and this is expected to continue in the future. In contrast with many other institutional roles, its performance by a particular individual is for a fixed time—four or, at most, eight years. To be admitted to this role, an individual must first become a candidate, usually nominated by the members of a political party, and then be chosen by a larger number of voters than any other candidate. He is elected before the term of his predecessor expires, so as to take over this role immediately on his predecessor's retirement. Later, before his own first term expires, he may again become a candidate and, if elected, continue to perform this role for another four years. To insure that the performance of the presidential role be uninterrupted, another individual is elected to perform a different kind of institutional role—that of vice president—which exists partly for the purpose of assisting the president, but mainly for the purpose of substituting for him, if he dies, is absent, or incapacitated before his term expires.

Now, while the social circle of a candidate for the presidency is composed only of those who nominate him and eventually vote for him, the social circle of a president is wider and lasts as long as he remains in office. All citizens of the United States are obliged to accept him as the one and only person to fill the role of chief executive. They must recognize his constitutional authority and conform with the norms which he lawfully promulgates, even though many of them may disapprove of him as the representative and leading member of a political party which they oppose or disagree with. But those who judge him unfit for his main public role cannot reject him; the only way of getting rid of him is to impeach him or elect another president to take his place after his term expires.

Many other social roles connected with that of the president are also institutional. Thus, he has an inner circle of cabinet members, whose function is considered so important for American society that, although a new president can and usually does substitute another person for the one who previously performed this kind of role, there must always be somebody functioning in each office. This applies also to many subordinate roles within each department of government. Thus, when administrative subgroups of a Federal department are located in different states, every such subgroup must always have an individual whose role is that of administrative head.

Furthermore, the President often has to cooperate with persons performing legislative or judiciary social roles within certain groups—the Senate, the House of Representatives, the Supreme Court—and their roles are also institutional. Different individuals perform them during certain periods, longer or shorter, but when a particular individual ceases to perform one of those roles, somebody else must enter the group and start to perform the same kind of role.

Another well-known institutional role is that of the Pope of the Roman Catholic Church. His total social circle is one of the oldest and largest in the world, independent of all territorial limits; it is supposed to include nearly 350 million members of the Church. And there must always be a Pope, since the role which he performs is considered indispensable for the Church. Unlike the President's, his role has no definite time limit, but lasts as long as he lives. After his death, his successor is elected, not by the popular vote of Church members, but by a small group of Cardinals. Since their task is an essential one, this group must be permanent; when one Cardinal dies, the Pope appoints another one.

The inner circle of the Pope includes, in addition to the assistants living in or near the Vatican, all the highest Church officials: heads of monastical orders, which extend all over the world, archbishops, bishops, nuncios, rectors of universities, etc., whose circles are territorially limited. The role of every one of these officials, as heads of long-lasting social groups, is institutional. And each of them has an inner circle of subordinates functioning within smaller social groups, and most of these subordinate roles are also institutional.

The connection between an individual who performs an institutional role and his long-lasting, united social circle is somewhat different when the role is hereditary; for in that case, the choice of his successor does not depend on his circle. Thus, after the death of a king, his legitimate heir becomes the new king. Even then, however, the heir has to be identified in advance as future king by his prospective subjects, or at least by an inner governmental circle, presumably representing the total membership of the kingdom. And his actual succession to the throne must be explicitly recognized, first in a public announcement (as in the famous French statement: "Le Roi est mort, vive le Roi"), later in a public ceremony, such as a formal coronation.

There seems to be a fundamental difference between an institutional role which an individual performs only after he has been selected and accepted by the same social circle within which his predecessor performed a similar role, and the kind of role which an individual starts on his own initiative, gaining gradually a social circle which did not exist before. Institutional roles are presumed to be stable and follow uniform cultural patterns. They are considered components of the permanent "structure" of a social group or of a united society. An individual who performs such a role is supposed to conform with the same standards and norms as his predecessor did; and this apparently precludes all original innovations. Thus, only roles which are not institutional allow innovations. This difference seemingly explains and justifies the old antithesis between "social statics" and "social dynamics."

However, we shall see later, when we investigate comparatively the evolution of social systems, that many institutional roles in the course of time permit, even require, innovations; whereas many new roles which are not institutional hinder future innovations. This is well exemplified by the roles of Hitler and Stalin. Hitler was supposed to promote the growth of German culture, Stalin the growth of all cultures within the Soviet Union; whereas, as a matter of fact, both of them, on gaining power, impeded the creative development of those cultures by repressing original innovations in literature, art, philosophy, and the social sciences.

CHAPTER 13

PERSONAL RIGHTS

1. THE SOCIOLOGICAL CONCEPTION OF RIGHTS

In defining the social role we stated that, in order to fulfil adequately his duties, a person must have certain rights granted to him by his circle. Therefore, we shall survey comparatively the various rights of individuals performing social roles before we survey their duties, because frequently the rights which are granted to an individual precede his duties (e.g. those of an infant or a guest in the home) and sometimes are preserved even after he has ceased to perform his duties (e.g., a retired university professor or a pensioned invalid).

We find considerable confusion concerning the meaning of the term "rights." This confusion, however, is not due to sociologists or psychologists, but to theorists of law and philosophers. Many of them treat "right" and "law" as inseparable, and limit "right" to what is enforceable by law. Indeed, in some languages the same term is used to denote both right and law (e.g., *Recht* in German and *prawo* in Polish).

However, the term "law" itself symbolizes several different concepts. Most jurists limit it to rules explicitly promulgated and actively supported by the government of a state. But even the basic Roman *jus gentium* was not reducible to this concept. Metaphysical philosophers and theologians added two more concepts: natural law and divine law. Furthermore, many historians and ethnologists have extended the use of this term to traditional rules included in customs and mores—e.g., "tribal law" and the so-called "customary law" of local and regional folk communities. Recently, sociologists of the French School have applied it to rules maintained by any organized social group which regulates the conduct of its members.

While, from the scientific point of view, we are not concerned with metaphysical or theological conceptions of law, we cannot ignore the fundamental similarity discovered by historians, ethnologists, and sociologists between the standards and norms promulgated and enforced by state governments and those accepted and supported by other kinds of collectivities. The conclusions from their investigations force us to give a much wider meaning to the term "right" than jurists do.

Here again we omit the conceptions of ethical thinkers concerning universal, "inalienable" human rights, for these are ideals, not scientific generalizations. What we do find is that normatively regulated social relations which include so-called rights are not limited to those relations which the government of a state controls. Essentially similar norms are accepted and applied by human collectivities which do not belong to any politically organized state, as well as by various groups of people whose social relations are not controlled by any political government, though they live within the territory of a state.

Therefore, the concept of *right*, to be useful to sociologists, must be redefined in such a way as to include within it not only the phenomena which jurists call rights, but all other phenomena which are like legal rights in every respect except that they are not subjected to governmental control.

Rights in this wider sense may be granted not only to individuals, but to social groups (e.g., to corporations by a state or to specialized associations of church members by their church). These may be called *collective rights*. Here we are concerned only with rights granted to individuals as persons, which we shall call *personal rights*. We need such a concept for heuristic purposes, in order to discover basic similarities and differences among the vast multiplicity of norms which regulate the actions of participants in social circles toward the persons who perform specific social roles.

A personal right may be defined as whatever, in accordance with the norms accepted by a person's social circle, the participants in this circle are *obliged to do for him*. When we say obliged, we mean not only that it is a participant's duty to do what the norm requires and refrain from doing anything that would conflict with it, but that the fulfilment of this duty is subjected to definite sanctions of the circle. These sanctions can be effective not only when the circle constitutes an organized group, but also when it is an unorganized aggregation of individuals, provided they are positively interested in the same person, recognize each other's obligations toward him, and act accordingly.

The existence of a personal right may be demonstrated in two ways. First, if a person's partner in a social relation fails to perform some duty toward him, other participants in this person's circle will assume the duty. For instance, when a child's mother or father dies, is sick, or deserts him, some other woman or man or several of them will take over the duty of looking after the child. Second, if a participant in a person's social circle does something to this person which conflicts with his duty, other participants will try to counteract this action.

As we shall see in comparing the rights of persons in specific roles, there is considerable difference in the importance of their rights. This is frequently correlated with the relative importance ascribed to the duties which they perform. When their duties are considered more important than the duties of those who collaborate with them, their corresponding rights are given priority over the rights of those others—e.g., the rights of industrial managers as compared with those of workers, or the rights of generals as compared with those of corporals. Such rights may be called *prerogatives*.

Sometimes, on the other hand, a person may have considerable rights with only minor duties—for instance, the absentee owners of large estates, the holders of stocks and bonds who do little but collect their dividends, and members of the leisure class who perform few, if any, productive activities on behalf of those who support them. We may call such rights *privileges*.

2. ARE THERE ANY UNIVERSAL RIGHTS?

It is difficult to generalize about the many diverse rights which individuals have in their various roles. But we may ask: Is there any universal category of essential rights which all persons have, whatever the roles they perform?

In answering this question, we must take into consideration, first of all, that rights are conditioned by the way in which the persons to whom they are granted are defined and evaluated by their social circles. We have seen that, in order to perform a certain role, an individual must be accepted by participants in a social circle as a valuable person. Hereafter, and so long as his role lasts, he is granted the right to have *his personal worth recognized*. This right may grow, if he consistently and effectively enacts his duties, but decrease or even disappear, if he behaves in a way which conflicts with the norms with which he is in duty bound to conform.

Recognition of his worth is implicitly manifested by the willingness of his circle to cooperate with him; and usually, as we shall see, it is also explicitly manifested by the symbolic expression of positive attitudes toward him. If somebody expresses a negative valuation of his person, the participants in his circle are supposed to object to such expressions. For instance, participants in a circle of polite companionship should defend each other against malicious gossip; admirers of a poet or an artist resent adverse criticism of him; followers of a prophet oppose any depreciation of his sacredness.

Every individual has such a right in every role, from a child in a small family circle to a famous hero in a circle of millions. But the kind and degree of recognition that is granted differ widely, depending on the roles which individuals perform and on the composition of their social circles.

In surveying the standards by which individual fitness for certain roles is judged (Chapter 11), we found that some individuals are considered highly valuable persons, fit for socially superior roles, while others are judged to be much less valuable, fit only for socially inferior roles. And the person's social circle may be composed of people who consider him their superior, or of people who consider him their inferior, or of people who consider him their equal.

In speaking of people who are "superior," "inferior," or "equal," we do not imply that there are any objective standards of valuation by which human individuals in general can be graded. Characterologists of various schools have found more than a hundred typical characteristics, each of which individuals possess in various degrees and all of which partly overlap. But in any case, sociologists should not use any evaluative judgments of their own. What they, as objective observers, actually find and investigate are *beliefs* that the individuals who perform certain roles are superior or inferior or equal to others. These beliefs are significant, for the rights granted to individuals by their circles are graded according to these beliefs. Superiority, inferiority, and equality are differences in social relations between individuals, not differences between the human beings as wholes.

3. RIGHTS TO PERSONAL PRESTIGE

Let us first examine the recognition of an individual's personal worth by a social circle whose participants consider him their superior. We call such recognized superiority "personal prestige." We find different sources and considerable gradation of prestige.

Seniority is one of the earliest and most persistent standards of personal superiority. It originated, as we know, in the role of the father who dominates his descendants; but it has often been extended far beyond the family circle. For instance, in some clans or tribes, particularly in Australia, a man of the older generation was considered superior to all men of the younger generation. This prestige of an old person is mostly rooted in the belief that the old are the bearers of the wisdom which is essential for all social domination and leadership and which it takes many years to acquire. This belief persisted for thousands of years in China and partly in Rome. It still persists in many Western collectivities, although usually after a certain age the old are no longer considered fit to perform the roles which they performed before. While the oldest persons usually have the greatest prestige, the youngest have no prestige at all; individuals of intermediary age are granted some prestige in smaller circles which include younger men who consider them superior to themselves. For instance, in a university "freshmen" have no prestige, but senior students have a little in undergraduate circles; instructors and lower-grade professors have prestige with the student body, but the highest prestige goes to members of the Senate.

Personal sacredness is another early and persistent source of prestige, sometimes connected with seniority. Such is the prestige of a shaman, a priest, a saint, a yogi in a secular circle of people who recognize him as endowed with a sacredness which they do not possess. Whether he is supposed to have acquired his sacredness directly by mystical contact with supernatural powers or had it transmitted to him by some other sacred person may be a secondary matter, so far as his secular circle is concerned. Where a hierarchy of the roles of sacred persons exists, like the priestly hierarchy of the Roman Catholic Church, this implies a gradation of prestige from the Pope through cardinals, archbishops, bishops, down to ordinary clergymen. Laymen lack the prestige of sacredness, and no layman can become a priest unless and until he has been consecrated by a priest. Similarly, no priest can reach a higher level until he has passed through a lower level and been raised by his superiors.

The belief in hereditary superiority which we discussed above (Chapter 11) is a familiar basis of personal prestige. It may be connected with personal sacredness. Thus, in India castes are hereditarily stratified. Every individual belonging to a certain caste, though considered inferior to individuals of a higher caste, has the right to be recognized as superior by individuals of the lower castes. His right has a religious foundation, for his inferiors cannot reject it without incurring mystical as well as worldly penalties. In short, there is a gradation of prestige from the Brahmans, with the highest prestige, down to the individuals who are just above the people of the lowest caste.

Hereditary secular class superiority in European kingdoms also involves a gradation of prestige. A member of the royal family has a higher prestige than a titled aristocrat with no royal ancestry. A titled aristocrat is considered superior to the so-called "small nobility" (*petite noblesse*) without titles. But an untitled nobleman is recognized as superior by a circle of "commoners" in a small-town or rural community.

A different kind of class stratification evolved, as we know, in large cities, especially in Western Europe from the Middle Ages on, and spread in modern times to other countries. In comparing it with the older hereditary classification, we find that both of them recognize the possession of wealth as a source of prestige. However, the term "wealth" is used with two different meanings. Frequently it denotes the ownership of what may be called "means of consumption," i.e., values which individuals and their families use to satisfy their wants—homes, furniture, clothes, food, vehicles for transportation—and values which enable them to obtain personal services from outsiders, educate their children, enjoy pleasant recreation, etc. It is also used to denote ownership of the means for production and distribution of products, which gives the owners power to control the actions of many producers and distributors.

It is the first kind of wealth which constitutes the general basis of class stratification in modern times, as those sociologists have discovered who try to measure what they call the "socioeconomic status" of families. For it enables the owner and his family to live on a high cultural level, to maintain companionate intercourse with other high-class people, near and distant, and to use their leisure time in performing various influential social roles.

Many European noblemen have inherited enough wealth to maintain this kind of life without performing any economically productive activity. In the United States, wealthy families living in the exclusive sections of large cities—e.g., Boston, New York, Chicago, and San Francisco—and in fashionable summer resorts maintain a high level of life, and have frequent companionate interaction with other such families, although the wealth they are using is mostly derived from the economic performances of others as industrial, commercial, or financial leaders. They have considerable prestige, as is indicated by their inclusion in the "social registers." This means that the right to prestige of each of them is supported by the others, just as in Europe the right to prestige of every noble family was supported, and sometimes still is, by other noble families. They do not need their superiority to be recognized by their inferiors. As a matter of fact, it is easy for them to prove their claim to superiority: They simply exclude from active participation in their social life all people of the lower classes except when their services are required.

If we survey small cities and towns, both in Europe and in America, we find everywhere some families which consider themselves superior to other local families in wealth and way of life, with mutually recognized prestige, although on a lower level and with narrower circles than the upper-class families mentioned above. And when we investigate families in both large and small cities, we usually discover that the class stratification which begins at the top with the wealthy families ends at the bottom with families barely able or even entirely unable to subsist without help. The wealthy families, therefore, sometimes at the instigation of religious leaders, are often induced to use some of their wealth for charity, so as to justify their claim to social superiority.

The prestige of the owners of means for the production and distribution of products is not based merely on the amount of wealth which they own, but also on the way in which they use this wealth when they function as entrepreneurs in industry, trade, or finance. We shall merely mention here the two main conditions on which this prestige depends. The first condition is the owner's *efficiency* as leader and organizer; his prestige increases if his enterprise successfully expands, and decreases if he fails or eventually loses his wealth. But his prestige depends also on the valuation of his role by other entrepreneurs, his employees, and his customers. If his function supplements those of other entrepreneurs, is supposed to benefit his employees and the public, he gains considerable prestige. But if he ruthlessly eliminates other entrepreneurs as competitors, so as to monopolize specific products and make customers pay high prices, or reduces the remuneration of his employees to a minimum in order to maintain or increase high profits, he loses prestige. This is why many nineteenth-century capitalists were called "pirates of industry" or "robber barons." Gradually, some of them under the impact of public opinion changed their technique, began to strive for popular approval, and even offered much of their wealth to foundations for promoting human welfare.

The gradation of prestige within organized military and governmental groups is also well known. Persons with higher prestige are supposed to have superior practical knowledge, ability, and efficiency than persons with lower prestige. Thus, in the army ordinary soldiers have no prestige; noncommissioned officers, low prestige; commissioned officers, higher prestige; and the prestige of officers rises up to that of the supreme military commander. The basis of the belief in the personal superiority of noncommissioned officers over soldiers is their longer practical training and experience. Commissioned officers are presumed to be personally superior to noncommissioned officers because they were educated for several years in military schools which prepared them for the adequate performance of their roles. The gradation of commissioned officers is, at least partly, based on the principle of seniority, under the assumption that the longer an officer performs a certain role, the better he is prepared for a superior role. Of course, there are also other standards which we will discuss presently, when we survey the recognition of merit.

Gradation of prestige in modern bureaucracies is also largely based on education and seniority, although the highest officials are usually selected and appointed by the supreme administrators because they have performed effectively some other important social roles which made them presumably fit for superior bureaucratic roles.

In our survey of social circles, we discussed the expansion of the social circles of individuals who initiated more or less new social roles and gained an increasing number of followers. The recognition of their personal superiority is obviously based on their creative achievement. The degree of this prestige can be estimated by the size of their social circles, as compared with the circles of others who have achieved something new in the same realm of culture—other poets, artists, prophets, economic leaders, statesmen, scientists, or inventors. Their prestige becomes relatively higher when their circles increase, and lower when their circles decrease in size.

This gradation of prestige in widely different roles requires some common term denoting the relative importance ascribed to persons performing certain roles in comparison with others. We cannot use the term "social class," for an individual who is neither a nobleman nor a wealthy man, but performs the role of poet, artist, priest, prophet, inventor, scientist, or university professor may have a much higher prestige in the circle of his followers than any aristocrat or capitalist in the same circle. Attempts to include in theories of social classes all the diverse gradations of recognized superiority have failed. Nor can we use the term "status," since the same individual may have different degrees of prestige in different circles, and his prestige in any one of them may increase or decrease. We shall use instead the term "rank." There is a scale of ranks in every social group with institutional roles—religious, military, administrative, industrial, commercial, or educational. Every person considered as belonging to a social caste has a certain rank above or below the ranks of those who belong to other castes and even to some who belong to the same caste. The rank of an innovator depends on the relative importance ascribed to his innovation. And so on.

4. Symbolic Manifestations of Prestige

How is the recognition of an individual's superiority explicitly manifested by a circle of inferiors?

We find, first of all, an old and very general way of manifesting this recognition by the use of terms locating each individual in relation to others. Most of the terms indicating gradation of prestige, including the terms "superior" and "inferior," "high" and "low," are derived from positions in space. Take, e.g., such expressions as "high clergy" and "low clergy," "high office" and "low office," "high status" and "low status." Social classes have been divided by Warner and Lunt into "upper-upper," "lower-upper," "upper-middle," "lower-middle," "upper-lower," and "lower-lower." Social stratification implies the division of people into strata, one above the other. And the term "vertical mobility" denotes passage of individuals from inferior to superior classes and vice versa.

This social meaning given to spatial terms is not altogether metaphysical; for when social superiors and social inferiors congregate, the former frequently occupy spatial positions above the latter. Already Herbert Spencer, in his study of "Ceremonial Institutions," pointed out how general this custom is. He ascribed its origin partly to the relationship between the victors and the vanquished in physical struggles. When the vanquished gave up the struggle and submitted, they were often compelled to lie down, kneel, or crawl, which made them helpless and put them at the mercy of the victors. But there were other sources of such manifestations of submission to superiors. In many religions, the greatest gods are located in heaven or live, like the Olympian gods, on the tops of mountains. In general, high places are apt to be more sacred than low places, and only persons endowed with sacredness can approach such places or stay there.

Whatever their origin, spatial manifestations of prestige are found almost everywhere. Typical examples of inferiors lowering their bodies in the presence of or in contact with superiors are found in many religious groups. When a priest, a holy representative of the deity, stands and gives divine blessing to laymen, the latter prostrate themselves, kneel down, or at least bend their heads. Common subjects of the Emperor of Japan not so long ago prostrated themselves or knelt and lowered their heads when they saw him. Subjects of European kings and emperors also often knelt when they came to beg for mercy or for special benefits. The customary courtesy to a king or queen is a survival of this age-old custom.

A well-known example of the higher position reserved for a social superior is the royal throne; below this are chairs or standing-room for the immediate subordinates of the king, while other subjects keep at a distance. In churches with a priestly hierarchy, priests during religious ceremonies occupy places graded in space according to their rank, and in nearly all denominations priests or ministers stand or sit somewhat above the level of laymen. At public meetings a platform is often reserved not only for speakers, so that the audience can see and hear them, but also for individuals who are socially superior to the other participants.

Such vertical gradation of space is often supplemented or supplanted by a different kind of symbolism: spatial separation of social superiors from social inferiors. This probably goes back to the belief that an individual's sacredness could be profaned if people devoid of sacredness touched him or even approached him. It was clearly manifested in relations between the highest and the lowest castes in India and in the spatial isolation of sacred kings, e.g., the Emperor of China or of Japan. But it was applied also to some secular social relations, e.g., racial relations. The segregation of "whites" from "colored" people is probably a survival of this old attitude.

When people of unequal degrees of prestige congregate, spatial proximity and distance are used as symbols of prestige. At a ceremonial meeting, the degree of prestige of participants is symbolized by their spatial nearness to the person with the highest prestige. At a private dinner, the host has his exclusive seat, and the nearness of the seats of the guests to his seat is a measure of their prestige. The gradation is more complicated when men and women are entertained together, for then the hostess also has an exclusive seat opposite to that of the host, and the nearness of men to her seat and of women to his seat are measures of prestige of the men and women, respectively. This spatial symbolism is most complicated at ceremonial dinners in capitals. Knowledge of several gradations of rank connected with the various official roles (executive, legislative, juridical, military, diplomatic, and ecclesiastical), as well as of class gradation and of prestige based on supernormal cultural achievements, is needed to plan the seating in such a way that persons of higher rank will sit somewhat nearer to the person whose rank is highest of all than persons of lower rank.

Of course, spatial manifestations of prestige are not the only ones. Many verbal expressions of this recognition are used: honorific nouns and adjectives, oral or written statements exalting innate personal greatness or superior achievements, good wishes for the superior's future—e.g., "God guard the Tsar," "Long live the King," "Heil Hitler." Sometimes works of art also manifest this recognition, such as idealized portraits of kings or dictators, often exhibited and reproduced, as typically the many thousands of portraits of Stalin distributed all over the Soviet Union and satellite countries.

In view of the belief that the socially superior person has the right to be recognized as such, those who share this belief defend him against any derogation of his person. Thus, when kings were recognized by their subjects as supremely valuable, any explicit negative valuation of a king's person was considered a criminal offense against his majesty (*lèse-majesté*), and the offender was liable to punishment. We know how dangerous it was in Germany under the Nazi regime to express any negative judgment about Hitler, Goering, or Himmler; or in Russia under the Tsarist regime to blame the Tsar; or under the Communist regime to criticize Lenin, Stalin, or any other influential member of the Communist Party, as long as the party recognized his superiority. Frequently such an offense was, and still is, considered proof that the offender is a traitor. In an organized religious, military, or industrial group, open negative valuation of a person of high rank by somebody of low rank is often treated as an act of rebellion.

5. The Right of Inferiors to Have Their Merit Recognized by Superiors

Recognition of personal worth by social superiors is also found wherever a gradation of rank exists. It presupposes that the inferior individual has been regularly and effectively performing the duties which his superiors require him to perform or has even done something supererogatory, exceeding their requirements. The idea that he has the right to recognition is expressed in such statements as that "he deserves it" or "he merits it."

Praise is a familiar, though short-lasting, symbolic manifestation of such recognition. Children are praised by adult participants in their family circles, pupils by their teachers, servants by their masters, brave soldiers by their commanders, loyal followers by their leaders, efficient subordinates in industry or trade by their superordinates. Praise may be privately communicated by a superior in contact with his inferior, but it is much more significant when expressed in the presence of others.

More important and influential are the long-lasting manifestations of recognition of merit, e.g., degrees granted to students upon fulfilment of their duties. These degrees are supplemented in colleges and universities by "honors" granted to students for supererogatory work above their required duties.

Well known are the decorations given to military officers and soldiers in Europe and America and to civil servants in most European countries. Such decorations are symbolically graded according to the importance of the meritorious deeds, the efforts, sacrifice, or danger which their performance requires, especially in warfare. But in many countries they are also graded according to the rank of the persons who receive them. For instance, before World War I in the German army there were numerous varieties of decorations or "orders," graded in importance; each variety had several degrees, and the more important varieties or the higher degrees of the same variety were reserved for officers of the higher ranks. The French *légion d'honneur*, which is granted to both warriors and civilians, has five grades, and only persons of higher rank can receive the higher grades. The gradation of civilian decorations according to rank was until recently most obvious in diplomatic sets: Only ambassadors could receive first-grade decorations; ministers, second grade; attachés, third grade; and consuls, the fourth grade. In kingdoms where the old class stratification survives and kings grant their subjects "orders" as symbolic manifestations of recognition of merit, certain orders are reserved exclusively for upper-class persons.

In traditional bureaucracies, honorific titles were granted to state employees by their superiors. For instance, fourteen such titles, symbolizing gradations of merit, existed in Tsarist Russia. Their gradation usually coincided with the stratification of ranks; in any case, only high-ranking bureaucrats were honored by high titles.

A different kind of recognition of merit is based on the length of past services. Thus, a military officer, a civil official, an industrial employee, a teacher, if he has served many years, is evaluated more highly by his superiors than another who has served for only a short period of time. The recognition of his merit is often symbolized by honorific awards or the celebration of his anniversary; and frequently he is granted other rewards, especially economic ones, such as a raise of salary or a pension, if he can no longer perform his role.

The recognition of merit may be accompanied or followed by promotion to a higher rank. Such is usually not the case if the individual ceases to perform his role and retires—e.g., a "professor emeritus" or a soldier who leaves the army, unless he has been incapacitated during his military service and the army assumes the task of preparing him for a civilian occupation. On the other hand, when social roles, especially institutional roles, are graded in rank, fewer roles of higher rank are accessible than roles of lower rank. Thus, in an industrial plant, roles of foremen are much less numerous than those of workers; roles of superintendents are fewer than those of foremen; and so on, up to the unique role of manager. The same obviously applies to the gradation of roles in the army from soldiers through noncommissioned officers, commissioned officers, to generals, to the commander-in-chief; or in a universal church from laymen through parish priests, to bishops, to archbishops, to the head; or in an American university from students through instructors, to full professors, up to the president. Consequently, each promotion from a lower to a higher rank requires the selection of a particular person from a number of candidates. The basis of this selection may be recognition of merit for prior performance of lower-rank roles. If promotion requires educational preparation for the higher-rank roles, those candidates are selected who in the opinion of educators have performed most effectively their roles as educands.

6. The Right to Personal Esteem by Equals

When the social circle within which an individual performs his role is composed of participants who consider him their equal, neither he nor they are obliged to submit to domination. His cooperation with each of them is voluntary, and social control is mutual, not one-sided.

Of course, equality is relative, not absolute, but minor inequalities may be ignored. Thus, in extracurricular activities of college students, seniors, juniors, and sophomores often act as equals. Skilled and unskilled workers in a factory sometimes interact as equals when they cooperate in opposition to managers. Commissioned officers, ranking from lieutenants to majors and even colonels, treat each other as equals or nearly so, when they cooperate unofficially in companionate intercourse; so do university teachers in unofficial meetings. Physicians or scientists who collaborate in forming and maintaining professional associations, though they do not ignore the gradations of rank of such institutional roles as those of president, vice-president, and secretary, yet in personal contacts with each other treat all professional members as equals, in contrast with nonprofessional outsiders. Individuals and families of the same hereditary rank accept the principle of equality, even when their wealth is very unequal.

But individuals who perform similarly patterned roles differ personally in the ways in which they act. Recognition of an individual's personal worth by a circle of equals is based on the spontaneous and effective fulfilment of his duties on behalf of others. Such recognition is called *esteem*. Esteem differs from prestige in that it does not imply that other participants in his circle are not supposed to perform the same kind of role; on the contrary, his performance is considered a model, an example which others ought to imitate.

Thus, in a circle of polite companionship a man (or a woman) who as host or guest regularly acts in perfect accordance with the best rules of etiquette and always helps others enjoy companionate meetings is highly esteemed. A physician is esteemed by other physicians if he has considerable medical knowledge and skill, uses it regularly for the benefit of his patients rather than for his own benefit, and spontaneously cooperates with his fellow physicians whenever cooperation is needed. A scientist who carries on productive research in conformity with approved methods and is willing to collaborate with others for common goals enjoys esteem in the opinion of his fellow scientists. Similarly, a university professor who is a good scholar and a stimulating teacher and also maintains harmonious cooperative relations with his colleagues is esteemed by his faculty circle. A student is esteemed by his fellow students not so much when professors give him high grades (though this counts, if he uses his superior knowledge to help others), but chiefly when he is recognized as a valuable leader and collaborator in extracurricular activities.

Generally speaking, esteem by a circle of equals is founded partly on perfect or nearly perfect individual conformity with cultural standards and norms which participants in his circle consider essential for the kind of role which all of them perform, and partly on what we may call his *altruistic* conduct on behalf of other participants. When sociometrists—Moreno and his followers—measure the valuation of an individual as a "socius" by listing the number of participants in collective activities who spontaneously manifest their willingness to cooperate with him in preference to others, such preference may be considered a test of esteem based on recognition and expectation of the individual's altruistic conduct.

An individual who is esteemed has the right to expect that participants in his circle will oppose negative valuations of his person which conflict with their positive valuation. In democratic countries, this right is supported by the law of slander and libel, which protects every individual, whatever his rank, against unjustified explicit depreciation of his person.

We shall now survey briefly other categories of personal rights and indicate how they are connected with the right to recognition of personal worth. We begin with the right to safety, manifested in physical protection.

7. RIGHT TO PHYSICAL SAFETY

This right is most obvious and universal in the roles of children. Every child, once accepted as a potentially valuable participant in social life, has the right to be protected from influences which endanger his life or health. His body is supposed to be guarded against extreme physical changes in his natural environment, dangerous animals or machines, and hostile or careless men. This is usually done by keeping him in a safe place within the home. In communities where the belief in mystical evil forces persists, his life has to be protected from them. Protection of health from sickness and the appropriate treatment when he is sick is also the right of every child.

And yet not all children's bodies are equally well guarded. The protection that is granted to them depends upon their valuation in adult circles. A child who is positively evaluated only by its family circle has less protection than a child who is considered valuable by all the participants in the community. Children in a modern democratic town receive much better protection and care, with the help of public officials, physicians, and nurses, than children in a scattered tribal community. Where a hereditary class stratification exists, especially if connected with a gradation of wealth, children of upper-class families are much more thoroughly and efficiently protected than children of lower-class families. The most radical contrast is between the protection given to the child of a king and that given the child of a manual worker.

This right to bodily safety persists as individuals grow from childhood through adolescence to adulthood. Though during this growth some duties of the adult circle are taken over by the individual himself, who learns how to avoid certain physical dangers, mystical evils, and sources of sickness, yet no individual is ever entirely safe or able to avoid all dangers, especially as new dangers are continually emerging. Every individual has, at least in principle, the right to be protected from diseases dangerous to life. This task is performed by medical specialists, though as a matter of fact the realization of this right is still frequently affected by inequalities of rank and wealth. Protection from physical dangers is one of the tasks which certain technologists perform. The architects who construct dwellings and public buildings try to make them relatively safe from natural catastrophes; likewise, builders of ships and roads, engineers inventing and planning trains and automobiles, and the organizers and producers in machine industries safeguard workers from accidents.

Safeguarding lives from human enemies has become increasingly difficult. Of course, in all communities throughout history every participant has the right to be protected from being murdered by another individual. This protection is not always effective, as we know; for it is not easy to prevent murder, unless every individual is continually guarded by others, and only persons of very high rank can afford to be so guarded. The usual method employed to prevent murder is to make every potential murderer aware that he will be punished if he commits murder, but many believe that they will be able to escape punishment. Only by developing fully social cooperation among all participants in a community can this danger be eliminated.

But individuals, especially warriors, cannot be safeguarded from the danger of being killed or wounded by militant members of a hostile collectivity in the course of warfare. Thus warriors have no right to bodily safety: Their roles necessarily involve the risk of being killed or wounded in struggles against enemy warriors, although in so far as possible they are supposed to protect each other during these struggles. They are also supposed to prevent other participants in their community or society from being injured by enemy warriors. Their task was particularly difficult during those wars in the past when aggressive military groups purposely attempted to destroy foreign societies, as did Tamerlane's army and the Nazis. It is even more difficult now, in consequence of the invention of atomic and hydrogen bombs.

8. Economic Rights

These rights are found in all human collectivities during all historical periods. But before surveying them, we must clearly distinguish between the approach to economic phenomena used by economic theorists and the sociological approach.

Economists investigate primarily actions dealing with the material values which men produce and use to satisfy their wants. Sociologists investigate primarily social actions dealing with men as values. Thus, an economic system is a system of relationships between actions of producing, consuming, buying, selling, borrowing, lending, etc., no matter who performs these actions. A social system is a system of interaction between two or more men.

Economists have extended their theory to all human actions, provided those who perform them receive some economic values from others. They include, for instance, such actions as writing poetry, composing and playing music, teaching, functioning as legislators, judges, public officials, or military officers. The individual who performs such actions is presumed to sell them as services; those who give him material values to be used for the satisfaction of his wants or money as the symbol of such values are presumed to buy these services. Now, this approach may be adequate for the study of economic values and actions abstracted from the valuation of men as concrete persons by other men, but is entirely inadequate for comparative study of individual participation in social systems.

Although some individuals are more, others less dependent, every individual throughout his life depends for his "living," i.e., the satisfaction of his wants, upon the aid of others who grant him certain economic rights. His rights are prior to his duties; he must be regularly helped to live before he can regularly perform any actions on behalf of others. Every small child in a family is, of course, fully dependent; so is the lady of leisure. A farmer is less dependent, but even he must have his rights recognized. In the first place, no farmer (except a settler in an uninhabited land) can use his farm unless the right to possession is granted to him and protected by others; second, almost every farmer needs the aid of a wife or some other woman, often also younger family members; third, most farmers use implements produced by others and techniques learned from others; fourth, he together with his family must have explicit or implicit rights to consume his own products, otherwise many of his products may be taken away from him (e.g., as during the Middle Ages by the lord of a manorial estate or right now by the Communist government in Soviet Russia); fifth, he needs the right to exchange the products he does not consume for goods he wants, but does not produce.

Economic rights are of two types: rights to ownership or a share of ownership of long-lasting values which continue to exist, though repeatedly used—e.g., land, buildings, or machines—and rights to repeated acquisition of values which are needed for the satisfaction of wants, but cease to exist after they have been used—e.g., food, fuel, or personal services. Although there is no sharp dividing line between them, we may call the first type "rights to property," and the second type "rights to income."

A comparative survey of economic rights indicates that usually a person is granted those rights which his social circle considers necessary for the adequate performance of this social role. "Economic security" means that an individual can expect his social circle to support his rights as long as he continues to perform his role and sometimes even after he has ceased to perform it, as in the lifelong security of retired people on a pension.

It is easy to understand why economic rights are always granted to individuals whose roles involve such specifically economic activities as producing or exchanging material goods, organizing production or exchange. This obviously applies to the roles of workers, foremen, superintendents, managers, and owners of factories; the roles of tradesmen, from small local merchants to salesmen, buyers, assistants, managers, owners of large commercial corporations; the roles of bankers, their associates, and employees; and the roles of rural landowners, their tenants, and employed workers. All of these have rights which are considered essential for the performance of their roles, but these rights are very unequal.

A wealthy capitalist has property rights to his capital and to the factory or store in which his capital is invested. These rights are now usually supported by the government of his state and sometimes by associations of capitalists. But this is not enough. In order to perform his role, he needs the regular cooperation of his employees. To obtain this, he must grant them definite economic rights. He can do it only because he has the right to the monetary income from the customers who buy the products of his factory or the goods which his store sells. He divides most of this income among his employees; and the rights of the latter are graded according to their rank—e.g., in a factory, from the head manager down to the unskilled workers. Such gradation exists also when the industry is not owned individually, but collectively.

The rights granted to inferiors depend on their superiors. Thus, the owner or manager of a factory usually decides how much economic income workers need in order to perform their technical roles. These decisions are often arbitrary in many private factories and in the forced labor camps of the Soviet Union. But wherever labor unions are organized to protect the rights of workers, managers have to take their demands into consideration.

Many individuals, however, are granted economic rights, though their roles do not include economically productive activities. First of all, there are the "high-class families" discussed above, whose wealth is inherited. Their rights are supported by other wealthy families, so as to enable them to maintain a high level of life and preserve their prestige. This gives them considerable influence, either through contact with powerful political leaders or because some of their members are economic producers.

But economic rights are extended to many other roles. Thus, a priest or minister of religion is granted by his parishioners economic rights which he needs in order to perform regularly his duties, though these duties contribute nothing to the economic possessions or income of the parishioners (unless he assumes in addition to his religious duties the task of a leader in economic cooperation, as a few of them do). A university professor has a salary, though (if he teaches philosophy, history, sociology, literature, art, music, astronomy, or mathematics) his teaching is economically useless. Only if he teaches applied economics, engineering, or some other practical subject is his teaching economically useful, for he then prepares students for economically useful roles in the future. Certainly, a poet, an artist, or a musician performs no economic activities whatsoever, and yet he is granted economic rights by the circle of those who appreciate his creative works, so as to enable him to do more creative work without wasting his time and energy on technical production or trade. A soldier or military officer has economic rights, though the remuneration he gets, especially in time of war, obviously cannot be considered an adequate compensation for risking his life and his health and being subjected to great physical discomfort. The duties of a congressman or administrative officer are social, not economic, unless he deals with state finances. A physician has to be economically supported by his patients in order to perform his role, but saving or prolonging human lives is not an economic activity.

These economic rights granted to persons who perform noneconomic roles are also partly graded according to rank. A bishop has greater rights than a parish priest; a full professor has a larger salary than an instructor; a famous poet, artist, or musician obtains more money from the public than one who is little known; a general is paid more than a soldier. This remuneration is a recognition of personal worth, not merely a way of making the individual perform his superior role, as is obvious when an individual is granted economic rights in recognition of past merit after he has ceased to perform his role. However, quite a few social and political leaders, scientists, scholars, and poets perform their roles without any economic reward. Finally, even individuals who perform economically useful roles sometimes obtain no economic compensation— e.g., unpaid treasurers of associations, volunteer social workers, founders and supporters of charitable institutions. Of course, in such cases the individual is assured sufficient economic rights in some other role.

Another general type of economic right—the right to use public property—will be investigated in connection with the study of social groups.

9. RIGHT TO SYMPATHETIC UNDERSTANDING

When an individual communicates to others symbolically his observations, feelings, or volitions, he expects to be understood and to provoke some response. Indeed, mutual understanding through symbolic communication is an essential condition of social solidarity. But differences in the content and meaning of symbolic communication will provoke various kinds of response. We shall begin with what may be called *sympathetic* understanding.

In discussing the relations between a child and its mother, we mentioned that the child early manifests its feelings of pain and pleasure and that the mother should not only understand and sympathize with it, but manifest her sympathetic understanding so that the child will be aware of it, as well as alleviate its pain or promote its pleasure. As we have seen, such sympathetic understanding is also a primary mutual duty between brothers and friends. It is the most essential mutual duty in erotic relations.

When a child is connected by social relations with other adults on whom its development as a desirable person depends, it usually has the right to some degree of sympathetic understanding from each of these adults. This right is exacted by subjecting the child's symbolic communications with every adult to positive or negative sanctions. Similarly, when an individual has a number of "brothers," every one of them is expected by the others to sympathize with him.

Well-known manifestations of this right are found in the roles of adult participants in primary groups (in Cooley's sense of this term). When something very painful or very pleasant occurs to an individual participant, he (or she) has the right to expect a manifestation of sympathy from his circle—be it a large family or a circle of neighbors or acquaintances. Thus, after the circle learns of the death of an individual's father, mother, husband, wife, or other close kin, every participant is obliged to share in the common mourning. If a happy event, like a wedding or the birth of a child, is announced, every participant should join in ceremonial rejoicing. In some modern communities, the birthday or nameday of every member is a happy day, and he can expect other members to manifest their sympathy through greetings and good wishes, sometimes even through gifts. In some influential social roles these rights extend to much wider circles. Thus, in many kingdoms all subjects were supposed to participate in mourning the death of a king and in joyful celebrations of a royal wedding or the birth of an heir. Birthdays or namedays of kings and queens were often state holidays.

At meetings of the partners in relations of polite companionship, sympathetic understanding has its limitations: No participant in such a meeting is supposed to communicate to others painful experiences or feelings of his, for every such meeting is organized for purposes of common enjoyment. But every participant, while he functions as the temporary leader in conversation, has the right to expect from the others manifestations of sympathetic understanding of everything he communicates to them.

More important historically, but more difficult to realize, is the right to sympathetic understanding granted to poets, painters, sculptors, actors, composers, concert musicians, and singers by circles of readers, observers, or listeners. The chief right which such an artist has, according to his admirers, is the right to prestige based on positive valuation of his works by aesthetic standards. This is the right which his circle actively supports by helping him gain recognition and defending him against negative criticism. But an essential condition of the full appreciation of his art is sympathetic understanding of the experiences, ideas, and feelings which he expresses. Every participant in his circle is expected to manifest symbolically such understanding. Even when, as a matter of fact, he cannot understand, he must at least pretend that he does by following those who presumably do and reproducing their manifestations. This is typically represented in theaters, opera houses, and concert halls, where connoisseurs take the lead in expressing approval and the public follows them.

10. Right to Have Authoritative Judgments Accepted

This is a right which certain persons claim when they communicate their judgments to others and expect them to agree. It is actually realized when supported by a social circle of people who accept these judgments as valid. Frequently such rights are also supported by organized groups.

Authoritative judgments may be theoretic (scientific or philosophic) or evaluative and normative (e.g., ethical or aesthetic) or a combination of both (e.g., religious).

A teacher who communicates theoretic judgments to a circle of students usually assumes that he has the right to have all of his students agree with these judgments, since his authority is based on knowledge which they lack. This right is sometimes supported by the circle of students themselves. Thus, the disciples of an ancient philosopher voluntarily selected him and followed his guidance; and even in a modern school, students may be allowed to choose a teacher whom they expect to impart to them the kind of knowledge they want to acquire.

The right to have evaluative and normative judgments accepted is granted to individuals who function as authoritative *advisers*. Here the right is often supported directly by the circle of those who believe that they, as well as others, need advice as to what is right and wrong, and voluntarily seek it from "sages" who are both wise and good. Such are the rights of prophets and preachers who are not members of organized religious groups, of political ideologists who are not participants in a government, and of all kinds of moralists.

We are familiar with the authoritative writers of books on etiquette whose judgments are voluntarily accepted by many thousands of people. Some popular advisers to the lovelorn have quite a following. A musicologist, a historian, or a critic of literature who, in the opinion of amateurs, has superior knowledge of aesthetic standards with which musical composers, players, or writers tend to conform is considered by this circle as endowed with the authority to evaluate such works; and every participant in his circle is supposed to accept his judgments as valid. During public exhibitions of paintings, individuals who are recognized by the public as superior connoisseurs of art select the paintings which they consider the best, and their judgments are accepted by the public.

More influential are those judges whose statements are supported by an organized group. In an organized school, students have to take some obligatory courses, accept the authority of appointed teachers, and prove that they accept it by passing examinations. In organized religions with well-established dogmas, systems of cultus, and ethical principles, laymen are required to agree with the judgments of priests or be branded as heretics. The right of state legislators is supported by administrative groups who

force all citizens to accept the evaluative and normative promulga-
tions about human conduct which are embodied in the laws.
Professional groups of physicians hasten to support the authority of
their fellow members.

Some social thinkers identify authority with power. But the term
"power" has a very different meaning. We say that a social agent
has power when he can compel people to do what they do not want
to do or prevent them from doing what they want to do. Some
authoritative judges do, indeed, have power in this sense; and
others—typically legislators—are supported by individuals or
groups who have considerable power. Obviously, however, those
authoritative judges mentioned above who have only circles of
voluntary followers lack coercive power. Even priests of organized
religions have little power in those areas where, as in the United
States, many different religious groups coexist, and none of them
has governmental support. Nor do physicians whose authority is
supported by professional associations have much power over their
circles of voluntary patients. On the other hand, many powerful
agents are not accepted as authoritative judges by the people over
whom they exert their power.

Nor should authority be confused with competence. Competence means ability to fulfil one's own duties, but not the superior
knowledge or wisdom needed to judge the performances of others
or to tell them what they ought to do. A nurse may be competent
to perform specific functions, but the authority to decide what
ought to be done for a patient rests with the physician. Many
individuals are considered competent artists, but are not endowed
by the public and other artists with the authority to estimate works
of art comparatively, since they lack the adequate knowledge of art
and of aesthetic standards which a critic is supposed to possess.

11. Right to Obedience

This right is the primary foundation of personal power. Its origin
may be traced back to the roles of parents in family circles.

We saw that it is the duty of a child to obey its mother; and it is the mother's task to induce her child to fulfil this duty. As long as she performs it successfully, it may be left entirely to her. But if her growing children frequently disobey and associate with the disobedient children of other mothers in companionate play, individual disobedience may become open or latent rebellion against motherly domination. In such a case, the mother can usually obtain aid from her husband, brother, sister, or some other adult. This implies that, from the point of view of her family circle, it is her right to have her children obey her orders and that other family members are obliged to support it.

We notice, however, that in most communities obedience to mothers is much less exacting than obedience to fathers. In these communities, the child's duty to obey its mother is usually limited to those orders which are approved by the father, whereas its duty to obey the father is unconditional, applied to every command of the father. Furthermore, the father's right to obedience is often supported not only by the family circle, but if necessary by other fathers in the community, sometimes even by older sons who expect to become fathers and to gain gradually the same right in relations with their future children. With the development of the state, this right may be supported by the government, as in ancient Rome.

In many preliterate societies, however, and in some societies with highly developed cultures—e.g., in China—there is no need for men outside the family circle to support actively the father's right to obedience. For this right is sanctioned by supernatural powers—totemic beings, spirits of ancestors, or other gods. Individuals from early childhood learn about these mystical powers under the guidance of older family members or even priests; they learn that the right of their father (or grandfather, if still alive) has been delegated to him by divine or semidivine beings and that disobedience will be inevitably punished and obedience rewarded in this life or the next. Later, in discussing the role of king, we shall see what influence such beliefs in supernatural sanctions have upon the obedience of their subjects.

Another example of social roles which include the right to

obedience is that of masters in relations with slaves. Slaves are originally strangers to the community, sometimes enemies who have no rights whatever. None of them could survive unless an influential community member granted them permanent protection and support. When he does so, he becomes an absolute master who can exact unconditional obedience. If a slave disobeys, the master can treat him again as an enemy stranger, inflict upon him any punishment he wants, with the aid of obedient slaves or community members.

Very familiar, widely spread, and influential is the right of a military commander to have his subordinate warriors obey his orders. The problem is: Who supports these rights? Of course, a group of warriors possesses physical powers which can be used to coerce others to perform or refrain from performing various kinds of actions. However, as a private individual the commander would have no physical power over the social circle of his subordinates; and, unlike the master of slaves, he cannot rely upon community members who are not warriors to aid him enforce his commands. If his subordinates refused to obey, he would be utterly helpless. Of course, his right to exact obedience from them may have been delegated to him by a superior commander. But here again the same problem arises: Where did the superior commander get his right to exact obedience? Unless the right has been delegated to him by a sacred king whom all his subjects, warriors as well as citizens, accept as endowed with magico-religious power, there is only one solution to this problem. The right of a military commander to exact obedience can be realized only if, and in so far as, supported by an organized group of warriors, so that every disobedience within the group can be prevented or repressed collectively by other members of the group. This implies that the group as a whole, small or large, simple or complex, must have a common purpose which can be achieved only by victory over enemies and that the group accepts the role of military commander as necessary for the achievement of this purpose.

If the right to obedience of a military commander is supported by a relatively large well-integrated group of warriors, it can be extended by compelling into submission people who are unable to resist the physical power of this group. This is how a military commander becomes a "war lord," a ruler of a population which must obey his orders, even if it evaluates him negatively and would like to disobey him.

Also well known is the right to obedience in administrative roles. In a bureaucratic hierarchy, it begins at the top and within the group of bureaucrats is accepted by subordinates at every level, since a disobedient subordinate can be dismissed by his superiors and lose his rights and opportunities for advancement. But its acceptance by the rest of the people who are subjected to administrative rule is a different matter. In fact, it is apt to be accepted by a considerable proportion of people, whenever a well-organized administrative system is supposed to maintain some kind of social order within the territory where the administrators function. This is demonstrated in democratic countries, where administrators are elected by the people and their functions subjected to the control of the public; but it has been found also in countries subjected to autocratic rule, as in the popular approval of the Roman administrative system under the empire and the preference manifested by French people for the administrative monarchical order when it became substituted for feudalism.

A different right to obedience is attached to the role of manager of an industrial group. It is ultimately rooted in property rights. Either the manager is also the owner of the industrial plant or he has been appointed by the owner—be it an individual, a corporation, or a public association—and granted the right to exact obedience from workers directly or through the medium of subordinate managers. In any case, his right is explicitly or implicitly accepted by the workers: This is the condition under which the workers are hired and continue to be employed. He has effective sanctions which enable him to exact obedience: Obedient workers receive wages and even have their wages raised, whereas disobedient workers can be fired. Inasmuch as the efficient functioning of an industry depends upon realization of the technological plans, it is the task of the manager to take care that the activities of the workers conform with the requirements of these plans; and his right to exact obedience in technical matters is essential for the fulfilment of his task. But this does not give him the right to exact the obedience of workers to orders which have no connection with the technical organization—e.g., to do the same work for lower wages, to risk dangers to life and health, to buy the goods they need in factory stores, to teach their children loyalty to the owners of the factory, etc. Collective rebellion against the enforcement of such orders has resulted in the limitation of managerial rights to obedience.

12. RIGHT TO PERFORM NEW ACTIONS

This right is important for individual life histories and the general history of culture.

Every child in an adult family circle has such a right in the sense that he is not only allowed, but encouraged to do something he has not done before, something *new* to him. His circle helps him remove obstacles to his activities and manifests positive appreciation of the results of his activities. This is essential for the acculturation and socialization of children as future active participants in the community. Most of it occurs under the guidance or even at the initiative of adults, and constitutes what is generally called "education." Usually only in association with other children can a child perform new actions without adult guidance; and sometimes these actions are spontaneously initiated by him. We may call this "self-education."

However, the range of new actions allowed and encouraged has definite limitations, though the limits differ in various communities. Attempts to initiate new actions are restrained "for the child's own good," if they endanger the child's physical or mystical safety. They are prohibited, if the child's actions can be injurious to adult property or peace. Girls are not permitted to perform actions reserved for boys, and boys are discouraged from doing anything which is the special task of girls. Children in general are not admitted to participation in most collective activities of adults, not only serious activities—religious, political, and economic—but even in companionate intercourse. They may be "seen, but not heard." At best, they can imitate such activities in their play. And the right to spontaneous new actions often decreases rather than increases with age. For instance, in many Polynesian, Melanesian, Amerindian, and African communities, children have considerable freedom; but as they grow older and begin to participate in adult activities, their freedom becomes curtailed.

In the role of a student in school, the right to acquire knowledge which is new to him and to use this knowledge in thinking and acting is the most essential of his rights. However, in most schools students are not expected to search for anything new on their own initiative without guidance. For their own good, they are supposed to learn only that which is "true," not that which is "false," to do the "right" kind of thinking and not the "wrong" kind. It is the student's teaching circle which decides what is true and what is false, what is right and what is wrong.

Only in recent times, especially in the United States, have these rights undergone considerable changes. According to the basic principle of progressive education, educands should be spontaneously acting rather than merely reacting to the active guidance of education. They are supposed to be granted freedom to choose for study topics in which they are interested and to do considerable active experimentation on their own initiative. This right to freedom is most fully developed in kindergartens and in many primary schools, much less in high schools, and probably least of all in colleges. In both high school and college, students have more opportunity for spontaneous new actions in extracurricular performances than in regular class work, especially if these performances are mere play. When students initiate any serious activity—economic, political, religious, or scientific—the guidance and control of faculty sponsors increases. This is highly significant.

When we survey the social roles of adults, we find that most of them have considerable rights to new actions only as participants in *play*. For play in general is not supposed to have serious results affecting the social order; nor is it meant to produce or destroy any important cultural values. Participation in play is voluntary; and although there are definite rules in every game with which participants have to conform, these rules are such as to allow every individual to initiate something new, if he wants and knows how to. But in his role as an industrial worker, foreman, or manager of an organized factory, a lieutenant, a governmental official, or housewife and mother, a person has little freedom to do anything new. Only during a holiday in a merry town with boon companions or at a nonpuritanical evening party has a man or woman the right to do things which are not permitted during his or her serious role.

However, in the course of history, the rights to spontaneous active innovations outside of play have been gradually increasing in roles which involve culturally productive actions, as technicians, sculptors, painters, musicians, religious leaders, social reformers, philosophers, and scientists. But this has been a slow process. Obviously these rights correspond to the duties which the innovators are supposed to perform within the social circles which accept them.

CHAPTER 14

PERSONAL FUNCTIONS

1. The Concept of Personal Function

In surveying the duties of individuals who perform certain roles, we must remember that an individual's relations with the participants in his social circle involve social cooperation with all of them and are presumed to be integrated. This implies that his duties are interconnected: The effective performance of his role depends upon his enactment of every one of them. For instance, a man's role as the head of a small family is effectively performed if he enacts all his duties toward his children and his wife. A woman entertaining guests at a dinner party has definite duties toward every guest which she must enact in order to perform effectively her role as hostess.

Consequently, whenever an individual fails to enact a certain duty of his, this impedes his cooperation with the participants in his circle. Thus, if a worker who is supposed to collaborate with other workers fails to do what they expect him to do, their collaboration is obstructed. If a man fails to provide his wife and children with the means of subsistence which they expect, his cooperation with them decreases. If a physician fails to cure some of his patients, he may lose actual or potential patients. There is a difference, of course, between failures due to unforeseen obstacles and those due to the individual's unwillingness or inability to do what his duty requires. In the former case, cooperation may be only temporarily interrupted; in the latter case, especially when failures occur repeatedly, the individual may be judged unfit for his role. And if an individual actually does something which his circle considers bad, harmful, conflicting with a duty of his, this results in social conflicts between him and other participants and has a disorganizing influence on his role. Such are the results of individual transgressions of basic rules of etiquette in companionate intercourse, of actions of a husband or wife which lead to divorce and dissolution of the family circle, and of actions of a manager who deprives some workers of their established rights.

This does not mean, however, that every individual who performs a specific role always has to conform strictly with all the norms which regulate his conduct. For, as a matter of fact, the cultural patterns of most social roles allow for variations, changes, and even some failures and transgressions.

In the first place, the ways in which particular individuals enact similarly regulated duties can vary considerably; some of these variations are approved and others tolerated by their social circles. For instance, in investigating the roles of students in a university, we found a wide range of variations. Students could select their courses out of a vast diversity of available courses, and the individual students in every class enacted their duties differently. Their actions were estimated by their teachers according to certain standards of efficiency; and these estimates were graded from high approval to moderate approval, and from mere tolerance to complete disapproval. The same student often acted more efficiently in one class than in others; and when a student failed to perform his duty in a class, he could compensate for his failure by assuming again the same duty and enacting it efficiently.

The origin of many differences in the performance of student roles could be traced back to the diversity of social roles which the students had performed during adolescence or even childhood. In some of them, the social circle provided a means of compensation not only for failures, but for transgressions. A child or adolescent who did something harmful to others was shown by educators how to restore social cooperation by doing something valuable on behalf of those whom he had harmed. This is a well-known practice in religious roles; sins can be compensated for by assuming and enacting supererogatory duties.

In the second place, an individual's failures or transgressions which interfere with the effective performance of his role may be ascribed to the influence of another role which he is performing. Almost every individual performs simultaneously several different roles, and certain requirements of one of them may be incompatible with requirements of the others. Such partial incompatibility of two roles which the same individual performs has been investigated by some sociologists and social psychologists. Here again we find considerable individual differences. Some individuals may give priority to the duties of one of these roles, others to the duties of the other role. Frequently, however, individuals avoid conflicts by limiting the duties of each role so as to prevent them from interfering with the basic duties of the other. This is the usual way when social roles are integrated into organized groups.

In the third place, when an individual performs a specific role for a long period of time, his duties may change during this period. For instance, some of the early duties of a mother or father toward their children are no longer required as the children grow up. On the other hand, an individual may have to assume in the course of time duties which he did not enact before, as a child does when he grows up or a person whose social circle increases in size.

And, finally, individual innovations lead to the development of new varieties of duties.

Therefore, in comparatively studying social roles, we should take into consideration all the duties which an individual enacts as long as he performs a specific role, and try to ascertain how these activities of his are interconnected. We shall call this dynamic combination of active duties his *personal function*. We use the adjective "personal" to distinguish the function of an individual from the function of a social group.

Now, we find a vast diversity of personal functions, depending first upon the composition, size, and integration of the social circles to which an individual belongs; secondly, upon the kind of actions which his duties require.

All duties in the sociological sense are social; i.e., they are duties toward other human individuals or collectivities whom an agent experiences and evaluates as *social objects*, essentially different from all other, nonhuman objects. But social objects vary considerably.

2. Particular Duties Toward Particular Individuals

In every social role, the performer has definite duties toward those individual participants in his social circle with whom he directly interacts. Thus, if his entire social circle is numerically limited and he can identify and get into direct contact with every individual within it, his function includes all the duties and only those which he enacts on behalf of these individuals.

We mentioned the duties of the male head of a small family toward his wife and children. But even if a man's family circle includes his own and his wife's parents, brothers, sisters, uncles, aunts, nephews, and nieces, he can still identify each of them; and when he interacts with any one of them, he is supposed to do something definite on his or her behalf. On the other hand, his wife also has definite, though different, duties toward him, her children, and the relatives of both of them. So has every one of the children, as it becomes a conscious and active person and gets into contact with its grandparents, uncles, aunts, and cousins, though its duties differ from those of its father and mother.

The role of a shaman or physician includes duties toward every particular individual who becomes his patient, but is limited to the circle of his patients and his assistants in curing them. Whatever duties he may have toward other people are components of some other role of his.

The function of a woman teacher in a circle of pupils is educational guidance of every individual pupil. The composition of her circle changes periodically; former pupils leave it, new pupils come in. She may also teach different subjects to separate circles of pupils. But in any case, as long as she performs her role, she continues to enact these duties toward particular pupils. Of course, her role is not independent; she is usually subjected to some social control of the parents of her pupils, of the school board, of the superintendent, if there is one, perhaps of the teachers' association to which she belongs. If she is in duty bound to submit to such control, this may affect her function, for instance, the content of the subjects which she teaches or the educational methods which she uses. Nevertheless, educational guidance of individual pupils remains her basic function, with only secondary variations or changes.

An owner of a small industrial enterprise has definite duties toward every individual worker whom he employs. So does a foreman in a small, separate section of an industrial factory, if he regulates the cooperation of the workers. All these duties constitute the personal function of the employer or the foreman within this circle, though of course the foreman's function is not independent, but controlled by the manager. Every worker also has definite duties toward his employer or his foreman and fellow workers. These duties constitute his function within this circle and are manifestly different from those of the employer or foreman. In a small cooperative enterprise without a dominant role of employer or foreman, every active participant is a worker whose function consists in definite active duties toward other workers. The continued fulfilment of all the personal functions is intended to result in an effective continuous fulfilment of the collective function.

A Christian clergyman, as head of a local congregation, also has definite duties toward each individual participant in his congregation. Thus, if infants or small children are admitted into the congregation, he admits each one of them individually by baptizing it. He usually prepares every admitted child for future active membership. When two participants in the congregation intend to marry, he sanctions their marriage. If a participant has sinned, his task is to induce him to repent and compensate for his sin. Finally, he has the duty to aid every dying participant to gain salvation after death, and to preside at the funeral. And every active participant has certain duties toward the clergyman and other participants who need his cooperation, though his total duties are obviously much less numerous and exacting than those of the clergyman.

3. GENERALIZED DUTIES WITHIN WIDE SOCIAL CIRCLES

When an individual's social circle is very wide, his function includes specific duties toward all the people who compose this circle, even those he cannot identify individually or interact with. Consequently, in enacting his duties he is supposed to conform with general standards and norms which are applicable to all participants who are expected to benefit by his actions, however they may differ individually. By way of example, we may refer to some of the social roles with wide social circles which we mentioned above.

The basic duties of the head of a government are toward the people who accept him and submit to his domination; his function is to benefit all of them. Considerable differences exist between such governmental functions, as we know. For instance, the President of the United States is only the supreme executive, while a sovereign king or dictator is—like Hitler, Mussolini, or Stalin—also the supreme legislator and judge. His duties toward the people over whom he dominates can also vary, depending on their rank, especially when he needs the support of high-ranking people more than that of low-ranking people. When there is a recognized hereditary class stratification, his duties toward the higher class are more exacting than those toward the lower classes. In countries with highly developed private industry, his duties toward industrial owners and managers may take priority over his duties toward the workers, under the assumption that supporting and promoting industrial development ultimately benefits all the people in the country and that their prosperity is due to the initiative of the "captains of industry." In a totalitarian state with a single party, the dictator's duties toward people who are full members of the party—Communists, Fascists, or Nazis—are much more important than those toward the masses of people who do not belong.

But, whatever his function, every political leader, as we mentioned before, must rely on an inner circle or several inner circles of assistants, and must also assume definite duties toward them. These duties, however, are supposed to be subordinated to his general duties, since the task of his assistants is to enable him to fulfil his function within his total circle. Yet assistants are often selected and promoted on the basis of their personal loyalty to the ruler rather than their efficiency. Many kings have entrusted important political functions to incompetent, though loyal, courtiers; and a few presidents have entrusted such functions to their old friends, regardless of their qualifications. Indeed, dictators, e.g., Hitler and especially Stalin, rejected and even killed assistants who considered governmental functions more important than personal loyalty to the dictator.

When we study the roles of prominent scientists, scholars, and philosophers, we find that each of them has a more or less wide circle of active thinkers in the same realm of knowledge who appreciate his contributions and usually also a circle of learners who study his works while preparing themselves for future roles of active thinkers. In modern times he seldom, if ever, gets into direct contact with most of the participants in these circles, who may be scattered over the whole world. Yet it is his basic duty toward all of them to make his products conform with those standards of epistemology, logic, and methodology which his fellow thinkers consider essential conditions of theoretically valid knowledge. But in order to produce such works and make them available to other thinkers, he usually needs sponsors to provide him with the necessary means of research and grant him economic rights to subsistence as well as an opportunity to have his works published. In the past, sponsors were mostly rulers. Nowadays, many active thinkers obtain such sponsorship in their roles of university professors; others from governmental groups or associations for promoting the development of knowledge; still others from the owners or managers of economic corporations. In principle, their duties toward their sponsors are supposed to be, and often are, only auxiliary to their basic functions on behalf of wide circles of active thinkers; but sometimes they conflict with them. Contemporary struggles for preservation and expansion of "academic freedom," i.e., freedom to develop new theories and to make them generally available, are attempting to overcome such conflicts.

4. DUTIES TOWARD A PERSON'S SOCIAL CIRCLE WHEN IT IS AN ORGANIZED SOCIAL GROUP

If an individual is a member of an organized social group, he is supposed to have certain duties not only toward other individual members, but toward his group as a whole.

We mentioned the duties of a priest or minister toward individual participants in his congregation, but these duties do not constitute his entire function. He must also regularly act as the leader in collective cultus intended to benefit the entire congregation, not only its individual members. Indeed, in organized religious groups with highly developed ritual, where ceremonial cultus of deities is essential to gain divine favor, no such cultus is considered effective without the guidance of priests endowed with sacredness; and this guidance is the most important duty of every priest. But the priest is not the only person who is in duty bound to carry on collective cultus. Every member of a religious group is supposed to participate; it is his duty toward the group to cooperate for the common purpose of propitiating the deity. Of course, a layman contributes to this purpose much less than a priest, though some laymen make more important contributions than others.

Often the duties of group members include technical and economic contributions to the construction and maintenance of buildings as centers of cultus. When a local religious group is one of many groups which together constitute a large and complex church, it is the duty of clergymen and influential lay believers to promote the collaboration of these smaller groups on behalf of the entire church.

But perhaps the most important duty of the members of a religious group is common defense against any group which is trying to disorganize it, destroy its values, or eliminate it altogether. This duty may take priority over duties toward individual members.

Frequently the defense is one-sided, e.g., the defense of Jewish groups against the hostile conquerors of Judea and in the Diaspora against Christians and Moslems; the defense of early Christian groups in the Roman Empire; and, later, the defense of new sects against the dominant churches. Recently this defense has had to be carried on not against other religious groups, but against powerful secular groups—e.g., in Germany against the Nazis, in Soviet Russia and satellite countries against the Communists.

Sometimes, however, the defense is two-sided: Members of each group may be convinced that the other group is dangerous to its existence and, consequently, that its members should counteract the danger by carrying on a "holy war" to eliminate the enemy group. This led to many violent struggles between religious groups with different beliefs and practices, since most religious believers are very loyal to their own group. Only the loyalty of members of cultural nationalities in modern times equals and sometimes even exceeds religious loyalty.

But in every long-lasting social group, at least some members assume duties toward the group as a whole. Thus, members of a state government have duties not only toward the citizens, but toward the state as a whole; and these duties are more exacting than those of the ordinary citizen, who individually is obliged to do little more than pay taxes and avoid offenses against the laws. But in times of crisis even the ordinary citizen has more important duties. During a war, all capable men assume military duty, defending their state against enemies at the risk of their lives, and even people who are not warriors assume extraordinary duties. Thus, in the course of World War II, every average American— even the ordinary housewife, farmer, and semiskilled worker—was supposed to undertake certain public duties as a contribution to the security of the United States.

While members of a political party in a democratic country most of the time do little for their party, as compared with their leaders, their duties become important during elections when, according to the famous saying, "Now is the time for all good men to come to the aid of their party." We know how relatively exacting are the duties of all Communist Party members wherever a struggle is being waged between their party and a democratic party. In a modern American university, the duties of members of the Board of Trustees, of the President, the Provost, the Comptroller, the Deans, and the leading alumni are primarily toward the university as a whole. The students are expected to manifest their loyalty very vigorously during interuniversity contests, especially football games.

5. DUTIES OF MEMBERS OF ORGANIZED GROUPS TOWARD OUTSIDERS

While every social group needs the active cooperation of its members for their own benefit, certain groups require some, or even all, of their members to assume duties toward people who are not members.

Such duties are often subordinated to duties toward members or toward the group as a whole. For instance, employees in a store or cooks and waiters in a restaurant have duties toward customers, but the purpose of those duties is to benefit the owners and employees themselves. And when leaders of a political party assume duties toward people who do not belong to their party, they usually do so in order to increase the size and power of the party.

In some groups, however, these duties are primarily intended to benefit outsiders and only secondarily the members, though as a result of them the group as a whole may gain prestige and influence. For instance, the duty of military groups is to protect not themselves, but civilians of their country from dangerous enemies; this duty obviously corresponds to the right to bodily safety which we discussed above.

When some members of a religious group assume the roles of missionaries and other members help them socially and economically, they sincerely believe that it is their duty to aid unbelievers gain divine benefits which only faithful believers share, even though the performance of this duty requires considerable efforts. Of course, the fact that in consequence of these efforts the religious group grows in size and expands into new areas is also important from the point of view of its loyal members, especially when groups of different denominations compete with each other.

The members of other religious groups, however, have assumed disinterested altruistic duties toward peoples of various religions, as the Y.M.C.A. and the Y.W.C.A. did during and after the two world wars, and also small groups of American Quakers in Europe. Likewise, various secular groups have been organized for the purpose of helping other people more effectively than their members could do individually. The work of the Red Cross shows how effective this collaboration can be.

Somewhat different are the duties of members of professional groups, e.g., associations of physicians, lawyers, teachers, etc. Of course, these professional roles existed before associations were organized, and individuals can still perform them, whether they belong to professional associations or not. The explicit purpose of such associations is to maintain high standards of personal fitness for professional roles, prevent anybody from performing such a role who is considered unfit, make every member conform with definite norms in enacting his duties, and stimulate functional collaboration between members. In principle, the basic duties of all members are toward those outsiders who need their professional services—physicians toward patients, lawyers toward clients, teachers toward learners. However, inasmuch as professionals need certain rights in order to fulfil their duties, every professional association is supposed to protect the rights of its members, and it is the duty of all members to collaborate in such protection. Indeed, some associations seem to be more interested in protecting their rights than in aiding outsiders.

6. DUTIES TOWARD ONE'S SELF

Since an individual's person is valuable to his circle, according to certain standards, it is his duty to keep it valuable and to guard against loss of prestige, esteem, or merit. His social circle expects him to do this; otherwise, they will be disappointed and consider the actions which they perform on his behalf to be wasted.

In certain roles, these duties are of great importance, as is clearly manifested in some religious beliefs. Thus, according to Christian dogmas, every individual as a creature of God is potentially valuable, but every one can lose his worth by sin. Therefore, it is every individual's duty to work for his own salvation with the aid of God and to refrain from sinning. The most extreme instance of the supreme importance attributed to this duty was that of the hermit who in early periods of Christianity assumed no active duties toward other men. Yet the religious function of the hermit had a social significance, for he was positively valued by those fellow Christians who knew about him, as a model whose striving for self-salvation should be imitated. Somewhat similar is the role of a Hindu yogi.

Another interesting example of duties toward one's self was the duty of a nobleman—or, more generally, a "gentleman"—to defend his honor against any kind of accusation, depreciative word, or even gesture which would lower his personal valuation by the circle of his equals or superiors. If the offender was his equal, he could defend his honor and prove how important it was to him by risking his life in a duel. This duty persisted among civilians in some countries as late as the first quarter of this century, especially among military officers, each of whom was obliged to defend his honor by challenging the offender to a duel, because any loss of honor by a particular officer would lower the prestige of his whole regiment. Even more exacting was the duty of a Japanese Samurai who, after losing prestige, regained it by sacrificing his life in *harakiri*.

The duty of maintaining personal dignity in appearance and manners is well known. We find it among priests of nearly all religions, hereditary upper-class people, officers in the army and the navy, high-ranking bureaucrats, diplomats, judges holding court, and university professors on ceremonial occasions.

We are familiar with the age-old duty of women to be "respectable." This duty demands rigid conformity with established mores and customs and avoidance of deviations or innovations which might raise doubts about a woman's respectability among men, but especially among other women who consider themselves authoritative judges as to what a respectable woman ought to do and ought not to do. For anything unexpected she does can stir up gossip; and gossip, as it spreads, easily becomes malicious. This is probably why Pericles is supposed to have stated: "The less said about a wife and mother, whether good or bad, the better." Of course, the importance attached to her respectability varies in degree, according to her husband's rank: "Caesar's wife should be above suspicion." And whenever she performs a social role outside of the family circle, her duty to be respectable becomes even more exacting. For instance, a woman teacher, in order to avoid the slightest doubts about her respectability, must be serious and earnest; in some communities even participation in light companionate play may lower her esteem.

Perhaps the best known and most explicit duties toward one's self are those of educands, especially university students. A student is being prepared for a future social role. After he assumes this role, his main duties will be toward other people; but his role as a student is different. Although he has some duties toward administrative officials, faculty members, fellow students, and is occasionally supposed to manifest loyalty to the university as his Alma Mater, his main, most important duty as educand is toward himself. He cannot become the kind of valuable participant in social life which he is expected to become after completing his education, unless he assumes the duty of making himself a valuable person and refrains from doing everything which might lower his worth. He is not supposed to do anything for his educators which will be of benefit to them (or he would be suspected of "apple-polishing"); what he is expected to do is to collaborate with his educators in developing his own personality under their guidance.

Somewhat different is the duty of a creative innovator toward himself. Although his innovations are expected to benefit all those who accept them and use them, and such is his ultimate duty; yet in order to fulfil this duty toward others, he must first assume the duty of developing his own ability to create valuable innovations. We call this the duty of *self-education*. It is a very hard, long-lasting duty, even when he has the voluntary help of competent cultural leaders.

7. CULTURALLY PATTERNED ACTIONS BY WHICH SOCIAL DUTIES ARE FULFILLED

When we compare the social roles of individuals, we find that the actions which they are expected to perform on behalf of others differ widely, depending on whether the role is performed within a small social circle, a large social circle, or an organized group. But in every case, they deal with certain values, and their function is to achieve results which will help others who deal with the same values to realize their purposes. In order to achieve such results, their actions must follow definite cultural patterns.

The best known of these patterns are those of productive material techniques. Thus, the function of a farmer is to produce values—especially vegetables and animals—which will be used by others for purposes of their own. This function requires that he should follow certain culturally patterned techniques of horticulture, agriculture, and animal husbandry. Since the values which farmers produce and the technical patterns of production vary in various areas and historical periods, considerable differences underlie the basic similarity in the functions of farmers.

The function of an independent craftsman is to produce material values which will be used by others, either for productive purposes (e.g., the products of a blacksmith by farmers, those of a weaver by tailors, and those of a lumberman by carpenters) or to satisfy their needs (e.g., wearing clothes, using furniture, or living in a cottage). A craftsman is considered in duty bound by the circle of those who use his products to follow definite norms of technical skill in his productive actions; otherwise, his products may not be fit to be used as intended. Therefore, in every community the roles of craftsmen require technical training, and only those who have such training are supposed to perform them; but the functions of craftsmen who specialize in producing certain varieties of material values and who use various culturally patterned techniques in the course of their production may differ widely from each other.

In cooperative techniques with considerable "division of labor," when many individuals contribute to a common product, it is not the circle of users, but the circle of fellow producers which requires that the individual should enact his specialized function in accordance with definite technical norms. This is exemplified by the cooperation of masons, carpenters, plumbers, painters, and perhaps some unskilled helpers who together build and decorate a house, and especially by the cooperation of planning engineers, industrial managers, skilled and unskilled workers in a modern factory. While from the strictly technological point of view the industrial production which goes on within a factory is a synthesis of physical and chemical processes, including movements of human bodies (not so long ago the workers were called "hands"), from the sociological point of view it is a dynamic combination of social roles performed by individuals who have been selected as presumably willing and able to enact specific personal functions useful to others in accordance with definite technical norms, or to organize such functions of others for the realization of common technical purposes. The investigation of such combinations of social roles within a factory is one of the main tasks of industrial sociology. Owners and managers of factories have become increasingly aware that an essential condition of effective technical production is the treatment of producers as persons, the stimulation of social solidarity among them, and the prevention of social conflicts. Thence the emergence of special social roles of "personnel managers."

Quite different are the culturally patterned functions of producing or reproducing (creating or recreating) nonmaterial, "ideational" values. Such are the functions of poets and novelists, of the publishers who reproduce their works for the benefit of readers; of dramatists and of the actors who reproduce their dramas for the benefit of audiences; and of musical composers and of the players who reproduce their compositions. In the realm of religion, prophets initiate new myths which are reproduced by their followers, communicated to new converts, and transmitted to successive generations. Prophets or priests start or adopt new ritualistic performances which become included in religious cultus and sometimes are regularly reproduced for centuries. Legislators promulgate general laws which judges repeatedly apply to particular cases. Philosophers construct new systems of ideas which are reproduced by their disciples and, later, by disciples of their disciples. Social reformers initiate new ideals of social cooperation which their followers try to realize.

We have already mentioned the functions of scientists who formulate new theories, have these theories reproduced by other scientists and students, and eventually problematized, tested, developed, modified, or rejected. The functions of painters, sculptors, and architects also belong here, inasmuch as they do not merely produce material objects, but create new aesthetic patterns, new ways of seeing and interpreting visible data. The function of inventors must also be included in this category, for they not only produce technical objects, but create new purposes and methods of technical production.

The vast diversity of these culturally patterned functions is, of course, well known. Not only do the functions of poets, musicians, painters, believers who participate in religious cultus, jurists, social reformers, philosophers, scientists, and inventors obviously follow very different cultural patterns, but within each of these classes numerous secondary varieties are found. The functions of lyrical poets, dramatists, and novelists differ in content, and each individual has his own style; nor can differences in language be ignored. The functions of composers of popular songs, of pieces intended to be played by individuals on various musical instruments, of symphonies, and of operas obviously differ. Several hundred religions have participants who share different beliefs and enact different rites; and within each religion some functional differentiation occurs in the performances of various believers. In the realm of scientific knowledge, there are at least thirty divisions. Although the basic epistemological, logical, and methodological principles are alike for all, the cultural patterns which scientific specialists in astronomy, chemistry, botany, zoology, geology, economics, linguistics, sociology, anthropology, and history follow differ considerably. Even more differentiated are the functions of technical inventors and of social innovators.

8. CLASSIFICATION OF SOCIAL ROLES BY THEIR FUNCTIONS

Our survey of the diversity found in each of the four components of social roles raises a sociological problem of primary importance. How can a general systematic theory of social roles be developed? Such a theory would require an adequate classification or taxonomy of all the social roles in the human world as social systems, just as a general biological theory requires an adequate classification of animals and plants as organic systems.

Now, such a classification can be developed after a comparative analysis of social roles discloses which of their four components is the most influential in the sense that all the other components depend upon it. Social roles could then be classified by the common distinctive characteristic of this main component, and then subclassified by similarities and differences of the other components.

Several sociologists have based their classification of social roles on one of the first three components which we have discussed. The best known are taxonomic generalizations about *persons* as defined and evaluated by participants in a collectivity. This kind of taxonomy seems relatively easy, for such generalizations are already current in most collectivities, and many of them are symbolized by common names—e.g., fathers, mothers, doctors, teachers, students, merchants, workers, managers, etc. These popular classifications apparently imply that all persons designated by the same common names are supposed to conform with the same standards and norms.

Another, more recent theory, according to which every role is performed within an organized group, classifies social roles by the "positions" of individuals in the groups to which they belong and which constitute their social circles.

The third, rather old classification of people in strata is based on a gradation of rights and privileges; the term "social classes" in the popular sense denotes such a stratification.

We have already mentioned the main weaknesses of each of these generalizations (see Chapters 11–13). Moreover, they have a common weakness. All three classifications of social roles—by the standardized definitions and valuations of persons, by positions in organized social groups, and by gradations in rights—use the term "status." Though its meanings differ, it has one universal connotation, that of a static, stable something that does not change except under external influences. But how can such a conception be reconciled with the historical evidence that new varieties of social roles have been continually emerging from previous roles?

Because all three components depend on personal functions and vary with them, we are inevitably led to the hypothetic conclusion that social roles can be classified only by personal functions. In the first place, by whatever standards an individual is defined and evaluated, his acceptance by a social circle as a person considered fit for a certain role implies that he is expected actively to fulfil definite duties. This expectation may be based on his presumed innate characteristics which are supposed to make him capable of enacting these duties or on his actions before he entered this social circle or on his actions after he entered it. But in any case, it is his definition and evaluation as a person which depends on his function, potential or actual, and not vice versa.

Secondly, the so-called "positions" of members in organized groups are also conditioned by personal functions. For if, in the course of the duration of a group, a specific personal function has been found necessary for its collective function or even its continued existence, it becomes an integral component of the institutional organization of the group.

Thirdly, in surveying personal rights, we found that they are presumed to be essential for the individual to perform adequately his duties. However, we noticed that privileged persons may have important rights granted to them without corresponding duties on their part. This may mean simply that these rights are granted in expectation of future functions, as in the case of a child, or in recognition of past functions, as in the case of an old retired person. But it may mean also that privileges are granted and supported without regard to functions by agents endowed with political or economic power. Without knowing the source of personal power and the way in which it is actively exerted—i.e., the functions of the agents who have this power—we cannot understand privilege.

How can this general hypothesis be used in classifying the enormous diversity of social roles found in various cultures?

We are facing here a problem analogous to that which biologists faced a century and a half ago. They succeeded in solving their problem by tracing the gradual evolution of many diverse families, genera, and species of organisms from earlier, simpler, and less diverse types of organic life. We believe that a similar approach will help us solve our problem.

9. The Evolutionary Approach to the History of Social Roles

There is no doubt whatever that in the course of history new varieties of social roles, differentiated by functions, have been multiplying. Compare, for instance, the vast diversity of specialized social roles performed by the inhabitants of the eastern part of the United States during the second quarter of this century with the roles of the pioneers in the same area during the second quarter of the seventeenth century; or the roles of the inhabitants of France or Western Germany at the beginning of this century with those which Caesar observed within the territory called "Gallia" or those which Tacitus described in his book on *Germania*.

However, comparative surveys of the development of many specialized varieties of social roles in particular areas during successive historical periods are not sufficient for drawing generalizations about the evolution of social roles throughout the world in the total course of human history. To make such generalizations, we must start with the assumption that the social history of mankind began with the formation of small and simple collectivities, which later gradually became integrated into larger and more complex collectivities. Then we must try to discover by comparative analysis what kind of social roles existed in those early small communities, how they became integrated, and how new varieties of social roles evolved during this integration.

We must discard, however, attempts to trace the evolution of human collectivities back to "animal society," for all such attempts must remain pure conjecture, since we have no factual evidence whatever concerning the period when human culture began to merge. Every human collectivity shares a culture, and all cultures are human products. We cannot go back any further than archeological evidence permits, and at this stage culture already existed. All human collectivities whose remnants archeologists have discovered, even if relatively small, were sufficiently large and continuous to develop and maintain some culture and transmit it from generation to generation. There must have been enough solidarity for common, long-lasting survival, which means that in all of them some rudimentary social roles existed. Of course, archeological evidence about social roles is only indirect, based on material artifacts; but it can be, and has been, supplemented and confirmed by direct observation of social interaction within relatively small and simple contemporaneous communities with material culture not much above the level of prehistorical communities.

Therefore, we shall begin with a brief survey of those basic social roles which are found in all relatively small, independent contemporary communities and which must have existed in prehistoric communities.

CHAPTER 15

ROLES IN TRIBAL COMMUNITIES

1. Primary Differentiation of Social Roles

A comparative survey of the nonliterate communities still accessible to observation and of those which archeologists reconstruct provides evidence that originally social roles were functionally differentiated by sex and age, and they remained so differentiated in all relatively small, long-lasting communities. Thus, theoretically no less than four kinds of social roles must have existed everywhere. However, even in the simplest communities which have been investigated there are usually seven roles; those of little children without distinction of sex, adolescent girls, adolescent boys, adult women, adult men, old women, old men. The roles of adults condition the others, since they fulfil the essential functions necessary for the existence of the community. Little children are considered future adults who in the course of their personal development will gradually learn to do what they are expected to do when they reach adult age. An old person is a former adult no longer able to fulfil the whole function she or he fulfilled in the past, e.g., a woman who cannot bear children, a man who cannot hunt, fight, or labor as effectively as younger men. In some communities, indeed, an old person has specific functions, different from those of adults; mainly, however, the evolution of social roles is due to the differentiation of functions of adults, and we shall now concentrate on this differentiation.

Of all adult functions, the woman's function of childbearing and child rearing is universally recognized as essential for the survival of every community. Consequently, the woman's role as a mother was probably the first to be culturally patterned, and the pattern has changed the least in the course of history.

2. Social Roles of Women as Mothers

In analyzing mother-child relations, we found that the fundamental duties of the mother toward her child, though differing in kind and degree in different communities, can be included under the same general categories: protection, support, promotion of physical development, and educational guidance. In analyzing conjugal relations, we noticed that the universal purpose of these relations is to procreate a valuable new generation; and this implies that a married woman is expected to have several children. From the point of view of this task of hers, her husband is primarily the father of her children, and her duties as a wife are integral components of her main function as a mother.

This is most obvious when her children are considered descendants of her own progenitors; but even when they are regarded as descendants of her husband's progenitors, her essential task as a wife is still to bear and rear children. Therefore, her sexual duties toward her husband are subordinated to her motherly duties. The same applies to her technical duties. We noticed that, while it is a duty of the wife toward her husband to prepare the goods which he needs for final consumption, and in many communities her technically productive activities are numerous and exacting, yet she is usually supposed to enact only those which can be enacted without seriously interfering with her duties as a mother. Since most of these duties require spatial proximity to her children, whatever she does must be done within or near the home where the children live. This leaves to her husband those activities which require prolonged absence from home—hunting, fishing, and pasturing cattle. In agricultural villages, where the husband assumes the main function of cultivating fields and taking care of the larger domestic animals, the wife acts as helper in harvesting crops and gardening, and in taking care of the small domestic animals and birds.

Her duties, however, are not limited to her children and her husband, except in those modern communities where a parental family forms a more or less closed unit with self-control of the relations between its participants. In tribal and folk communities, the mother and her children belong to a larger matrilineal or patrilineal family, or to two families, the one on the mother's and the other on the father's side. In a matrilineal family, she has definite duties toward her own mother and father, her mother's brothers and sisters, and her own brothers and sisters. For, inasmuch as her children and the children of her sisters are descendants of this family, she is in duty bound to bring her own children up under the guidance of the older generation and to cooperate with her sisters in bringing up their children. As she grows older, more experienced, and wiser, even when she can no longer bear children and enact the duties she enacted in the past, still as a grandmother she can guide the mothers of the younger generation and help them to educate their children. In a patrilineal family, her duties toward members of her own family decrease or cease after marriage, but she has to assume duties toward her husband's father, mother, and other relatives essentially similar to those mentioned above, because also pertaining to the continuation of the family through successive generations. When descent counts on both sides, she has duties toward members of her own as well as her husband's family.

As for her duties toward herself, she has to do on her own behalf whatever is necessary for the continuous fulfilment of her basic function and also whatever she cannot expect her social circle to do for her—e.g., feed and dress herself, protect herself against minor dangers, if she is able to do so, and maintain her personal dignity.

This raises the problem: What are her rights? The right to recognition of personal worth is universal. In many communities, the role of mother in general is exalted, as is most clearly manifested in religious myths. Several religions have goddesses which are conceived as mothers, sometimes as the original mothers of mankind or even of all living beings. And in some societies without such myths, human mothers are exalted, as we saw in connection with the celebration of "Mother's Day" in America.

Of course, not all mothers are considered equally valuable in all communities. We have already mentioned that a young man's parents in selecting his future wife base their choice on her presumed fitness for becoming a mother of desirable progeny. The daughter of superior parents is recognized as hereditarily superior to a daughter of inferior parents and is expected to transmit this superiority to her children.

After a married woman begins to bear children, her prestige steadily rises: the more valuable and numerous her children and the better she brings them up, the higher her prestige. If there is a limitation on the number of children which she and her husband can support, their quality becomes the basis of prestige. But, in any case, after her personal worth has been proved by the adequate performance of her motherly function, she has the right to have it recognized. She has, obviously, higher prestige than a childless woman, married or unmarried, or a younger woman with fewer or smaller children; if her children are boys, she is considered superior to the mother of girls. And, of course, if her children are destined to perform or are already performing socially superior roles, her prestige is much higher than that of a woman whose children perform only inferior roles. This is obvious when she and her husband belong to a hereditarily higher class; but even within the same class, the superior individual achievements of a child of hers gives her greater prestige. For instance, a peasant mother whose son becomes a candidate for priesthood rises in prestige high above the other peasant mothers in the same community.

This right to recognition of personal worth is actively supported by her family circle, which counteracts all attempts to lower her prestige by insult, slander, malicious gossip, etc. The other rights of mothers are closely connected with her function. Her right to personal safety is obviously indispensable. Her home must be a safe place for herself and her children; and it is the task of men to protect it from physical and human dangers. Magico-religious safety may depend partly on her, if she has magical power, as in those communities where every home has a sacred fire, a center of positive mystical forces, and the women keep these fires going. But when a mother lacks this power, she has the right to be protected, either by some woman endowed with it or by men, if the men dominate, as in early Rome, where the *paterfamilias* protected his wife and children through the family gods.

We have already mentioned her economic rights: She must be

provided with all goods which can be obtained only by territorial activities which would interfere with her motherly functions. She has the right to have her authoritative judgments accepted by her children, and the right to have her orders obeyed by them, though this right decreases as the children grow up and usually stops rather early, so far as her sons are concerned. When necessary for the fulfilment of her functions, she has the right to cooperation from other women of her family circle and from her children and husband, though men are not expected to cooperate with her in specifically feminine activities. And she should receive sympathetic understanding from other women in her family circle, some affection from her husband, affection and gratitude from her children.

Her sexual rights in relations with her husband vary considerably. They are usually more important in matrilineal than in patrilineal families; in many of the latter, all she can require is enough sexual intercourse to make her pregnant. As a wife and mother, she should always conform with traditional patterns in social relations. But this is not so in the realm of technique. If we leave out those technical activities which are reserved for men, most of the material techniques in tribal and folk communities were *invented* by women. This applies to all preparations of food and clothes (including tanning and shoe making), producing domestic implements, making baskets and pottery, weaving rugs, hoeing and gardening, and domestication of small animals. The fact that most of those feminine inventions were later taken over and developed by men is easily explained. Their further development by new inventions required specialization, which was impossible for women because of the multiplicity of their duties as mothers and wives. We shall see later how in the course of history specific roles of women gradually evolved from their motherly roles.

3. The Emergence of Nonmaterial Roles of Women

In some tribal and early historical communities, we find certain women's roles which are different and set apart from family roles. The most important from the historical point of view were magico-religious roles. In earlier times, women were usually supposed to be endowed with special mystical traits, some of which were essential for the performance of their motherly functions. Procreation itself was often considered a manifestation of mystical power. The same power enabled a woman to promote the fecundity of plants; and this is why horticulture in most tribal communities was the exclusive task of women. Other traits, however, were unconnected with these functions.

Some women had mystical contacts with supernatural beings inaccessible to men. If these beings were beneficent, like many female goddesses, such women functioned as *priestesses* who brought blessings to the whole community. But women might be mystically connected with dangerous, if not evil, beings. For instance, women rather than men had contacts with the moon; and the moon was dangerous, for evil forces in general roamed at night. Therefore, a woman who derived her power from the moon was also dangerous. Obviously, so was a sorceress or witch who had relations with evil spirits.

This does not necessarily mean that such women always used their powers to harm people; they may have propitiated the dangerous deities for the protection of their people. This was what, for instance, a Siberian shamaness was supposed to do or a "wise woman" in a rural community. Even a witch could function both ways: harm some people and benefit others. However, it was difficult to combine such magico-religious roles with those of mother and wife. Therefore, most of the women who performed them were unmarried, childless, or already old; and their roles became increasingly specialized during early historical periods in the more developed societies—Aegean, Cretan, Babylonian, Etruscan, and Roman.

Less important were the roles of unmarried women who carried on sexual intercourse with several men consecutively. They were found in tribal communities where free premarital intercourse was allowed, even encouraged. Such was the cultural pattern of sexual relations in Tahiti and among the Masai and the Nandi. In Africa, among the latter the young men who functioned as warriors lived apart from the married men. Young women visited them regularly and each time sexual intercourse was carried on between partners who freely chose each other. Sooner or later, the relation between two partners usually became exclusive; and, if a girl became pregnant, the partner who presumably made her pregnant had to marry her.

However, long-lasting sexual roles of women which did not end in marriage evolved only later. Sometimes they were connected with religious roles. Thus, priestesses who represented sexual goddesses—e.g., Astarte—had intercourse with men who came to worship these goddesses. But usually they had no religious implications and were performed either by women who were discarded as unable to bear children or by "foreign" women who were considered unworthy of becoming the wives of native men. They differ greatly, though the differences are often ignored by righteous social thinkers. At one extreme are the ordinary prostitutes on a low cultural level, who sell their services at any time to any men without maintaining a lasting relation with them. At the other extreme are the so-called "courtesans," women on a higher cultural level, the temporary mistresses of men who contribute to their support, but whom they select and with whom they maintain mutually satisfactory hedonistic relations.

4. The Differentiation of Men's Roles in Tribal Communities

We have already discussed a man's role as the father of a family. Just like the mother's, the father's social circle has diminished in the course of time, and his functions have decreased. In any case, however, his role was never as inclusive or exacting as hers. Since he was not bound to care for his little children, as the mother did, he was free to spend a considerable part of his life in relations with other men. Men's associations, as compared with women's, were more active. Thence the growing power of the men, their domination over women, and the masculine claim to superiority.

In most, if not all, tribal communities we find six main categories of masculine activities outside the family circle: magico-religious, technical, economic, moral, military, and artistic. Though it was possible for the same man at different times to participate in several or even all of them, yet after activities of a certain kind became more complex and required specialized knowledge and skill, only men considered fully competent could regularly perform them, and they had the right to expect whatever cooperation was needed from those who lacked this competence. This is how functional specialization of the social roles of men seems to have originated.

Since there is not much reliable knowledge about the history of tribal communities, it is difficult to ascertain how specific roles evolved in any particular community. But when we compare many communities, we see that some show more functional specialization than others and that the activities which specialists perform are more developed and better integrated than those which do not require specialization. Consequently, we can hypothetically conclude that the functional specialization of masculine roles is not a primitive, universal characteristic of human communities, but a later historical product.

5. Magico-religious Roles of Men

In most tribal communities hitherto studied, nearly all the men after reaching a certain age acquired from the older men some magico-religious lore and skill which women could not share. This was usually manifested by periodical rites of initiation from which women were excluded.

This common magico-religious lore did not lead to any specialization among the men. Every man could use the lore and skill he learned for his own benefit and that of his family; he had the right to ask for the aid of other men whenever he needed it, and the duty to give aid whenever needed. In some communities, however, where considerable conflict occurred between clans and families, this magic was used as much to harm others as to aid them. Indeed, sometimes magic, especially secret magic, was the main or even the only way in which hostility was allowed to express itself.

Very different from these purely individual activities were the ceremonial activities cooperatively performed to protect the tribe against evil powers (especially enemy magicians) and to derive benefits from the good powers. These activities were considered so important that they had to be carried on under the guidance of competent men who functioned as organizers and leaders of the less competent men. Originally this function seems to have been performed by experienced old men who by virtue of age were presumed to have all the necessary wisdom. Such was typically the case in Australian tribes during the yearly ceremonial meetings. Even among the old men, however, because of differences between clans, some specialization existed. Members of each clan had special bonds with their own totemic ancestor, and only they could obtain the aid of this ancestor for the benefit of the tribe.

Another source of specialization in the magico-religious activities of men was due to mystical contacts between particular individuals and particular supernatural beings. Thus, as in the religion of some Amerindians, where there were many such beings, a young man could try to establish contact with one of them by spending time in isolation and waiting for a dream or vision, although not every man was successful. If successful, he gained the lifelong assistance of this being in performing some special activity—e.g., curing a certain kind of sickness, helping hunters find some species of wild game, leading travelers safely over dangerous areas, etc. In many other tribal communities, however, all important magico-religious functions were regularly performed only by a small minority of specialists. This was due to a combination of two factors: mystical individual superiority and superiority of knowledge acquired through education.

Thus, most Siberian tribes had shamans whose main function was protecting people, especially their life and health, from evil powers and gaining the help of good powers. A shaman was supposed to be inherently different from ordinary men and was endowed with unusual ability to get into connection with mystical powers. But in order to use this ability for the benefit of others, he had to learn from an older shaman his traditional magico-religious lore and skill—and this took years. Eventually the competent shamans within a tribal area took care to prevent inherently incapable or ignorant men, and especially evil sorcerers, from assuming the roles of shamans.

In some tribes, religious functions were monopolized not by individuals, but by associations. Exclusive magico-religious societies with secret lore developed. Membership in such a society was a privilege, sometimes inherited, sometimes acquired by gifts, but often attained only by passing special tests. Members were graded not merely by age, but by knowledge and sacredness which were not innate, but transmitted from the higher to the lower grades by special ritual. The upper-grade members of such associations exercised complete control over the magico-religious life of the community. Similar associations were sometimes formed in several neighboring tribes and kept some contact with one another.

The final stage of this evolution was the development of roles of *priests*. We find priestly roles in many small tribal communities, where their social circles are limited to the people of the community, and their functions are performed within these circles. But, as we shall see, these roles expanded and came to be performed in wider fields; and numerous social roles of great historical importance evolved from them. Nevertheless, such roles have retained certain basic characteristics which all of them have in common.

In the first place, the role of priest, unlike that of magician or sorcerer, is a public role. Everything a priest does is supposed to benefit not only individuals, but the community as a whole. This is obvious in all the public ceremonies in which he functions as leader. Even his duties toward individual members of the community—their protection from evil powers, their authoritative religious and moral guidance, the repression or prevention of impurity and sin—are also duties toward the community. For a magically pure, religiously pious, morally righteous individual is a benefit to the community, while a magically impure, sinful, criminal individual is a danger to his community.

In the second place, only priests, not laymen, judge who is fit for the role of priest. To be recognized as fit, a candidate for the priesthood must pass through a rather long period of education by priests. In the third place, only priests, not laymen, are competent to decide what the duties of priests are.

As to the rights of the priest, they are related to his duties and therefore also indirectly determined by priests. According to the norms which priests consider binding for laymen, a priest should be granted by laymen all those rights without which he could not adequately perform his sacred functions.

6. The Technical Functions of Men

The technical activities of men outside the home differ widely in different tribal communities. Some of them can be performed by individuals alone, with the occasional aid of other individuals, when needed. But some always require the cooperation of several men—e.g., hunting big game, deep-sea fishing, clearing forested areas for gardens or agriculture, irrigation, large-scale cattle raising, construction of large buildings, especially the men's ceremonial houses. Even though every adult man participates occasionally in all kinds of technical activities which other tribesmen perform, yet there is usually some degree of specialization, at least in leadership. The men who possess any superior skill acquired by learning regularly function as leaders.

Sometimes men supposed to be endowed with special magical lore are entrusted with the production of objects which must have certain magical characteristics. Thus, building a boat may require not only technical skill, but the use of magic to make the boat safe. Producing hunting implements or military weapons also often needs magic in order to make them effective. And such magical lore is usually monopolized by certain technicians and transmitted to their selected disciples or descendants.

However, the development of technical specialization is generally connected with the growth of economic exchange, for exchange implies that various technicians produce more than they need of certain goods so as to obtain in exchange goods which they do not produce. Therefore, although specialization has developed fully only in cities as commercial and industrial centers, some economic exchange is already found in most tribal communities.

7. ECONOMIC FUNCTIONS IN TRIBAL COMMUNITIES

In surveying social relations between men connected by kinship bonds, we noticed that their mutual duties include offering and receiving gifts and services. According to some cultural anthropologists and sociologists, offering gifts is the primary source of exchange in general as the essential economic activity; for the receiver of a gift is expected to reciprocate by offering a gift to the original giver, and eventually the principle of equivalence of gifts given and gifts received is established. But gifts can be exchanged not only for gifts, but for active services; and, moreover, services can be exchanged for services. In many communities certain men function as organizers and leaders of these types of exchange. For instance, in some Northwestern Indian tribes which anthropologists have investigated, the head of a clan collects from time to time contributions from all members of his clan and arranges a ceremonial meeting during which these contributions will be offered as gifts to members of the other clans. This has been called "potlatch." Sooner or later, the head of every other clan arranges a similar meeting and offers gifts to members of other clans. The more numerous and valuable the gifts offered, as compared with those received, the higher the prestige of the head of the clan and of the clan as a whole.

More general and important have been the functions of men who control material property from which goods satisfying human needs are derived—areas with wild game and useful plants, pastures and cattle, cultivated land—and who regulate the technical activities producing these goods, as well as the distribution of products among the producers. Such is the old economic function of the father of a patrilineal family who has supreme control over the family property. It is he who decides what every family member, including himself, should do and what values every family member, including himself, should receive for his own benefit. However, this economic function is dependent upon the social function of the father, who is supposed to evaluate positively the other family members and recognize their personal rights.

No such dependence is found in the economic functions of masters over their slaves. A master has not only supreme possessive rights over the property on which his slaves work, but an unlimited right to control the lives of the slaves. Slavery did not exist in all tribal communities. It originated in aggressive warfare. Slaves were at first prisoners of war who were spared and put to work, and their descendants were also slaves. Eventually, slaves were imported from other communities by trade. But, in any case, slaves as foreigners or descendants of foreigners originally had no rights whatsoever within the community. It was the master who protected them from human and mystical dangers and made it possible for them to survive by working on his property. If they were valuable to him only for economic purposes, he could use them continually for such purposes. He could compel them to perform productive activities exclusively for his own personal benefit or the benefit of his family, and had absolute control over their products; it depended on him how much or how little share in these products he awarded to them for their services. Of course, it was to his advantage to give them enough to keep them alive and active.

Nevertheless, in most communities masters did assume voluntarily certain social duties toward their slaves, especially hereditary and domestic slaves who became valuable to them not only as economic chattels, but as participants in personal relations. This began in some tribal communities and continued in more complex societies—e.g., in Greece and Rome.

A different kind of economic function evolved from intertribal trade, i.e., exchange of products with inhabitants of foreign communities. This was naturally slow in developing, because of the general mistrust of "foreigners." Even when the people of a community needed foreign products, they often tried to avoid direct contacts with the people who produced them by using the curious method called "silent trade." Two tribal groups periodically brought the products which they wanted to exchange to the borders of a "no-man's-land" sufficiently distant to prevent any personal contacts. One group took its products to the middle of this no-man's-land, left them, and moved back. Then the other group brought its products to the same place, inspected the goods already there, left goods which it considered their equivalent, and moved back. Then the first side moved in again, inspected the goods the second had left, and if they seemed less valuable than its own, took some of its own back. The others then moved in, perhaps added more goods, and waited for the first ones to return what they had taken away or else take some of its goods away. This primitive form of bargaining continued until one group took the other's goods and left its own.

In most tribal communities, however, foreigners who brought goods for exchange were admitted, but only after some bonds were established between them and the natives. For instance, they offered some gifts not for trade and were invited to share food; this created a magical connection between them. Or, as in the case of the Trobriand Islanders who periodically carried their products by boats to inhabitants of other islands and exchanged them for the products of the latter, trade with considerable bargaining was preceded by giving and receiving ornaments for decoration which were practically useless but endowed their bearers with personal prestige, such as necklaces and bracelets.

Eventually, if an individual with some experience in bargaining and means of transporting goods established lasting personal bonds with influential foreigners and gained their confidence, he could repeatedly function as a traveling trader who with his assistants carried abroad the products of his fellow tribesmen and brought back foreign products. The role of traveling tradesman differs from the role of a *merchant* who lives among his own people, buys and exports their products abroad, imports and sells to them foreign products. It differs also from the role of a merchant who settles in a foreign country, exports its products to his own country and sells them there, imports products of his own country and sells them to the foreign people. In either case, the merchant's role requires the use of money and is therefore a later result of social evolution.

8. MORAL FUNCTIONS

What term should we use to denote the activities performed by some men in tribal communities which are usually called "political"? The term *political* is derived from *polis*, which means city. But the functions which we have in mind were performed long before cities appeared and are still performed in most tribal and rural communities which have no urban centers. Another possible term is *legal*; but the word *law* usually means a norm sanctioned by a state or at least by some organized group, whereas not all the norms with which participants in a community are supposed to conform are subjected to such sanctions.

The word *moral* has the same root as mores and originally meant simply that which conforms with the *mores* of a community. Although in popular use it has an evaluative connotation (moral is supposed to be good, immoral to be bad), yet sociologists can use it, just as they use the term *mores*, without such connotations. Thus, what we call the moral function performed within a tribe consists in maintaining the mores of the tribal community, mostly by preventing or settling conflicts arising out of transgression of the norms which regulate social interaction between community members. While conflicts between individual partners in lasting social relations, especially progenitors and descendants and kin of the same generation, are mostly prevented or counteracted by the integration of such relations into social roles, this does not solve the problem of conflicts between people who are not connected by such bonds—e.g., members of different families or clans, inhabitants of separate local settlements. Such conflicts can be very disturbing to the tribal community, particularly when solidarity within a family, clan, camp, or village is strong, and each group sides with its own members against outsiders; for then interindividual conflict leads to intergroup conflict.

In most tribal communities the solution of such conflicts is entrusted to individuals endowed with high authority, whose judgments are supposed to be accepted by all loyal community members. These individuals recognize the basic principle that tribal solidarity should take precedence over the solidarity of any group within the tribe, be it a genetic group, like a family or a clan, or a local group, and that consequently a way must be found to reconcile conflicting claims of such groups which arise out of conflicts between their members. There are different ways of solving such conflicts in different communities; but all of them have something in common. If a member of one group has transgressed a social norm and harmed a member of another group—killed or injured him by evil magic, stolen or destroyed his possessions, had sexual intercourse with his wife, etc.—his group must compensate the other group for this harm.

The individual whose function it is to decide what should be done in such a situation is usually a chief of the tribe; but he does not function alone. He has an inner circle, mostly composed of heads of the various groups which are included in the tribe: heads of clans, of large patrilineal families, or local groups. He may be merely the leader of this selected circle, which agrees to accept his decision. Or, on the other hand, he may also perform an important magico-religious role; if so, this obviously enhances his authority. But in no case does this function of his imply that he can use force to have his decisions accepted and applied. Indeed, in quite a few tribes an explicit distinction is made between the role of a "peace chief" and the role of a "war chief."

This moral function of the chief and other leading members of a tribe is not necessarily limited to preventing and counteracting conflicts within the tribe. They may also employ positive means for promoting tribal solidarity by stimulating cooperation between families, clans, or local groups.

9. Roles of Warriors

Before surveying warfare on the tribal level, let us recall to mind the fact that war is not a universal phenomenon. As Malinowski said: "War is not an essential heritage of man . . . cannot be related to biological needs or immutable psychological impulses." There is no "instinct of pugnacity," as some social philosophers (e.g., Hobbes) and later social Darwinists believed.

To avoid confusion, we should distinguish between *war* and mere physical *fighting*. War is culturally patterned. Interindividual fighting in defense of various personal values sporadically occurs between children as well as between adults; but it is usually repressed or limited by the customs and mores. Individual physical rebellion against social groups is always repressed. Sporadic fighting between smaller groups within larger groups—e.g., families, clans, or local groups within a tribe—is negatively valued by the larger group, which tends to prevent or counteract it. And many tribal communities are purposely isolated from their neighbors so as to prevent fighting. When a tribe migrates and enters another area which is occupied by a different tribe, mass fighting usually occurs, but does not follow definite standards and norms.

War in the sense of purposeful struggle between groups always implies the existence of social roles of warriors. Every warrior has a social circle which considers him a valuable person because of the function which he performs. His function is usually performed in cooperation with other warriors and may be more or less important as compared with theirs. This function is violent struggle intended to end in victory over an enemy. Victory is the final proof of its successful performance and raises his prestige, while defeat lowers it. Since victory is supposed to benefit his own circle, it is his duty to do his best to achieve it, and he has the right to expect whatever help he needs for its achievement. These are the similar characteristics of all warriors' roles; the differences will become obvious when we survey the roles of warriors in tribal communities and compare them with those in more complex, urbanized societies.

The most general type of intertribal warfare consists in entering foreign territories, avoiding or overcoming resistance, and bringing back trophies and other proofs of bravery. This type is carried on mostly by young men, sometimes individually, more often in small groups. The achievements of such young men were of benefit primarily to their family circles.

Such was, for instance, the headhunting which was regularly

carried on in many tribal communities, from the Dyaks in Borneo to the Joruba Indians in Brazil. The head of an enemy was considered the most valuable trophy because it had a magico-religious significance: its possession gave not only prestige, but mystical power to the warrior who obtained it and his family. Its worth depended on the sex and age of the individual from whom it was taken: a child's head was the least valuable, a man's head more valuable than a woman's, and the head of a prominent man the most valuable. When a young warrior brought home such a trophy, it proved his maturity and superiority; he gained the admiration of the girls and was now free to marry. Sometimes the headhunting was carried on in groups. A curious cooperation developed between the Dyaks and the Malay pirates who invaded the shores of Borneo. The Dyaks wanted heads for prestige, the pirates economic gains only; thus, they could join together without any competition between them.

We have already mentioned the raids of Masai and Nandi warriors upon their neighbors in Africa. They were carried on exclusively by young men, but chiefly for cattle, which was divided between their families. It was not the economic value of the cattle that mattered most to them; it was victory at the risk of their lives in spite of the resistance of the original owners. The cattle represented mainly a trophy, proof of victory. Every young man who contributed to this victory manifested bravery in the struggle against the enemies and thereby gained prestige for himself and his family, as well as admiration from the girls. Only after participation in a victorious raid could he marry and cease to function as a warrior.

In intertribal warfare among the Amerindians, the warriors were also mostly young men, though usually under the guidance of an older, more experienced leader. They did not hunt heads; although in many tribes scalps were valuable trophies, personal prestige was most important. Thus, among the Plains Indians, warriors raided foreign territories and seized such valuable domestic animals as horses; but horses, and also human prisoners, were prestige-giving trophies. During an intertribal battle, the highest prestige was gained by a "coup," i.e., approaching an enemy and touching him at the risk of one's life. Indeed, sometimes when the warriors of one tribe lacked adequate military weapons, warriors of the other tribe waited until they obtained their weapons or even gave them some. As Goldenweiser has said: "These persistent warlike activities, which meant so much to the ego of a Plains brave, and to the vanity of his bride or spouse, cannot really be compared with modern wars. . . . They should rather be envisaged as ceremonial byplay." We might call it "sportive warfare."

Such warfare was perhaps most fully developed among Arabian tribes before Islam resulted in their unification. It was subjected to standards and norms which became the main source of what later was called "chivalry." This included respect for brave enemies who, if defeated or disabled, were offered hospitality with honor. In general, intertribal wars were not destructive wars, but rather struggles for prestige, and the standards and norms applied to them included also romantic respect for women. There is a story about a tribal village which was surrounded by enemies and saved by four women who went out and stood on the four sides of the village. The enemies could not attack them and moved away. Some of this sportive, chivalrous warfare survived in the struggles between medieval knights; but by that time, with the development of feudalism, war had acquired an entirely different significance.

The social roles of tribal warriors mentioned above did not require any specialization, obviously not when performed mostly or even exclusively by young men. And they were not public roles like those of leaders in magico-religious ceremonies, priests, or peace chiefs. They were not intended to benefit the tribal community as a whole, only the warriors themselves and their family circles, even though the prestige they gained as victors raised the prestige of the tribe. As a matter of fact, their military activities were entirely separated from their peacetime participation in the tribal community; indeed, in some communities after they returned from a raid, they could not rejoin the tribe until they had undergone a magico-religious purification.

Most significant from the point of view of later developments was the solidarity of warriors as they became organized into groups. Such organization required effective leadership; and as the groups grew, the social roles of their leaders became increasingly important. While warfare was going on, every warrior owed loyalty to every fellow warrior, especially to the leader, who also had the supreme duty to be loyal to all of them. Every one had the right to have his bravery recognized, but the leader of a victorious group got the most prestige. If they took valuable prey, everybody had the right to share it; but the rights were unequal, depending on their respective contributions, and the leader had greater rights than his followers. Naturally, since the very existence of such a group of tribal warriors depended on the tribe to which its members belonged, their mutual loyalty was subordinated to their common tribal loyalty.

When, in contrast to these roles of tribal warriors which were not permanently specialized, we investigate the warriors' roles which required lasting specialization, we find two very different types of the latter.

On the one hand, in many areas during certain periods there were organized groups of specialists in warfare who did not belong to any larger society and owed no lasting loyalty to anybody but their own group. They were predatory warriors who lived mostly on their prey, e.g., German war leaders with their followers during Caesar's time and later, medieval "robber barons, and Chinese private war lords. Well known were the pirates in the Mediterranean and later in the China and Malayan and Indian seas. More important from the historical point of view were the mercenaries, special organized groups of warriors detached from their own societies and serving anybody who hired them, living partly on their regular pay, partly on loot. Their functions in classical antiquity have been described by famous historians, especially Polybius. In modern times, the roles of the Italian "condottieri," as leaders of military groups hired by Italian cities, are the best known, though many mercenary troops in other parts of Europe served state rulers temporarily for pay, particularly during the sixteenth and seventeenth centuries.

When warriors began to function regularly as the builders and guardians of *states*, their roles became public roles. We know that states grew by the gradual integration of several tribal communities inhabiting a certain territory and their subjection to centralized rule. A historical survey of the formation and continued existence of states shows that, with a few minor exceptions, such a unification was achieved under the supreme authority of *kings*. Therefore, we must investigate their functions in order to understand the evolution of social roles beyond the tribal level.

10. AESTHETICALLY PATTERNED FUNCTIONS

In all nonliterate communities some men—and also some women—perform various kinds of activities which follow definite aesthetic standards and norms.

The best known are activities producing works of plastic and decorative art. Many of these works produced in a distant past have been discovered by archeologists—e.g., the famous representations of animals in the caves of the Cro-Magnons, probably the oldest of all. Numerous sculptures, artistically shaped instruments and tools, decorated pottery, mostly made by women, rugs (also made by women), and the decorations on buildings and tombs have been collected and preserved. Moreover, anthropologists and folklorists have observed many contemporary activities producing such works, and this has helped them reconstruct similar activities performed in the past.

Other kinds of aesthetically patterned activities found in many nonliterate communities include songs, individual and collective, and some instrumental music, usually very simple, consisting mainly in rhythmic drumming. Dancing is also widely spread and sometimes well regulated. Thus, during collective sun dances in some Indian tribes the dancers specialize in certain movements, and all of these movements are harmoniously integrated. In some communities dramas are enacted on ceremonial occasions. Telling stories is almost universal and it is supposed to follow recognized standards and norms.

In surveying comparatively these activities, we find a significant distinction. Most of them were, and in some tribes still are, inseparably connected with magico-religious functions; in other words, they are sacred. The plastic art of cavemen had a magico-religious influence, as did sculptures representing mythical beings. Decorating buildings and making instruments, rugs, and clothes to be used during religious ceremonies were also activities endowed with some degree of sacredness. The sun dances are sacred; so are many tribal songs and most dramas. Transmitting orally to the younger generation culturally standardized mythical stories, whether in verse or in prose, is necessary to perpetuate religious beliefs. In order to perform such important functions, considerable training and ability were required, and usually only a few individuals had enough time and energy to devote to their effective performance.

By contrast, purely secular activities did not need any special, superior ability. Decorating objects to be used only for practical purposes in everyday life was one of the numerous tasks almost every adult woman performed. Many dances and songs were mere play—often sexual play—without any magico-religious meaning. Men in their leisure time frequently indulged in telling stories, fictitious or semifictitious, purely for amusement. In the course of time all these secular activities increased in importance, while the sacred activities gradually decreased.

11. How to Study the Historical Evolution of Social Roles

As we have seen, in tribal communities men's roles were more differentiated functionally than women's roles. The emergence of new varieties of social roles above the tribal level was primarily due to the further functional differentiation of men's roles; the differentiation of women's roles occurred later and was much more limited. Consequently, in the following chapters we shall concentrate on the history of men's roles and then devote a special chapter to the history of women's roles. Later we shall survey the evolution of roles of children and adolescents, which are obviously dependent upon the evolution of roles of adults.

CHAPTER 16

THE SOCIAL ROLES OF KINGS

1. KINGS AS RULERS OF STATES

The most important historical trend on which the evolution of social roles above the level of tribal and rural communities depended was the integration of communities into *states*. Almost everywhere such integration was preceded, accompanied, or followed by the emergence of the social roles of persons who acted as rulers of all the people inhabiting the territory of a particular state.

Here are some well-known examples of such rulers found in various cultural areas and in various historical periods: the pharaohs of Egypt; the kings of Babylonia, of Assyria, of Persia, of Judea, of early Rome, of Sparta, of Macedonia; the heads of Hellenic states; Roman emperors; later Byzantine emperors in the East; Holy Roman emperors in the West; kings of England, of France, of Spain, of Bohemia, of Poland, of Denmark, of Sweden, of Norway, of the Netherlands, of Belgium, of Saxony, of Bavaria, of Prussia, of Italy; Dukes of Burgundy; Grand-dukes of Hessen-Darmstadt; emperors of Austria; tsars of Russia; emperors of China; mikados of Japan; maharajas of separate states within India; Dalai-Lamas of Tibet; kings of Siam; Moslem sultans; the Incas of Peru; kings of the Aztecs, of Dahomey, of the Zulus.

The roles of these rulers differed in many respects, depending particularly on the size of the states over which they ruled (compare, e.g., Sparta or Judea with nineteenth-century China or Russia) and on the degree of their sovereignty (compare, e.g., the sovereign rulers of France or England in the seventeenth century with the rulers of the German kingdoms or dukedoms which were subjected to some domination of the emperors of Germany at the end of the nineteenth and the beginning of the twentieth century. Nevertheless, when we compare the roles of these rulers, we shall find enough similarity to apply the same general terms to them. We may consider them all as "kings," since this is the most widely used term for such roles.

Our problem then is: What are the main functions which kings perform? And here we notice considerable disagreement among the investigators who have developed general theories based on comparative historical studies. According to some of them, the fundamental, original function of all kings was religious, rooted in their superior sacredness. This function was, indeed, of primary significance in many kingdoms during those periods when magico-religious beliefs dominated all kinds of culturally patterned activities. But with the growing secularization of social life and culture, it lost much of its influence, though it did not completely disappear, since organized priesthoods supported kings who sponsored religious cultus. Compare, for instance, the roles of pharaohs, kings of Babylonia, or mikados with the roles of eighteenth-century European kings.

Other investigators ascribe primary importance to the function of kings as war leaders, since states usually grow by military conquest. No doubt, many kings functioned as conquerors, e.g., the kings of Assyria, of Persia, Alexander of Macedonia and his followers, tsars of Russia. On the other hand, conquering war leaders and their heirs often became kings, e.g., the leaders of Teutonic and later Scandinavian invaders, Saracen conquerors, Ghengis Khan and his successors.

But conquest alone was not sufficient to integrate communities into states, certainly not if the conquerors destroyed the conquered communities, as most Assyrian conquerors did during the period of their aggressive expansion and later some Tartar invaders, especially Tamerlane; or if they expelled the original inhabitants from the invaded area. The permanent integration of conquered countries could be achieved only if after conquest some lasting cooperation between the conquering and the conquered peoples developed and they began to share common cultural values, especially religious beliefs and rites. This was, for instance, how England became gradually united after the Norman conquest, and how various Western Slavic communities became integrated into long-lasting states—Bohemia and Poland.

Such permanent integration implies that the conquering war leader or his successors assumed the task of keeping peace and order among his subjects and was recognized by them as endowed with the supreme moral authority needed for this task. The history of the Roman conquests illustrates this very well. The roles of the early Roman kings disappeared because they were unable to maintain inner unity within the kingdom, and their functions became divided among religious, military, and political leaders. Gradually, powerful military conquerors assumed the roles of rulers and imposed their power upon the political functionaries. After many struggles between them, the victors were accepted as lifelong rulers, "imperators," guardians of the "Roman peace," and finally with the support of the priesthood were proclaimed divine.

Maintaining peace and order within a state has been considered an essential function of all rulers by political and legal thinkers from Plato and Aristotle to this day. Undoubtedly, no state can exist without such order. But the function of maintaining it can be and has been effectively performed also by republican governments, though republican states evolved much later than royal states. Moreover, throughout history many republics either became incorporated into kingdoms or changed back into kingdoms. For instance, Greek republics were absorbed into the Kingdom of Macedonia; the Roman Republic changed into an empire; France in the course of eighty years changed from a republic to an empire, from empire to kingdom, from kingdom to republic, then to empire, again to republic. Germany installed a republican government for the first time after World War I, and fifteen years later a dictatorship was substituted for it; the Union of Soviet Socialist Republics which took the place of the tsarists' empire soon became a dictatorial empire; the Spanish Republic which was substituted for the kingdom changed into a dictatorship after a few years. It seems, therefore, that it was and sometimes still is easier to maintain social unity and order within a kingdom than within a republic. Why?

Probably because of the age-old attitude of the masses of people which predominates when they no longer live in self-sufficient, isolated communities, but in wider, more complex, and changing environments. They wanted—and often still want—not only transcendental gods on whom their whole lives ultimately depended, but also benevolent, wise, powerful human individuals whom they could identify personally and on whose help and guidance in important matters they could rely. To them, a king, emperor, or dictator was much more than the political head of the government: he was protector and promoter of the most important cultural values which all his subjects shared. He was also the military defender of his people against foreign enemies, capable not only of expelling hostile invaders, but of preventing invasions—most effectively by attacking enemies on their own territories and subjecting them to his control.

Of course, if he failed to perform these important tasks, he was considered unworthy of being king, and somebody else had to assume this role, as often occurred in early religious kingdoms—in China, where the failure of an imperial dynasty resulted in the formation of a new dynasty, and in France, where the inactive Merovingian kings ceased to be kings and were superseded by Charles the Great and his successors.

Thus, a comparison of the roles of kings at various periods and in various areas indicates that they include more or less different combinations of the three main functions mentioned above: *religious, military,* and *political.* Let us survey briefly how each of these functions was performed.

2. THE RELIGIOUS FUNCTION OF KINGS

The religious function of a king as ruler of a state, at least in early periods, was analogous to that of a priest in a tribal community. The obvious difference was that, since a kingdom included several communities, sometimes with different religions, a king had to have a much greater mystical power than a mere tribal priest.

Consequently, the source from which he derived his sacredness was either a god superior to all tribal gods or several gods who controlled various sections of the kingdom.

We find diverse conceptions of the sacredness of kings. Some kings were temporary incarnations of a god who had left his body when he became incapable of performing his function and entered other bodies. Some kings were descendants of gods—typically the mikados. Others were directly endowed by gods with the divine essence, which they transmitted to their heirs. This essence might be inherited on the female as well as on the male side, e.g., in Egypt; consequently, not only kings, but queens, i.e., daughters or mothers of kings, could be divine. Some kings were sacred priests, mystically connected with gods and carrying on their religious cultus. When there were women priestesses, the high priestess was also sacred and might be a queen. Most kings were chosen by gods as their representatives on earth, e.g., the Hittite kings, kings of Babylonia, of Assyria, of Persia, and emperors of China. They were endowed by gods with authority and entrusted with the task of organizing the cultus of the gods and making men act in accordance with the divine will. A few kings, especially certain Roman emperors, proclaimed themselves gods in their own right, though even they usually assumed that they were granted mystical power by the gods and transmitted it to their successors. With the development of organized churches and their expansion beyond the limits of particular kingdoms, kings, sometimes also queens, became consecrated by the priesthood and presumably gained the divine favor, provided they functioned in conformity with divine standards and norms, as formulated by theologians.

But, whatever the source and degree of his divinely derived power, the king was supposed to use it for the benefit of his people. If he had direct magico-religious control over nature, it was his task to influence natural phenomena in such a way as to preserve and promote the welfare of his subjects. Even in more developed religions, when the control of nature was vested entirely in gods, it was the king's function to obtain the help of gods on behalf of his people.

Another religious duty of his was the protection of his subjects against the mystical evil powers inherent in the natural environment and against the human magicians who tried to harm them. This duty was especially important in times of warfare. Some kings, especially in early periods, could not actively participate in warfare, for this would have profaned their sacredness; they either accepted or selected secular war leaders. What they actively did was to bring magico-religious protection and aid to the warriors of their own state and to counteract all attempts of hostile priests or magicians to make their own warriors secure and dangerous to their enemies.

Obviously, however, no king could perform his magico-religious function alone; he needed the continual help of an inner circle of priests—the more so, the larger the territory of his kingdom and the more numerous its population. We find, therefore, in every well-developed royal state a ceremonial mass cultus carried on by a group of priests in the religious center where the king presided and in several scattered centers, even without the presence of the king, for the explicit purpose of benefiting the kingdom as a whole.

Natural catastrophes had to be prevented or stopped, not by the king alone but also by collective appeals of the priests and the people for divine protection. In kingdoms where agriculture prevailed—as it did in most of them—seasonal collective ceremonies were intended to help the king persuade the gods to use their power over nature to promote the growth of plants and animals throughout the kingdom. Inasmuch as one of the oldest tasks of shamans and priests was to cure the sick, priests continued to perform this task in every section of the kingdom with some support from the king. Though the king was supposed to gain divine protection for his warriors, religious rites with the aid of priests were also considered necessary to insure the divine help in both defensive and aggressive warfare. Furthermore, the cooperation of priests was also necessary to achieve religious unification of the people, inasmuch as the communities within a kingdom often had their own tribal or local deities with somewhat different religions. Consequently, as kingdoms grew, the roles of priests (sometimes also those of priestesses) became increasingly complex and differentiated. Eventually new social roles evolved from them in an important evolutionary trend which we shall discuss in the next chapter.

3. THE MILITARY FUNCTION OF THE KING

As we have seen, in order to perform his *religious* function the king needed the cooperation of a circle of priests; the masses of his subjects believed that priests were indispensable as mediators between them and powerful gods, and consequently followed their guidance voluntarily. Where the king's military function was concerned, he needed not only the cooperation of a circle of leaders, "commanders," but also that of a relatively large organized group of warriors. To be a warrior required considerable training and a willingness to risk death, physical suffering, or imprisonment; consequently, warriors had to have some compensation for the dangerous duties which they undertook. It was not so necessary when they merely defended their own tribal or rural community against foreign invasion; for, as we have already seen, it was one of the essential duties of all men to defend their women and children. But when they had to defend the whole kingdom, with most of whose population they had few personal relations, or when they carried on aggressive warfare and invaded foreign territories, they had to be granted definite rights in remuneration for their duties.

Prestige granted as recognition of bravery was the most general of these rights. We noticed it in Amerindian communities with long-lasting mutual conflicts and in pre-Islam Arab communities, where the ideal of the chivalrous warrior emerged. When the warriors became a hereditary class, they gained considerable prestige, e.g., the medieval European knights, the Samurai in Japan, and the Kshatriyas in India. There was usually a gradation of prestige from upper nobles, immediate assistants of the king, down to minor nobles, especially in feudal times. Even when the hereditary warrior class was not numerous enough to defend the kingdom or to conquer foreign countries and had to be supplemented by warriors recruited from the lower classes, prestige was still granted them; we have already mentioned the decorations which modern kings give to warriors as rewards for distinguished service.

It is well known, however, that prestige alone is not enough to induce royal subjects to act as warriors. *Economic* rights had also to be granted, such as the feudal rights of the hereditary nobility to land and to economic services from the people who cultivated the land. The king as supreme ruler, "suzerain," was supposed to own all the land within his realm, but he delegated the ownership of sections of this land to his "vassals" under the condition that they be always ready to cooperate with him as warriors when such cooperation was needed. Whenever a foreign country was conquered and permanently incorporated into the kingdom, the conquering military leaders, especially those who settled in the foreign territory, were often granted economic mastery over the inhabitants of certain parts of this territory, provided they remained royal vassals.

Even when the king with the help of military assistants recruited warriors from the masses of his subjects, they had to be economically supported so as to be adequately trained and able to perform effectively the functions required of them in wartime. If they invaded a foreign territory, they were usually allowed to appropriate by force some goods owned by the inhabitants of this territory, just as tribal warriors did when they invaded the areas of other tribes. However, in the course of history quite a few rulers, in addition to or instead of recruiting their own subjects, hired groups of well-trained warriors of foreign origin who specialized in warfare as a permanent occupation and served any ruler who offered them adequate remuneration. These were called "mercenaries." Some pharaohs used mercenaries of Greek origin; so did Cyrus, who struggled against his brother Artaxerxes Mnemon for the throne of Persia. Xenophon, an officer in Cyrus' army, described its function in his famous book *Anabasis*. Several Roman emperors hired Teutonic warriors. Rulers of Italian city-states, when struggling against each other in the fifteenth and sixteenth centuries, hired groups of warriors under the competent leadership of so-called *condottieri*; since little hostility existed between members of these groups, they developed military tactics which enabled one group to win victory over another at little cost to human lives. Likewise, rulers of the German states involved in the Thirty Years' War used groups of military specialists, and the kings of Poland used foreign mercenaries in repressing rebellions of the Ukrainians and the Cossacks.

4. THE POLITICAL FUNCTION OF THE KING

The function of maintaining social order among his subjects in times of peace is an extension of the moral function of peace chief within a tribe. The king can do it effectively because, in addition to the moral authority rooted in his sacredness, he has the power of physical coercion as war lord.

His oldest and primary duty is to protect his subjects from the harmful actions of other subjects. This prevents violent struggles not only between individuals but between clans and villages and even tribes. Such struggles originate when the group to which an injured individual belongs takes cooperative revenge upon the offender and his group. It is therefore the king's self-assumed task to pursue the offender: "Vengeance is mine" says not only the Lord-God, but also the human lord. Doing harm to a subject of the king is a crime, an offence not only against the individual who is harmed, but against the sovereign authority of the king. Consequently, in most royal states kings function as supreme judges of criminals or delegate this task to subordinate judges. Of course, the underlying idea is that punishment of the criminals prevents further crimes.

This protection of subjects from harm has been extended by kings to travelers within the territory of their kingdoms. A king's subject from one community, entering the area of another community, was supposed to be safe; so was a foreign traveler, if the king or his delegate permitted him to enter the territory of the kingdom. On the other hand, inhabitants of the kingdom had to be protected from dangerous strangers. Therefore, a foreigner was admitted and protected only if considered to be a valuable person. This dual duty of protection resulted in the complete control of travelers by rulers, exemplified in the permits granted to travelers who are recommended by competent natives. This control has culminated in our modern passports, issued to subjects who intend to travel in foreign countries. In many kingdoms the protection of travelers was limited to roads, resting places, and special urban centers. "Trespassing" in other places was strictly prohibited.

Usually, however, kings did not limit themselves to protection of their subjects from the injurious actions of others. They also used their authority and power to enforce the active performances of duties in social relations, when the nonperformance of his duty by one partner was considered harmful to the other. Thus, rulers compelled sons who neglected duties toward their parents to perform those duties (as, e.g., in Babylonia, Judea, and Rome). Later they used compulsory sanctions to make wives perform duties toward husbands, husbands toward wives, and parents toward children, and to force partners in land ownership to cooperate with each other. Historically, the most important use of the king's authority and power to enforce the performance of duties was the support of contractual agreements. This is how *civil law*, as distinct from *criminal law*, evolved.

Manifestly, it was impossible for the king alone to carry on the functions of criminal and civil judge: he had to delegate them to subordinate judges, although he often remained the supreme judge to whom his subjects could appeal if the decisions of minor judges seemed wrong.

The king had to face other difficulties in performing these functions. As in the course of territorial expansion a kingdom gradually came to include a number of communities with different cultures and different patterns of social relations, the king sometimes found that the kind of protection he gave to his subjects was not what some particular communities wanted. His punishment of community members who injured members of other communities often disagreed with the age-old pattern according to which foreigners were treated as dangerous enemies. And when rulers prohibited witch-hunting and considered those who killed witches as criminals, this seemed to be protecting witches, instead of the victims of the witches. When a king enforced the performance of certain duties, these duties were often not regarded as binding by his subjects in various local communities. For instance, supporting creditors against debtors was sometimes considered unjust, especially when the creditors were strangers and the debtors local people. Compulsory regulation of relations based upon the ownership of land often conflicted with the traditional mores, since in various communities the rights of owners differed; thus, we find community ownership, family ownership, and individual ownership, and each kind might be exclusive or shared. The ruler's regulations concerning family relations (parent and child or husband and wife) do not always agree with the traditional patterns of such relations.

Consequently, we notice a growing trend toward superimposing standards and norms upon the same types of social relations throughout the territory under the king's control, thus eliminating differences between communities. In other words, kings increasingly functioned as *legislators*, either explicitly formulating legal norms applicable to social relations of a certain kind in all communities or giving juridical decisions in particular cases which were supposed to be models to be followed by the judges in all communities. The universal principle underlying these rules and decisions was that the king, being free from prejudice, independent of the personal ties which connected every subject of his with the other participants of the community in which he lived, and not bound by any particular local customs, could dispense impartial *justice*. Moreover, he either was himself a bearer of superior wisdom, originally derived from the gods, or was assisted by bearers of wisdom, originally priests, later secular thinkers. Consequently, he knew better than his subjects what was good for them.

Still, he tried to avoid radical conflicts between the new legal order and the traditional social order, with the help of assistants who were acquainted with the customs and mores in the various regions of the kingdom. If we survey the legal Code of Hammurabi, the first royal code ever put into writing, we find that it included a relatively limited number of laws, probably only those which did not conflict with the mores. Historically the most important and extensive legal system was that of the Roman law, which extended throughout the Roman Empire and introduced essential uniformity into the specific social relations of various peoples with widely different cultures, and yet left many regional customs and mores untouched. The reintroduction of Roman law by the monarchical states of continental Europe, as feudalism weakened, superimposed a growing uniformity upon the vast diversity of local and regional customs and mores; a similar result was achieved in England by the juridical uniformity of the "common law." New legislation imposed during the nineteenth century—the Napoleonic Code in France, Austria, Russia, and especially the Prussian legislation— carried this uniformity further than ever before. Obviously, the factual application of these legal systems required the active cooperation of many officials.

Another important task of the king was to promote economic unity and collaboration within his kingdom. It supplemented or supplanted his early mystical function of controlling nature on behalf of his subjects. Thus, in Egypt and Mesopotamia, where inundation was needed for agricultural production, the king through his assistants controlled it, especially when it required cooperation between communities. He often sponsored craftsmanship, trade, and the exchange of different goods produced in particular sectons of his kingdom, as well as the importation of products from other kingdoms in exchange for products of his own kingdom. These functions were also largely delegated to assistants. Finally, in a large kingdom efficient transportation by land or war was helpful, sometimes essential, for the unification of more or less distant communities under royal control.

The complexity of these executive functions, as distinct from religious, military, legislative, and juridical functions, is exemplified already in ancient kingdoms by the role of vizier in Egypt under the XVIII dynasty. It was the vizier who "carried on the administrative side of the royal function" with the help of assistants. His task was "to attend to home boundaries, allotment of land, inundation,

canals, orders for second crop . . . the arrears of taxes, the griev-
ances of the local governors, the robberies in the provinces, and
quarrels. . . . In the temples, he examined the shortcomings of
offerings . . . and division of tribute." In modern states these
functions are, of course, becoming more and more complex.

5. THE RIGHTS OF KINGS

The rights of kings included all those which he needed in order
to perform his functions. Since he functioned as the representative
of a god, or gods, his rights were supported by the god, or gods,
whom he represented: they were "divine." Indeed, the term
"divine rights of kings" was current in Europe up to the beginning
of this century. Of course, he had no such rights if he was not
divinely appointed, and he could lose them if he failed to enact his
duties or acted in a way which conflicted with them.

First of all, of course, he had the right to be recognized by his
subjects as the supreme, the most valuable and important person,
at least within his own kingdom, if not in the world. Numerous
ceremonial manifestations of this recognition are found in all
kingdoms: periodical religious cultus of the king, as in Japan or the
Roman Empire; public ceremonies during the king's coronation as
heir of his predecessor, at his marriage, on the birth of an heir;
yearly celebrations of important past events in the king's life,
especially his great achievements; and, finally, ceremonial mourning after his death. Another manifestation of this recognition was
the prohibition and punishment of any outward behavior or verbal
statements which profaned the king's sacredness or implied criticism of what he did, for "the king can do no wrong."

However, in order to perform all his duties the king not only had
to possess an inherent ability by virtue of his divine nature or divine
inspiration, but (being at least partly human) needed some educational preparation. As a matter of fact, the education preparing
royal heirs for their future function was probably the first planfully
organized *general* education in history. It was carried on under the
guidance and control of the heir's parents by men of

wisdom—priests, experienced warriors, later also jurists, and sometimes philosophers. We know about the education of various pharaohs, Persian kings (from Xenophon), Alexander of Macedonia (under Aristotle), some Roman emperors, khalifs, and European kings.

Once a king was well prepared for his role as supreme political authority, he had the right to have his juridical and legislative judgments unconditionally accepted as absolutely valid, unless they conflicted with the judgments of his priestly circle, which they seldom did. And, obviously, his orders had to be unconditionally obeyed by his warriors and those civilian subjects to whom they were addressed. It was the task of his military and political assistants to exact this obedience.

Well recognized and universal were the king's rights to personal safety. Such safety could be permanently imposed only if he resided in a place which was both religiously secure (inaccessible to evil powers) and physically secure from human enemies. This required that the royal residence be located in an area which was sacred, because it included a holy center of the religious cultus carried on by priests, and also physically strong, because protected by his warriors. All historical kings possessed secure residences in such areas, even if they occasionally traveled under adequate protection over their kingdoms or acted as leaders of aggressive warfare outside of these kingdoms. The king's residence, or what eventually became a royal castle or palace, was a sacred home for him and his family, almost as sacred as a temple, and in addition was protected by royal guards.

The economic rights of a king were very inclusive, in view of the extent and complexity of his duties. He had to promote the welfare of his subjects, support his warriors, and stimulate economic exchange. Neither he nor his priestly circle could perform any economically productive activities, which would profane their sacredness; and his political assistants could not support themselves by their own activities, for this might impede their essential functions. Thus, the king and his assistants were entitled to all the economic rights which they needed for the adequate performance of their roles.

In some kingdoms, the king was considered the owner of all the property of his subjects—e.g., the Zulu kings. As a matter of fact, however, kings had exclusive ownership and control of only limited portions of the total property within their kingdoms; priests, military leaders, political assistants, agriculturalists, eventually craftsmen and merchants, controlled most of the property. Nonetheless, the king shared some possessive rights with them—especially under feudalism, where—as we noticed—he was theoretically the sovereign owner of all land, but had transmitted most of the rights of ownership to his vassals. In any case, he had the right to share the income which his subjects derived from their property—in other terms, the right to tax them.

How large a proportion of property and income do kings use for their own benefit, and how much for the benefit of their subjects? This is difficult to ascertain. Since the king is obviously too important and sacred to perform any profane activity, he is surrounded by servants who satisfy all his wants and those of his family. There has been considerable luxury and splendor in many a royal palace, with hundreds of servants besides military guards to protect him. Since he entertained important visitors from various parts of the kingdom and often also foreign envoys, the splendor of the palace enhanced his prestige. Moreover, the royal palace was also often an administrative center, including numerous assistants whom the king also had to support.

6. The Historical Evolution of Social Roles Following the Formation of Kingdoms

In comparing the social roles which existed in early kingdoms —say, 4,000 years ago—with those which exist in the modern world, we find that a vast multiplicity of new species evolved during this period. This evolution became wider and faster after the integration of communities into states, partly because of one fundamental difference between royal states and tribal or rural communities: the existence of capital *cities*.

The area in which the king's residence was located was generally known as the *capital* of the kingdom. The inhabitants of the capital included priests, who regularly performed religious rites in temples for the benefit of the kingdom, and also those nobles and political assistants with whom the king was regularly in personal contact. But it included also the people who produced or imported the cultural values which the king, the priests, the warriors, the administrative officials, and the king's servants needed, but could not produce themselves. It was what we may call the sociocultural center of the kingdom, as is typically exemplified by Babylon, Niniveh, Teheran, Peking, early Rome, Alexandria, Constantinople, Paris, Vienna, Prague, Cracow, Kiev, and Moscow. Many of these grew, and their metropolitan areas expanded widely. Some cities remained sociocultural centers even when the roles of kings disappeared—e.g., Athens, Rome during the long period between the early kingdom and the empire, Paris during republican periods, Moscow since the Bolshevik Revolution—or when the kings became mere symbols of political unity—e.g., London, Amsterdam, Copenhagen, Stockholm. Moreover, when large new cities grew in countries without kings—e.g., in the United States—they also became sociocultural centers.

The long duration and growth of such centers and the emergence of new cities is very important from the point of view of the evolution of social roles, for nearly all the new varieties started in cities.

In surveying this evolution, we must distinguish the following main trends:

(1) The historical differentiation of *religious roles*.

(2) The historical differentiation and multiplication of *military* roles.

(3) The historical differentiation and multiplication of *political* roles.

(4) The creative evolution of the *aesthetic* roles of artists, men of letters, and musicians.

(5) The inventive evolution of *technical* roles.

(6) The evolution of *economic* roles.

(7) The creative evolution of secular *intellectual* roles (those of "men of knowledge").

(8) The evolution of *educational* roles.

(9) Closely connected with those evolutionary trends, which were started by men, is the historical evolution of the social roles of *women* during the last four centuries.

We shall devote special chapters to these evolutionary trends.

Only by analyzing such a development can we develop a functional typology of social roles.

CHAPTER 17

THE FUNCTIONAL DIFFERENTIATION
OF RELIGIOUS ROLES

1. THE PUBLIC FUNCTIONS OF PRIESTS IN CAPITAL CITIES

From earliest times, every capital city included at least one temple where a number of priests regularly performed religious functions, and sometimes it had several temples devoted to the cultus of different deities or even to the cultus of the same deity, if the city was too large for one temple to accommodate all the inhabitants who wished to attend the same or similar religious cultus. As kingdoms grew and the functions of priests in capital centers became increasingly complicated, some specialization was necessary.

First of all, in every large temple or in every city with several temples of the same deity, there was a high priest who controlled the functions of his subordinates. As we have already mentioned, the primary task of priests as assistants of the kings was to promote the security and welfare of the kingdom as a whole. Some priests, including the high priest, had considerable magico-religious power, which they used individually or cooperatively on behalf of the kingdom and against the influence of evil mystical powers. For instance, in Babylonia the most important priests were powerful magicians.

We noticed that, wherever agriculture prevailed, yearly seasonal or monthly ceremonies were regularly carried on by priests to insure the growth and harvesting of the crops. These ceremonies, planned and regulated in advance, year after year, required a calendar based on astronomical observations. Consequently, some priests in large kingdoms—e.g., the Egyptian, the Babylonian, the Chinese, and the Mayan—apparently specialized in such observations and developed calendars.

Priests, and sometimes also priestesses, performed another important task: they predicted future events which would affect positively or negatively the lives of the king and his subjects, and they advised the king how to prepare for such events. These predictions were obtained in various ways: by mystic intuition—e.g., that of the sybils of ancient Rome; by knowledge directly derived from the gods—e.g., the Delphic oracle; and by observation of sacrificial animals or human beings. However, the most important and widely spread basis for prediction was the study of the sun, the moon, the stars, and the planets; and this led to the development of *astrology*. Astrology was closely connected with the astronomical observations used in making the calendar and thus led eventually to astronomy. Since the heavenly bodies were components of a divinely controlled universe, the development of astronomy remained in the hands of the priests—typically in Babylonia, China, and Egypt.

Inasmuch as religious cultus had to be carried on within limited spatial locations, it was a task of the priests to select and circumscribe these locations. This was not done arbitrarily. For, according to well-known beliefs, found already in tribal communities, spatial areas differed widely from the magico-religious point of view. Some were sacred, inhabited or at least controlled by gods or other divine beings; others were impure, dangerous, inhabited by evil beings: but most of them were profane, with no magico-religious significance. Obviously, only sacred areas could be centers of cultus. The priests who planned an organized cultus within the territory of a kingdom had to know which sections of this territory were sacred and which were mystically impure or merely profane. This meant that some of them, at least, had to be *geographers*; moreover, in certain kingdoms they were expected to advise the king, his military commanders, and his political assistants in the selection of proper areas for their activities and in the avoidance of dangerous areas. This function was called *geomancy*; it was most highly developed in China, where it lasted up to this century.

Another priestly function was planning new temples in cities and supervising their construction. Even the construction of palaces for kings had to be supervised by priests, so as to insure their sacredness and protect the kings from evil influences. And in most kingdoms, special tombs for the sacred kings had to be raised, like the pyramids in Egypt. Therefore, certain priests specialized as *architects*. Furthermore, the selection and circumscription of areas reserved for temples, palaces, and tombs, as well as the planning of large-scale constructions, required mathematical calculations, at least arithmetic and geometry. And since the growth of astronomy also needed mathematics, priests were probably the first systematic mathematicians, although the use of arithmetic in taxation and commerce no doubt developed separately.

2. THE PRIVATE FUNCTIONS OF PRIESTS

The functions of priests, however, were not limited to public performances intended to benefit the kingdom as a whole. Temples were not only sacred buildings where ceremonial cultus was carried on by the priesthood, but also centers where individual believers sought the help and guidance of priests, sometimes also of priestesses. These individuals were primarily inhabitants of the city where the temple was located, but often also pilgrims from more or less distant areas. They sought to gain divine favor and protection from evil powers, to obtain divine sanction for their family relations, to insure the birth of valuable children and have them accepted into the fold of the faithful, to secure salvation for the dead, to expiate their own sins and thus avoid the anger of the gods. They usually offered gifts to the temple.

The tasks of priests in kingdoms were, thus, similar to those performed by tribal priests, but some of their methods were new. In certain temples where women were subordinate priestesses, men could gain mystical benefits from the deities by carrying on sexual intercourse with these women. More important historically were the innovations introduced in enacting one of the oldest tasks of shamans and priests—protecting the health of the people and curing the sick. Priests in urban centers learned the traditional techniques used in various sections of the kingdom and cooperated in trying to develop more effective *medical* practices, combining appeals to the gods with natural remedies. In certain temples, some priests specialized in this function, and eventually temples were built where the main functions of the priests were medical.

3. PRIESTS AS WRITERS

To perpetuate these innovations and continue the regular performance of such diverse and complex functions, oral tradition no longer sufficed. Therefore, in nearly every large, long-lasting kingdom some kind of durable visual symbolism was invented by the priests and first used in their temples. Eventually, this symbolism was developed into what we call "writing." Sometimes the origin of writing may be traced to movable symbols used as a means of distant communication between kings and their assistants (e.g., the Incas); but in any case its full development was primarily due to the priests, though, once developed, it was also used for secular purposes, political and economic.

This was how hieroglyphic writing, purely religious, developed in Egypt. Later it became somewhat simplified as so-called "hieratic," and finally completely secularized and popularized as demotic. Cuneiform writing, less complex than hieroglyphic, was developed in Babylonia. Chinese writing remained very complex for centuries, requiring many years for a scholar to learn fully how to use it.

Such written symbols spread beyond the country where they were invented and became accepted with modifications in other countries where different languages were spoken, also mostly on the initiative of the priests. Thus, Babylonian cuneiform writing became accepted by Assyrians, and later by Persians in a much simpler form. The sources of Greek, Roman, and Sanscrit symbols—all three relatively simple—are uncertain; but in any case they must have originated outside of these areas. The Roman alphabet, used by the Roman Catholic Church, spread throughout Central and Western Europe in religious and later also in secular writing. The Greek alphabet continued to be used for centuries by Greek Orthodox churches and the Byzantine emperors and their assistants. In the ninth century Cyril and Methodius, who converted some Slavic peoples, translated parts of the Bible into their language, using the Greek alphabet with certain changes. This alphabet persisted for centuries in all Eastern Slavonic churches and was eventually adopted in secular writing in Russia, Ukrainia, and White Ruthenia.

Even when writing came to be used for secular purposes, the writers ("scribes") were through centuries trained by priests, in Babylonia, Egypt, China, India, Judea, medieval Europe, and Eastern Europe until the seventeenth century.

The universal, primary task of religious writers was to preserve for posterity the basic standards and norms which authoritative priests followed in enacting their specific functions and to make these standards and norms available to all regional and local priests throughout the territory of the kingdom. Another task which they assumed quite early was to describe important events which occurred within the kingdom, so as to pass this information on to future generations. Their writings became *chronicles*, and chronicles eventually gave way to methodical history.

But the most vital function which priests performed was that of *theologians* who substituted a coherent religious doctrine for the divergent local and regional beliefs within the kingdom. This was sometimes done by integrating the most influential of these beliefs, as in ancient Egypt, where some old tribal deities gradually became recognized as deities of the kingdom with distinct, but mutually supplementary, mystical powers. Another means for religious unification was the development of a complex, inclusive, and consistent religious system in the expectation that it would be substituted for the older, less developed, and inconsistent religions. In this way many famous religious doctrines were formed—e.g., Judaism, Brahmanism, Buddhism, Zoroastrianim, Taoism, Christianity, and Islam. This function of the theologians found expression in *sacred books*, which multiplied in the course of time.

4. PRIESTS AS EDUCATORS

Already in tribal communities the final stage of education, preparing the younger generation for participation in their community, was often carried on by the older men during a short period of "initiation." The emergence of special roles of shamans and priests endowed with magico-religious wisdom was accompanied by longer periods of apprenticeship of candidates for such roles under the educational guidance of active shamans or priests. With the growing complexity and differentiation of priestly roles in urban centers, especially after the development of writing, the education of future priests became increasingly exacting, difficult, and long lasting, while the preparation of laymen for participation in religious life remained short and easy, since they were subjected any way to the control of priests. As a matter of fact, priests were the first to start *schools* for professional education (typically in Egypt and Babylonia). Every candidate for a priestly role had to be educated by several teachers. It took years to teach him how to read and write and to impart to him basic knowledge about the gods and the standards and norms intended to regulate religious cultus and human conduct, and to train him how to enact the duties that he would have to enact after the completion of his education.

The minimum education was given to those candidates who were expected to function as local priests in circles of laymen within the territories of the kingdom. Naturally, more educational preparation was required of candidates for the role of regional leader in control of local priests. Take, for instance, the differences in Christian countries between the education of parish priests and that of bishops. A small minority of priests were educated to perform specialized roles similar to those of their teachers in educational centers, so as to take over their roles after the older teachers died or to help organize new educative centers when the growing kingdom needed more priests.

Although no ordinary layman was expected to learn what future priests were being taught, the education of kings, queens, and their assistants was assumed by priests. Every prospective heir of a kingdom or prospective wife of a king was educated by priests or women trained by priests, usually under the tutorship of a prominent priest endowed with superior knowledge. Of course, kings were also taught warfare and politics, but religious teaching predominated in early days and in Asiatic kingdoms up to the twentieth century. We noticed that in ancient kingdoms royal scribes, whatever their function, were taught to read and write by priests in temples; nobody but priests taught adequately reading and writing in Sanscrit in India, or Slavonic writing in Eastern Europe up to the seventeenth century, or Latin writing in most Western European kingdoms up to the thirteenth century.

Originally, political education was also carried on by priests. In Babylonia and Egypt, the legislators and the jurists were trained by priests. In India, the Laws of Manu were written by priests; and in medieval Europe, participation in the faculty of law was conditioned by previous education under priestly guidance.

5. The Roles of Religious Innovators

In surveying the expansion of social circles (Chapter 12), we spoke about the prophets of new religions who gained increasing circles of followers. Our problem now is: How does a religious innovator gain followers within a kingdom? And here we notice an important distinction. If as yet there is no integrated religion which participants in the kingdom share, a theologian who starts such a religion and wins followers can easily gain the sponsorship of the ruler, as did the theologians who initiated the cult of Ammon in Egypt (though their names are unknown), and much later Zoroaster in Persia.

But if such a religion already exists and has the support of an organized priesthood, only minor innovations which conform with its basic doctrine are accepted by the priests and eventually approved by them as valuable according to existing standards. The most significant of these innovations are supposed to be due to mystical contacts of the innovator with gods, and their approval is manifested by explicit appreciation of the innovator as a holy person—e.g., a Hindu yogi or a Christian saint. Indeed, the life histories of saints, especially of the founders of various monastical orders, provide a key to the understanding of the range of innovations which were allowed by the organized priesthood. Minor theological innovations were also permitted when they helped apply the recognized doctrine to new problems.

A different situation arose whenever a religious innovator did not conform with the established doctrine or explicitly opposed the domination of the organized priesthood. He was considered by the priests to be a dangerous rebel; his future and that of his followers depended upon the priests' power of social control, particularly their influence on the political and military rulers. Compare, for instance, the treatment of Jesus with that of Buddha, who was the descendant of a powerful family; or the treatment of early Christians by such Roman emperors as Nero with their later treatment by Constantine; or the rapid spread of Buddhism under the sponsorship of King Asoka with its later disappearance from India.

When kings opposed the excessive control of the priesthood, they often supported rebellious religious innovators—e.g., Wesley and Luther. This, however, did not always have a lasting effect. For example, the new religious doctrine, nearly monotheistic, which Amenhotep IV supported disappeared after his death under the pressure of the organized Egyptian priesthood. The support of medieval heretics by the kings of Provence led to the Albigensian War in which rulers who conformed with the doctrines of the Roman Catholic Church invaded Provence and eliminated the heretics.

When certain religious innovations were prohibited by the rulers, they might still be preserved by secret religious associations founded by the innovators—e.g., the early Christian associations or the various heretical groups of the Middle Ages. Many religious innovations persisted and even developed, in spite of coercive repression, when the innovators and/or their followers escaped into territories where they were relatively free—e.g., the Calvinists from England and Holland, the Huguenots from France, and several German sects who came to the United States, the Mormons into Utah, and the Russian Dukhobors into Canada and California.

When, on the other hand, the rulers of a state permit religious innovation, the roles of innovators usually multiply. A historically unparalleled example is that of the United States during the last hundred years, when more than two hundred new religious groups emerged, some of them on the initiative of foreign prophets, but most on the initiative of native prophets, including some women.

6. THE ROLES OF PRIESTS AS MISSIONARIES

In contrast with the integration of religious beliefs and practices within a kingdom and the emergence of religious innovations which either conform or conflict with such systems, another historical trend has been going on for more than twenty centuries: the expansion of religious systems beyond the domain of the kingdom where they originally developed. While this sometimes followed military conquest, it was frequently achieved by peaceful methods. In any case, however, this function was usually delegated to specially prepared priests. These priests moved into a foreign territory whose inhabitants had a different religion (or several different religions) and assumed the task of converting these foreigners to their own presumably superior religion. Such was their "mission," and the term "missionaries" has been used to denote their specific roles. Thus, Buddhism, Roman Catholicism, Greek Orthodoxy, and Islam expanded far beyond their original territories.

Obviously, foreign missionaries were hardly welcomed by the native priests, shamans, wise men, or wise women. Their success usually depended upon their ability to convert or at least persuade a foreign ruler that their religion could help unify his kingdom. Thus, Roman Catholicism was accepted by the Frankish conquerors of Gaul, the Teutonic invaders of Iberia, influential rulers within Ireland, the Scandinavian invaders of Normandy, and the kings of Bohemia, Poland, and eventually Hungary, while Greek Orthodoxy was accepted by rulers of states which much later became parts of the Russian Empire and by the kings of Serbia and Bulgaria. The adoption of Islam by the Tartars and the Turks seems to have been voluntary, though its spread throughout Persia, Afghanistan, and Africa was largely due to Arab conquest. The expansion of Buddhism outside of India, where it originated, was certainly due to missionaries, who probably gained the support of rulers in Burma and Indochina; and it was approved or at least tolerated (though not actively supported) by the emperors of China and Japan.

The expansion of Christianity beyond Europe was largely conditioned by the military and political expansion of European states into colonial areas. Thus, the Christianization of Latin America obviously followed conquest, for the Catholic priests who functioned as missionaries had the powerful backing of the kings of Spain and Portugal. The penetration of Christian missionaries into other colonial territories was also partly sponsored by governments, e.g., in India, the Philippines, Central and Southern Africa. The permission granted to Christian missionaries during the nineteenth century to function within the Chinese and Japanese empires was mostly due to their protection by Western powers. When this protection could no longer be maintained, Christian missions were almost completely eliminated in Japan during World War II and completely throughout China during the last four years.

Of course, many missionaries entered foreign areas, especially tribal areas, without governmental sponsorship or protection. Quite a few of them lost their lives, but others slowly and gradually gained converts and formed organized groups. Their acceptance by the natives was often quicker and easier when they introduced not only religious beliefs and rites, but also efficient secular practices. It is significant that the most successful modern missionaries in tribal areas were trained physicians or agriculturalists.

With the multiplication of religious denominations during and after the Reformation, missionaries of different Christian groups began to compete for converts within certain territories. An interesting example was the penetration of various Protestant missions—Lutheran, Calvinist, Arian (Unitarian) into the Kingdom of Poland during the sixteenth century. Of course, when the ruler accepts one denomination and rejects the others, there cannot be much competition. Thus, although Protestant denominations did not disappear from Poland, they could no longer compete with the Catholic Church when it was accepted by the government in the seventeenth century. Vice versa, Catholic missions had little success in England after the government espoused Episcopalianism. Right now, no Protestant missions function in Spain, and they do not make much headway against Catholicism in most Latin American countries. But they still compete energetically in the United States, Canada, and most Western European countries, and the Methodists have been particularly successful in the United States. On the other hand, the Mormons, Jehovah's Witnesses, and the Christian Scientists have gained converts in Europe to religions which originated in the United States. But no missionaries of any denomination are allowed to function freely in the Soviet Union or the satellite countries.

CHAPTER 18

THE DIFFERENTIATION OF ROLES OF WARRIORS

1. TERRITORIAL DIVISIONS

As kingdoms grew in size through conquest, and conflicts between them multiplied, the military as well as the political functions of kings became so complex that they had to be delegated to the subordinate rulers who controlled territorial sections of the kingdom. This is how feudalism evolved in China, Japan, Persia, and medieval Europe. Within their territories these subordinate rulers were not only war lords, but keepers of order in peacetime, endowed with rights to obedience and economic rights analogous to those of kings. However, they remained vassals of their kings, ready to cooperate with him and, whenever necessary, to recruit and train soldiers from among their subjects. Of course, some powerful vassals tried to become sovereigns themselves.

In any case, we know that during feudal times kings and vassals developed efficient methods of educating the younger generation to become warriors and eventually leaders of the auxiliary warriors whom they recruited.

A different type of territorially located role of warrior developed in the cities—first of all, in the royal capitals. As the state grew and came to include many cities, the inhabitants of each city organized for common defense against aggressive enemies, with or without the help of the king. This local defense began already in ancient Greece and Greek colonies, continued in the Hellenic kingdoms and in the Roman Empire, and later still throughout Europe when cities became independent of the feudal lords. Some kings utilized this military organization of the urban inhabitants to overcome various conflicts which impaired their efficient functioning during the period of feudalism. But urban organization also enabled several countries not only to get rid of the domination of royal vassals, but also to weaken that of the king himself, as in Switzerland, in some measure in the Netherlands, but particularly in England.

2. DIFFERENTIATION OF THE SOCIAL FUNCTIONS OF WARRIORS

While the main social function of warriors originally consisted in serving kings as conquerors and defenders who built and maintained royal states, some warriors gradually assumed different functions.

As certain religions expanded, especially Christianity and Islam, wars acquired a religious significance. Although the priests opposed military struggles between faithful believers, they could not prevent them altogether. Therefore, they tolerated those which were justified by ethical standards. They agreed that manifestations of disloyalty to the consecrated ruler, all violent invasions by hostile neighbors, and the robbery of traveling merchants had to be repressed. In medieval Europe, "being unable to prevent war, the Church christianized the warriors." It developed what has been called a "Code of Chivalry," with which all Christian warriors were expected to conform, combatting all evil and defending all good. A somewhat similar conception developed among the Moslems.

But among both the Christians and the Moslems, the most important task of chivalrous warriors was to defend their own religion against dangerous unbelievers. This led to religious or "holy" wars; for defense of one's religion may require aggression, so as to incapacitate unbelievers or convert them by force. Thus, the wars started by Moslem warriors in the seventh century were from their point of view holy wars; so were the medieval Crusades, from the Christian point of view. Rebellious heretics had to be repressed by war whenever they could not otherwise be converted, as was exemplified by the Albigensian War fought by medieval knights on both sides. The development of Protestantism brought fresh religious wars to Europe. For instance, when John Huss the Heretic was condemned to death by the Catholic Church, his Czechish followers—the Hussites—carried on a defensive warfare for years, as did the Dutch Protestants against the dominion of Catholic Spain. Perhaps the best known is the Thirty Years' War, which was predominantly, though not exclusively, religious. In recent times, several holy wars have been started by Moslems in colonial areas.

Another social function of warriors evolved in consequence of the development of modern nationalities, i.e., societies united by distinctive literary national cultures. These cultures grew at the initiative of intellectual leaders, sometimes under the sponsorship of kings—e.g., French, Spanish, English, later Russian. Sometimes, however, they expanded, like various religions, beyond the range of particular states (e.g., in Italy from the fifteenth century on), or developed under republican governments (e.g., in the United States), or were subjected to the control of dictators (e.g., in Nazi Germany and the Soviet Union), or grew in rebellion against rulers who supposed [sic] and imposed foreign cultures (e.g., in Ireland, Poland, and Czechoslovakia).

These societies will be investigated later; but here we must mention the roles of warriors who without state support have functioned on behalf of the societies to which they belonged, either as aggressors or defenders. For instance, in consequence of military invasions by Russians, Prussians, and Austrians, Poland at the end of the eighteenth century became divided into three politically separate parts. Polish warriors, under the leadership of Pulaski and Kosciuszko, tried in vain to defend their nationality against the superior military power of the invaders. Nonetheless, the Poles preserved and even developed their national culture and resumed military struggles for independence, unsuccessfully in 1830 and 1863, successfully in 1914–18 with the help of Western European powers and especially of the United States. Irish nationalists for centuries organized unsuccessful rebellions against English domination until they obtained independence in 1920.

3. SPECIALIZATION OF WARRIORS IN AGGRESSIVE AND DEFENSIVE TECHNIQUES

This old and well-known evolutionary trend began with the use by warriors of new aggressive weapons and new means of defense which were invented not by warriors, but by technicians. The use of these inventions by warriors for military purposes obviously differed considerably from their use by merchants and industrialists for peaceful purposes. After the discovery of metals, first bronze, then iron and steel, swords and spears began to be used to directly injure enemies, and warriors specialized in their use, especially swordsmen. A high degree of skill was required to kill or wound another well-trained swordsman, and this was much appreciated in combats between members of enemy groups. Sometimes the best fighters were selected and fought each other before their groups started to fight, the victor gaining prestige for his group. This skill developed most fully, however, when dueling became a custom. An individual challenged to a duel another man who had offended him, and by so doing defended his honor. The man who was challenged could not refuse, lest he be branded a coward. The duel was fought in the presence of witnesses who acted as umpires and decided the outcome. Eventually special teachers began to train warriors and even civilians in swordsmanship, for though other weapons came to be used in duels, swords always remained the predominant weapon.

Another kind of specialization, which persisted for thousands of years and was connected with the use of spears and swords, was that of warriors who rode horses, or "cavalry men." As long as military struggles led to direct encounters between enemies, the cavalry had obvious advantages over the infantry. Not only the use of the proper weapons, but also the ability to ride and direct the horses required considerable training. The Mongolian invaders of Eastern Europe certainly learned how to ride from childhood. So did the medieval knights. In Central and Western Europe, special regiments of cavalry were organized, and it took years to achieve good horsemanship, especially for officers. The Italian condottieri, the Prussian Black Hussars and Uhlans were famous riders.

The specialization of warriors in the use of military weapons which can kill enemies at a distance began with archery. Bows were originally for hunting game, but eventually became adapted to warfare. As late as the thirteenth century, groups of skilled archers were trained to participate in struggles against enemy archers and cavalry. Of course, the invention and application of gunpowder provided the most efficient weapons enabling warriors to kill enemies at a distance. It led to the steady development of artillery as a special branch of the army and increased the power of infantry against cavalry. And the effective use of these weapons still requires specialized military training. Still greater specialization is required for warriors to use effectively the new aggressive weapons invented during the last thirty years, which are incomparably more destructive than those used in the past.

The effectiveness of means of defense is conditioned by the kind of aggressive weapons which enemy warriors use. Thus, the walls built around cities and medieval castles, combined with various techniques for preventing enemies from breaking through the walls, climbing them, or burrowing under them, were effective for centuries, though they could not protect the inhabitants of the surrounding areas—villages or small towns—from invaders unless by admitting them into the city before the invasion. With the development of artillery, defensive walls lost most of their usefulness.

Shields were employed quite early as a means of protecting individual warriors from aggressive enemy weapons. They developed into the complete panoply of the medieval knights; sometimes even the horses were shielded by armor. Here again the invention of guns made this kind of protection practically useless. Modern long-range, large-scale destructive weapons have raised new and difficult problems of defense. Apparently, the only effective defense is to destroy these weapons before they reach their targets.

4. SPECIALIZATION BASED ON WAYS OF TRANSPORTATION

Warriors who invade foreign areas have to transport their weapons and whatever other objects they need, frequently also their means of subsistence. Usually the invasion and such transportation as necessary are made by land, but sometimes by water.

Other persons besides warriors are interested in entering foreign areas—kings, priests, political assistants, merchants, and eventually explorers.

The invention of wheels and their use on chariots for transporting kings and commanders, and on wagons for transporting weapons and other material objects, required passable roads. And, as a matter of fact, most roads (typically Roman roads) were originally built for military purposes and used mostly by warriors. Apart from the fact that building roads requires special skill, eventually even professional engineering, the functions of warriors who can regularly use roads (e.g., the Roman legions) differ from those of warriors who have to move through a wilderness or at best use footpaths.

These, however, are relatively minor differences as compared with the fundamental difference between transportation by land and transportation by water, especially by sea. The sea has had a great influence on military expansion, as illustrated by the expansion of Phoenicia, resulting in the formation of Carthage; the colonial expansion of Athens; the invasion of Rome by Hannibal; the destruction of Carthage by Rome; the Roman conquest of Brittany, of Egypt, and of the western part of Asia Minor; the invasion by Scandinavian Vikings of various areas of Western Europe; the conquest of Central and South America by Spaniards; and the development of the British colonial empire.

Of course, the mere building and sailing of ships is not a military activity, but it can be explicitly planned for military purposes, i.e., to facilitate the invasion of a foreign area by transferring a large number of well-armed warriors, overcoming any obstructions to landing and the resistance of warriors located near the foreign shore. Or ships may be used to gain the possession of goods which foreign merchants are transferring by ships. This has been called "piracy," when done by private warriors for their own benefit; but sometimes the warriors are functioning for the benefit of their states. Many ships have been built and used exclusively to carry on struggles against enemy warriors using their ships for military purposes. This is why ships came to include aggressive weapons and are protected against the weapons used by the enemy, and why the specialization of warriors regularly functioning on ships has steadily increased. We now have the navy separated from the army, and naval schools which give naval warriors a long and thorough training both in the use of weapons, and in skill in sailing.

A historically unparalleled evolutionary trend, so far as speed and range are concerned, has been the specialization of warriors in the use of airplanes. Although air transportation by balloon was invented more than a century ago, and by the end of the last century balloons began to be used—not very effectively—for military purposes, not until the beginning of this century were efficient airplanes invented. Already during World War I, well-trained pilots used them, mainly for purposes of observation, and struggles between enemy pilots started. While during the period preceding World War II the rapid development of airplanes by new inventions was largely intended to promote peaceful traveling, their adaption for destructive purposes was also speeded up, especially after the war started. By now, barely fifty years after airplanes were invented, we have warriors who specialize in their use for aggressive and defensive military goals. The air force has at last been separated from the old special divisions of army and navy, and a distinct school started for educating specialists in air warfare.

CHAPTER 19

THE EVOLUTION OF POLITICAL ROLES

1. POLITICAL FUNCTIONS OF THE KING

We saw that the role of king included several functions which have been termed "political": that of supreme judge, applying established moral standards to social relations among his subjects, so as to counteract or prevent transgressions and conflicts; that of supreme legislator, promulgating general principles superimposed upon the diversity of customs and mores prevalent in the various communities within his kingdom; and that of supreme administrator, regulating the active cooperation of his subjects. We noticed that the performance of each of these functions usually required the aid of many assistants, except in feudal kingdoms, where the king delegated most of his political functions to his vassals. In the course of history, the roles of the king's assistants became increasingly differentiated, the more so the larger the kingdom, the greater the diversity of its population, and the more complex the relations among its inhabitants. And we must ask: What happened to the roles of the assistants in those states in which the supreme power of the king decreased or disappeared altogether?

2. EVOLUTION OF THE ROLES OF JUDGES AND LAWYERS

The main task of judges and lawyers is to apply established legal systems to particular cases. Judges were originally delegates of the kings and they still are wherever the king still retains his power. But in the Greek democracies and in the Roman republic, the magistrate was simply an administrative officer. He presided over the administration of justice, but the judgment was rendered by representatives of the people. The term "judge" was not applied to the presiding magistrate by the Romans until, in the imperial period, he became judge of the law and the facts. Now in most countries except those under the English law, the judge decides about the facts as well as the law in civil cases. In criminal cases the decision about the facts is often left to a jury of laymen. In the United States, most judges are elected by popular vote.

As their duties became more complicated, the early magistrates turned for advice to men who were well acquainted with the law; and from about 300 B.C. on, we find a growing class of lawyers, or persons versed in the law. Gradually they assumed the roles of representing private persons who brought suits before the courts or were hailed there to defend themselves in civil or criminal suits. They also represented the interest of the state in criminal matters as prosecuting attorneys. By the end of the thirteenth century, lawyers had become recognized as a professional class, and this profession has become a steppingstone to political office, especially in England and the United States. Women have also been admitted to practice in many countries.

Usually the requirements to become a lawyer are now strictly regulated and controlled by the state. As the law has grown, lawyers have tended to specialize in certain fields; some take chiefly criminal cases, while others refuse to handle such matters. Among those who take only civil cases, we find specialists in different branches of the law, e.g., wills and probate, trusts, corporations, taxes.

3. Evolution of the Roles of Legislators

In every large, long-lasting, expanding state, many changes occur which require the introduction of new laws or modifications of the older legal code. In order to deal with these changes, some persons must act as legislators, whether assistants to the king or members of a republican government.

In principle, the introduction of a new law or the modification of a legal code implies the agreement of the legislators, though even in the ancient kingdoms such agreement was by no means universal.

Some legislative assistants of the king often favored only those laws which would benefit a certain class, or group of subjects, or the inhabitants of a certain area of the kingdom, while others opposed them and demanded instead laws which would benefit a different class or group, or the inhabitants of another area. Thus political *factions* were formed, each trying to gain the support of the king and get its demands enacted into law. The faction which had the most powerful support in the royal court emerged as the victor. As we can easily imagine, these factional conflicts in royal courts affected considerably the legislative function.

Political factionalism in republican states also evolved quite early. For instance, it existed at some periods in Athens, but was most influential in republican Rome where, under the impact of struggles between military and political leaders, the Senate was usually disrupted by factions. Under the Roman Empire, the emperor controlled the Senate and often, under the influence of factional leaders, imposed legislation on behalf of different classes or groups of subjects.

We are familiar with the factionalism in the United States, where lobbyists, i.e., active representatives of so-called "pressure groups," attempt to induce influential members of the state legislatures or members of the Congress to promote the promulgation of laws which will benefit these groups.

More important historically was the organization of political *parties* whose active members plan to control not merely the promulgation of particular laws at a particular time, but general legislative trends for a long period of time. We shall later investigate political parties as social groups. Now we are concerned with the roles of the political leaders who initiate the formation of political parties and contribute to their growth and expansion, in particular with the roles of legislators who accept the common goals of the political parties to which they belong and attempt to realize these goals.

No political parties existed in feudal times or immediately thereafter. The permanent legislative bodies in certain countries were originally composed of the upper aristocracy, the upper clergy, and professional assistants selected by the king from the bourgeoisie. The lower social classes—the petty nobility, the merchants and craftsmen in cities, and even the peasants—often resented the legislation of this dominant, exclusive set, and eventually rebellious leaders organized political groups for the purpose of having the interests of these classes recognized by the legislators. These leaders led the fight for universal civil rights in England and France, in Italy from the middle of the nineteenth century, in Russia from the last quarter of the nineteenth century, etc. On the other hand, the higher classes also had leaders who tried to maintain or regain their legislative supremacy.

These struggles finally led to the formation of legislative bodies composed of elected representatives. However, the distinction between the political leaders functioning mainly on behalf of the higher classes and those functioning mainly on behalf of the lower classes still persists—e.g., in England and even in the United States, where the Democratic Party (with the exception of the Southern Democrats) stands for "the common man." In contemporary France, with many parties, the situation is more complex, for many political leaders function partly on behalf of the lower classes, partly on behalf of the higher classes. Of course, no such distinction exists where all the legislators belong to one party, as in Nazi Germany, in Italy under Fascist leadership, and now in the Soviet Union under Communist leadership.

Once a political party is organized, the task of the political leaders consists mainly in gaining more followers and preventing the party from losing adherents to a competing party. Special methods have been developed to perform effectively this task. There may or may not be a top leader, but in any case particular areas of the country, especially the large cities, have their own party leaders, or "bosses," each with assistant leaders to deal with the inhabitants of the area and try to prove to them that it is to their advantage to adhere to the party. What the boss obtains while performing his function—whether only prestige, or prestige and power, or economic rewards—is a different and complicated problem.

Now, when we consider the roles of legislators in countries where they are elected by political parties, we notice that they are becoming increasingly diversified. First, we often find two legislative bodies, the participants of one having higher prestige or more authority than participants in the other, even when the majority of both must agree in promulgating most of the laws. Thus, in the United States we have a Senate and a House of Representatives, and in England a House of Lords and a House of Commons, the former a survival of the old dominant upper-class legislature, though in recent times its legislative power has decreased.

Furthermore, as problems requiring legislative solutions multiply and become increasingly complex, numerous and diverse proposals, or "bills," are introduced during every session of the legislature, and it is almost impossible for a legislator to know and understand the significance of all of them. Consequently, some legislators have to specialize in studying certain problems and presenting the results of their studies to all the legislators. This is why a number of special committees are organized in every legislative body.

In countries with more or less autonomous divisions—like the United States, with one or two elected legislative bodies in every one of the forty-eight states—the roles of local legislators are quite numerous. The same is true in Canada, Australia, in some Latin American countries, in Germany before the Nazi regime, nominally in the Soviet Union with its numerous "republics," and in some measure in the Communist satellite states. Of course, the degree of autonomy which legislators in the different divisions are granted and the kinds of laws they are allowed to pass vary greatly.

4. Evolution of Administrative Roles

The mere promulgation of laws is usually not sufficient to make people actually conform with the standards and norms formulated in those laws. Some agents must be endowed with authority or power, or both, to control the conduct of the people who are ordered to conform. Kings obviously had authority and power. As their kingdoms grew, they were forced to delegate most of it to administrators. The Roman emperors delegated administrative authority to officials located within definite territorial areas—the *praefecti, vicarii, ractores, curiales,* etc.—and graded their powers according to the size of the areas which they controlled. Such a territorial gradation persists to this day, wherever the supreme administrator is still a hereditary king, an autocratic dictator, or an elected president. If the state is large, it is divided into sections and subsections, and the administrators of subsections are subordinated to the administrators of the sections within which their subsections are included. For instance, in royal Prussia there was a *Landrat* (country administrator), above him a *Regierungspräsident* (district administrator), and on top an *Oberpräsident* (provincial administrator). A similar division and gradation, though with different terms, was introduced by the Nazis into the whole territory of Germany and also the conquered countries.

In Russia under the Tsarist regime, administrators of small-town and rural communities were subjected to provincial "governors," who were in turn subjected to higher administrators who controlled the larger regions, such as Poland, the Ukraine, the Caucasus, and Trans-Caucasus, and vast sections of Siberia. Under the Bolsheviks, such divisions and gradations have become much more complicated, for the entire territory of the former Tsarist Empire has been divided into Soviet Socialist Republics with the Russian "Federated Republic" on the top; within each republic, especially the Russian, were "autonomous" regions and districts. Of course, all the administrators of these republics, regions, and districts, must be members of the Communist Party, and all of them are subjected to the supreme control of the small group centered in the Kremlin.

Along with territorial gradation, there exists a functional specialization and multiplication of administrative officials. This is the so-called "bureaucracy" which several sociologists are now engaged in studying. The term bureaucracy implies that superior administrators and their subordinates occupy bureaus or offices, where their specific functions become regulated and integrated, and also that they constitute organized groups. The term has been applied to the organization of authoritative heads of religious, industrial, and commercial groups; but it is usually limited to government groups which exert considerable power.

This sort of bureaucracy was already well developed in Egypt. Referring again to the role of the Egyptian vizier and his administrative assistants, we see that the function which they performed consisted chiefly in regulating activities essential for the economic welfare of the kingdom. Their main tasks were to stimulate technical production and commerce, to regulate economic relations among its inhabitants, and to support the economic rights of the king. This indubitably required considerable specialization on the part of those assistants who controlled irrigation, promoted the production of certain goods, transportation by land and sea, or the exchange of goods produced either within the kingdom or abroad.

In general, neither priests nor warriors were equipped to regulate such activities. And throughout history, in every state, the regulation of technical and economic activities has been the function of specialized administrators and their assistants. Some kings delegated to competent assistants the organization of industrial activities only when no private enterpreneurs undertook them, but governmental regulation of private business within states, including the control of foreign trade, has always existed and still persists. In various states, it decreased during certain periods, but later increased again, as typically in Great Britain during the last century and a half. Governmental control culminated in the Soviet Union, where private business has been eliminated, and the absolute control of all production, exchange, and consumption is assumed by the Communist rulers, involving a vast multiplicity of roles of administrators and their assistants.

In modern times, the collection of taxes is a practically universal duty of political administrators, since without a large income no government can subsist and perform its collective functions. The construction of roads, originally undertaken by the military authorities, has been taken over by administrators, and is now most fully developed in the United States.

Another well-known, almost universal function which administrators perform is the execution of judicial decisions. Especially in the realm of criminal law, such execution often requires the use of force. At first force was provided by the warriors, but eventually special agents were appointed—policemen—who enlist many assistants. Now, in every modern country the police constitute a special branch of administration. They give the necessary support to judges, enable administrators to control prisons, and protect the public at large from dangerous transgressions of legal norms. The police department reached a historically unparalleled growth in Nazi Germany and an even greater one in the Soviet Union, where it has been and still is used to eliminate, or "liquidate," all opponents of the supreme rulers as well as to repress crimes.

A different and historically significant function of administrators and their subordinates is the control of colonial areas which followed the colonial expansion of certain European kingdoms —Spain, Portugal, France, England, Holland, and Belgium. Regional and local administrators in colonies were subordinated to the highest administrator, who was appointed by the king and maintained an office with assistants in the capital city of the kingdom. The administration of the colonies from the home office persisted even after the kingdom became a republic, as in France, or when the king lost most of his power, as in England and Holland, or when a dictator assumed supreme control of the state, as recently in Spain and Portugal. However, colonial administrators have lost much of their power as a result of the growing rebellion of native peoples against foreign domination during the last forty years.

From the eighteenth century on, in many states a special "ministry of education" was organized, composed of administrators who controlled education throughout the state. Although education was initiated and for a time carried out mainly by the priesthood, all royal and even republican governments became concerned with the influence of education upon the educands.

They wanted education to impart loyalty, prevent disloyalty, and stimulate interest in those subjects which would be useful to the government of the state.

During the last fifty years, protection of public health has become another administrative function. Although obviously the curing of individual sickness is the function of competent physicians, public sanitation and prevention of the spread of contagious diseases requires the services of special administrators. Moreover, it has become obvious that the health of the lower classes is not adequately protected by private physicians, and some countries have therefore promulgated laws intended to secure such protection with the aid of public finances and a corps of special administrators. Several countries, e.g., Great Britain and the United States, have recently set up special administrative branches to promote public welfare and social security.

Each of these administrative functions requires the participation of numerous state employees, or "civil servants," who are sufficiently competent to perform their specialized tasks. They are graded into a hierarchy of ranks, from the chief, endowed with highest authority and power, down to the lowest assistants. Individuals of inferior rank are usually appointed by those of superior rank and promoted on the basis of merit; and, because of their special competency, their roles are presumed to be long lasting. Persistent efforts are being made to insure that not only the tenure of the lower officials, but even their appointment, depend on their qualifications, as proved by examinations or other tests of merit.

How numerous civil officials can be is best illustrated by Germany under the Nazi regime, when the number of governmental employees and other governmental workers on all levels soared to four and one-half million, excluding soldiers. In the United States the number of Federal administrators increased in seventy-five years from about 100,000 to more than 2,000,000. In the Soviet Union, three bureaucracies exert themselves side by side: one under the regular departments of the government; the second, the secret police; and the third, the party bureaucracy under Communist leaders. It is impossible to even guess how many Soviet citizens are functioning as administrators; but, considering that all industry is being administered under governmental rule, their number must far surpass anything so far known in history.

5. DIPLOMATIC ROLES

Although conflicts between states, especially wars, have engaged most of the attention of chroniclers and historians, nonetheless a considerable amount of cooperation has always existed also. Even the wars frequently ended in a peaceful settlement which required some cooperation from both sides. Furthermore, when two states had a common enemy, they often cooperated in a war against him. Economic cooperation in peacetime is an old and widespread phenomenon. And a relatively late, but interesting and influential type of cooperation, has been intermarriage between royal families.

How did these various types of interstate cooperation start? They obviously required agreement between kings as supreme rulers, and agreement must be based on mutual communication. But kings, until recent times, seldom met each other. What a king customarily did was to send a delegate, a representative, or—to use a modern term—an *envoy* to the other king to communicate his suggestions, plans, requests, or demands. After a conference, the envoy returned and informed his master what the other king was willing or unwilling to do. Or the other king might reciprocally send a messenger or delegate. Sometimes the delegates representing the two kings met somewhere to discuss their common problems and try to reach a tentative solution acceptable to both kings. In any case, when cooperation first took place between two kings as rulers of states, it was almost always the result of a decision reached by both through the medium of delegates.

Before the days of delegates, prominent travelers often acted as representatives of their kings. Especially if a kingdom was located at some distance, a king might ask a prominent traveler to visit the foreign king, offer him honorific gifts, and express high recognition of his greatness. When such a traveler returned, he sometimes brought back honorific gifts and expressions of recognition from his former host to his sovereign. Such visitors contributed to raise the prestige of their own rulers and to increase the understanding and knowledge of foreign rulers.

In modern times, with the spread of various religions, the development of means of transportation and communication, the growth of commerce and industry, the colonial expansion of Europe, and the migration of people into foreign areas, actual and potential contacts between states, near and far, have multiplied, and so has cooperation, but also the danger of conflicts. Consequently, the short-lasting functions of envoys are no longer sufficient, except for brief conferences on special problems. Instead there are long-lasting functionaries, ambassadors on the highest rank and somewhat lower ministers. These representatives of their states reside in foreign capitals as intermediaries between their own rulers—kings, presidents of republics, or dictators—and the foreign rulers, who reciprocate by sending their own ambassadors and ministers abroad to the countries which are represented in their capitals.

The function of an ambassador or minister is quite complicated, especially in times of international tension. He needs special assistants—attachés—to deal with the specialists of the foreign government, and other assistants who are sufficiently familiar with the language and culture of the foreign country to collect and transmit to his own government the information it may need. Furthermore, he must become acquainted not only with the political and social leaders of the country where he is stationed, but with the representatives of other foreign governments who are also stationed there. This is best achieved by regularly carrying on polite companionate intercourse as a guest and as a host. Inasmuch as the participation of women in this intercourse is customary, the wife of an ambassador or minister usually accompanies him and plays an important role in his social activities.

INDEX

INDEX OF NAMES

INDEX OF TOPICS